MW01625506

People of the Shoals

Native Peoples, Cultures, and Places of the Southeastern United States

Florida A&M University, Tallahassee
Florida Atlantic University, Boca Raton
Florida Gulf Coast University, Ft. Myers
Florida International University, Miami
Florida State University, Tallahassee
University of Central Florida, Orlando
University of Florida, Gainesville
University of North Florida, Jacksonville
University of South Florida, Tampa
University of West Florida, Pensacola

Native Peoples, Cultures, and Places of the Southeastern United States
Edited by Jerald T. Milanich

The Apalachee Indians and Mission San Luis, by John H. Hann and Bonnie G. McEwan (1998)
Florida's Indians from Ancient Times to the Present, by Jerald T. Milanich (1998)
Unconquered People: Florida's Seminole and Miccosukee Indians, by Brent R. Weisman (1999)
The Ancient Mounds of Poverty Point: Place of Rings, by Jon L. Gibson (2000)
Before and After Jamestown: Virginia's Powhatans and Their Predecessors, by Helen C. Rountree and E. Randolph Turner (2002); first paperback edition, 2005
Ancient Miamians: The Tequesta of South Florida, by William E. McGoun (2002)
The Archaeology and History of the Native Georgia Tribes, by Max E. White (2002); first paperback edition, 2005
The Calusa and Their Legacy: South Florida People and Their Environments, by Darcie A. MacMahon and William H. Marquardt (2004)
People of the Shoals: Stallings Culture of the Savannah River Valley, by Kenneth E. Sassaman (2006)

People of the Shoals

Stallings Culture of the Savannah River Valley

Kenneth E. Sassaman

Foreword by Jerald T. Milanich

University Press of Florida
Gainesville · Tallahassee · Tampa · Boca Raton
Pensacola · Orlando · Miami · Jacksonville · Ft. Myers

Printed in the United States of America on recycled, acid-free paper

11 10 09 08 07 06 6 5 4 3 2 1

All illustrations are by the author unless otherwise noted.

A record of cataloging-in-publication data is available from the Library of Congress.
ISBN 0-8130-2945-7

The University Press of Florida is the scholarly publishing agency for the State University System of Florida, comprising Florida A&M University, Florida Atlantic University, Florida Gulf Coast University, Florida International University, Florida State University, University of Central Florida, University of Florida, University of North Florida, University of South Florida, and University of West Florida.

University Press of Florida
15 Northwest 15th Street
Gainesville, FL 32611-2079
http://www.upf.com

Contents

Figures

Foreword

People of the Shoals tells the story of the Stallings Culture, American Indians who lived in the Savannah River valley 4,000 years ago. In this volume Kenneth Sassaman, a colleague of mine at the University of Florida and the acknowledged expert on these ancient people, skillfully weaves together information gleaned from numerous archaeological excavations to paint an engaging and close-up portrait of a southeastern society once lost to history.

The Stallings Culture was not unique. In ancient times many groups inhabited river valleys in what is now the southeastern United States. Communities of people moved in and out of those riverine settings, creating complex histories that can only be unraveled through careful excavations by archaeologists like Ken Sassaman.

Using the latest tools of the trade (methods of data collection and analysis that go far beyond shovels and trowels), Sassaman is one of a new generation of archaeologists who are providing us with unprecedented views of past life in those freshwater valleys. Fortunately for the Stallings people, he has chosen to study them and their several-hundred-year history, bringing them out of the past and into the present. Many other groups have yet to be investigated in similar detail.

In *People of the Shoals* Sassaman has crafted a book that describes numerous aspects of Stallings life and people, from feeding their families and finding suitable mates for marriage to honoring their dead. Along the way he leads his readers through the past and present archaeological projects that have uncovered events from four millennia ago. In doing so, he helps to trace the development of his discipline from its nineteenth-century roots to the highly complex science that it is today.

This is a wonderful and informative book, a readable synthesis that makes the Stallings people come alive for modern readers.

Jerald T. Milanich
Series Editor

Preface and Acknowledgments

Where the Savannah River descends from its elevated origins in the Appalachian Mountains and splays out on its rocky foundation near present-day Augusta, Georgia, an environment of unique character awaited the arrival of Native Americans. Modern impoundments have obscured its better qualities, hiding beneath still waters the many shoals and isles that made earth and river seem inseparable. For thousands of years shallow pools and riffles supported scores of fish and turtle species, as well as productive mussel habitat. Networks of boulders afforded both ready access to these aquatic riches and convenient stepping stones for fording the river. Bluffs rising on either side of the river offered refuge from the occasional floods that rendered otherwise idyllic surroundings inhospitable. Stands of hickory and oak throughout the adjoining Piedmont uplands complemented the river's potential to nurture human populations.

The bounty of the shoals and associated environs of the Savannah River long attracted Native Americans. If the number and diversity of artifacts from sites in the vicinity of Augusta are any indication, the area indeed was a mecca of prehistoric settlement. Virtually all known prehistoric cultures of the region are represented, from the early Clovis hunters who benefited from game crossings at the shoals to the Mississippian corn farmers who cultivated nearby floodplain flats. Evidence suggests that the first 8,000 years of prehistory involved only transient use of the middle Savannah River valley. The hunter-gatherers of these early millennia were mobile people whose annual rounds took them from the mountains to the coast. Their groups were comparatively small, their technology simple yet highly effective. Periodic bursts of innovation and the occasional interlopers did little to interrupt what was apparently a stable, highly successful lifestyle.

But stability had run its course, and eventually dramatic change shook the area. Beginning some 4,000 years ago, certain groups of hunter-gatherers relinquished the mobile lifestyle for a more settled existence along the river. The shoals became their homeland, their place of origin. Permanent settlements were established along the river's edge and on some of its larger islands. Distinctive new styles arose to invoke an ethnic identity apart from those of

Preface 1. Shoals of the Broad River near Columbia, South Carolina, with a close-up of the many shallow pools amid cobbles and exposed bedrock.

forebears and neighbors. For the next few centuries the middle Savannah area would be the unmistakable domain of the People of the Shoals.

Today, in the language of modern archaeology, these ancient people are referred to as the Stallings Culture. Their namesake is Stallings Island, a large, teardrop-shaped island 13 km up the Savannah River from Augusta. A gentleman by the name of Charles C. Jones Jr. brought this important site to public light in 1861. Jones was duly impressed by the mound-like accumulation of freshwater shell in the center of the island, but he was especially awestruck by human skeletons hidden beneath its surface. He speculated in 1873 that Stallings Island was a "huge necropolis," a monument to the ancients, "designed to perpetuate . . . the devotion to which the Indians of this region cherished the peace, the security, the memory of their dead."

Preface 2. View of Stallings Island in the middle Savannah River from the bank on the Georgia (west) side. Archaeological deposits are concentrated in the location of the three electrical pylons in the center of the island.

Jones's epitaphic sense of Stallings Island notwithstanding, it would be many decades before archaeologists would begin to piece together the details of Stallings prehistory. A large expedition mounted by Harvard University in the late 1920s showed us that Stallings Island was more than an island for the dead. Tons of domestic refuse were scattered throughout its heaps of shell and dark, loamy soil. Among the garbage were thousands of fragments of a low-fired pottery made from clay and Spanish moss. Lines of punctations marked the outsides of these sherds, some arranged in elaborate displays of curved and rectangular motifs. These traits proved to be the hallmark of Stallings Culture, the calling card by which archaeologists would recognize Stallings as a distinct people. Later, with the advent of radiocarbon dating, archaeologists would learn that this unusual pottery was among the oldest in North America, a discovery that propelled Stallings Culture into the limelight of world prehistory.

Other expeditions to Stallings Island came and went, teaching us a bit more each time. Even so, as knowledge accumulated, many basic questions went unanswered. Who were the Stallings people, and what delivered them to a settled existence on the river? How many people occupied Stallings Island, and for how long? What sort of relationships did these people have with one another and with their neighbors? What ultimately happened to the Stallings people?

Ironic as it may seem, Stallings Island itself has been the biggest impediment to advancing knowledge of Stallings prehistory. Most investigations were conducted using methods that destroyed or ignored evidence that archaeologists consider important today. For instance, food remains were not consistently collected. Neither were small artifacts, the by-products of tool manufacture, or data on the size and contents of the many pit features that Stallings folks had dug.

But even if all the excavations at Stallings Island were conducted in the most up-to-date, scientific fashion feasible, we still would have just part of the story, for it is only one of many sites. It is an important site, no doubt, perhaps of the enormous significance ascribed to it by C. C. Jones, but still only one site. In the surrounding area lie scores of other sites, including small shell middens, sites lacking shell, and quarries, along with one other large shell "mound." Each of these locations contains important pieces of the puzzle as to the origins, heyday, and ultimate demise of Stallings Culture.

Assembling these scattered pieces has been the chore of modern archaeologists. Prompted by development, vandalism, or just plain curiosity, recent work at several sites in the middle Savannah River valley has greatly enhanced our outlook on Stallings Culture. Success in this regard is due in great measure to the clarity of small sites. Unlike Stallings Island, which was occupied for many centuries and resulted in a complex matrix of shell layers, burials, and other features, small sites in the area have more limited occupational histories and thus greater clarity. In a sense, these are the snapshots of the past, time-lapse photos of the unfolding of Stallings prehistory.

Enough pieces have been assembled to relate a fairly detailed story about Stallings Culture. That is the purpose of this volume. From my perspective as an archaeologist, I have two stories to tell here. One, of course, is the history of the rise and fall of Stallings Culture. As we will see, this is a history of immense drama, not the bland recounting of hunter-gatherer lifeways to which we have become accustomed. Ironically, this rich and exciting history emerges from the minute details of everyday life: how Stallings people fed their families, found suitable mates, and honored their dead. From these details we learn how Stallings Culture arose among tensions between genders and ethnic groups, how its circumscribed, insular qualities pitted family obligations against cultural tradition. And we will see how Stallings Culture became the victim of its own customs, falling apart only to form again under new guise.

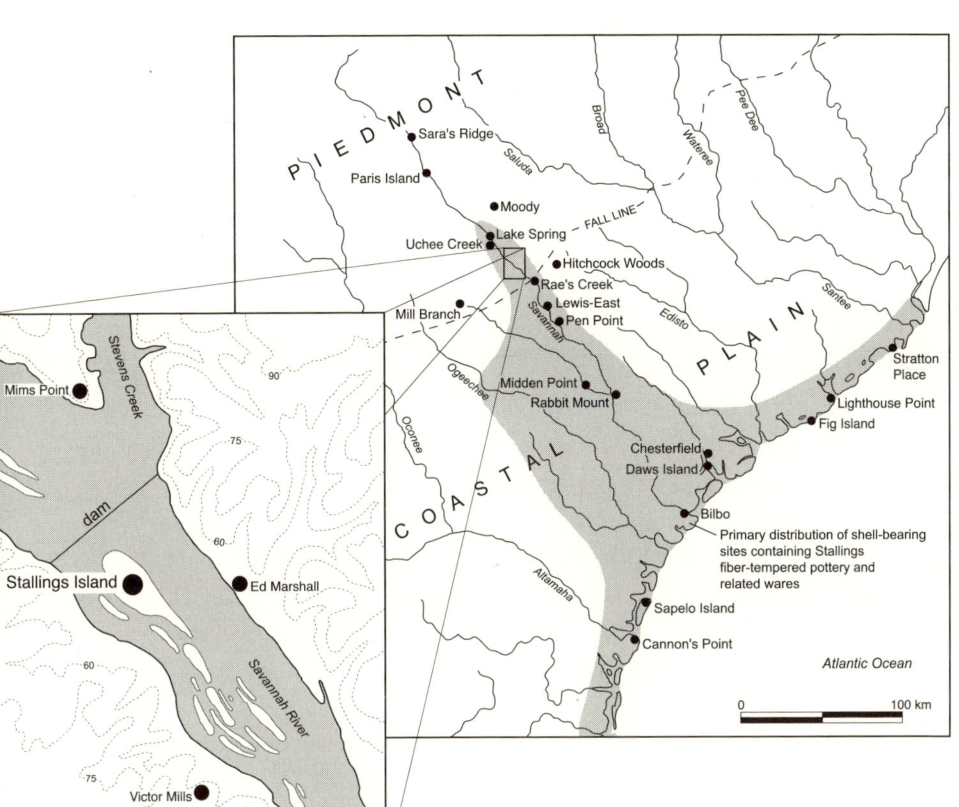

Preface 3. Map of the greater Savannah River valley and surrounding region (showing locations of sites mentioned in the text) and an inset topographic map of the middle Savannah River area (showing locations of Stallings Island, Mims Point, Ed Marshall, and Victor Mills sites).

The second story is about the archaeology that brings Stallings history to light. It is a tale of hard science, the painstaking excavating and analysis that enable detailed chronology, accurate dietary information, and the reconstruction of community patterning. And it is a tale of theory and humanism, for the potsherds and bones of prehistory cannot speak for themselves. The interpretations that I provide here are among the many alternative voices existing in today's archaeology. I do not pretend to have the complete, accurate story of Stallings prehistory, if such a thing is even feasible. Nonetheless, those generally familiar with hunter-gatherer prehistory in the Southeast will find many new insights in the pages that follow. My goal is to stretch the boundaries of interpretation without surpassing the limits of scientific plausibility. To the extent that I succeed in this effort, my wish is that the archaeology of the People of Shoals will inspire further humanistic study of other hunter-gatherer populations of the Southeast.

My intended audience is the interested public, fledgling archaeologists, and professional colleagues who enjoy a good story. I am compelled to specify my readership because two reviewers of a draft of this book were caught off guard by the casual tone of my writing. To those readers and others of like mind I offer assurance that the usual scientific treatment of Stallings archaeology is in the works. This book is not intended as a substitute for the technical reports that I am obliged to write as a member of a profession. But archaeologists have other obligations, too, notably to communicate with the public the results of our research (much of it, in my case, funded or licensed by public consent). Perhaps I should have issued the technical reports before writing a popular account, but that matters little to an archaeologist who finds it difficult to draw a sharp line between science and storytelling.

A Note on Chronology

Archaeological chronology since the 1950s has been constructed primarily from age estimates provided by radiocarbon dating. A number of factors cause radiocarbon age estimates to deviate from the actual age of the materials dated, so scientists have developed methods for calibrating radiocarbon years to calendar years. Throughout this book, all age estimates are given as calibrated radiocarbon years and are reported herein as years before present or, in shorthand, simply B.P. The actual difference between calibrated and radiocarbon age estimates tends to increase with age. For the period in question (some 5,800–3,600 calendar years ago), calibrated age estimates exceed the corresponding radiocarbon age estimates by as little as two and as many as eight (calendar) centuries. For instance, radiocarbon estimates for the oldest Stallings pottery are approximately 4450 radiocarbon years B.P.; the calibrated age estimates are almost 5100 years B.P. In another example, the abandonment of Stallings Island is dated to about 3500 radiocarbon years B.P., which is calibrated to about 3800 B.P.

For all age estimates, calibrated or not, a range of time is reported to reflect the probability that the event being dated actually occurred during the estimated time span. Although necessary from a scientific perspective, age ranges (for example, 4150–3830 B.P.) are difficult to convey in common language. For the purposes of this book, I choose to discuss ages simply as rough estimates of calendar years before present, generally to the nearest half-century, using qualifiers such as "approximately" or "about" when necessary. In the few cases where I use actual radiocarbon age estimates, both the actual radiocarbon age and the calibrated age are provided, with the appropriate statistical measures of probability.

The reader should not take any of this discussion to mean that archaeologists do not have a good handle on the actual ages of the cultures and events they hope to understand. The problem with chronology just discussed ultimately stems from the time differences between the rhythms of natural phenomena used for radiocarbon dating (in this case the atmospheric production of radioactive carbon) and the culturally determined units of measurement inherent in calendrical time. As the science of radiocarbon dating continues to improve, methods for relating radiocarbon to actual age will become more precise and more reliable. For now I trust current knowledge about calibration of radiocarbon dates to report here the best age estimates available (in calendar years before present [B.P.]) for the events of Stallings prehistory and concede that these estimates will change as further refinements in chronology are made.

Acknowledgments

I have been working on Stallings archaeology for some 15 (calendar, not radiocarbon) years and in that time have relied on the good resources of many people and institutions. None of the research reported herein would have been possible without the ubiquitous and generous support of the Savannah River Archaeological Research Program (SRARP) under the direction of Mark J. Brooks. I benefited from 11 years of working with the SRARP under the philosophy established by its founder, Glen T. Hanson: that compliance archaeology must be guided by research agendas. Most of the field projects involving Stallings sites were located outside the confines of the Savannah River Site, the 300-square-mile government installation that the SRARP is charged to manage archaeologically. That I had ample time and resources to work on these "extracurricular" projects speaks to the good wisdom of SRARP management and its U.S. Department of Energy sponsors to cultivate regional-scale knowledge to inform local research significance. Members of the home institution of the SRARP, the South Carolina Institute of

Archaeology and Anthropology (SCIAA), were equally supportive of these research efforts.

Other sponsors of my Stallings research include the National Science Foundation, National Geographic Society, American Philosophical Society, United States Forest Service, Augusta State University, and University of Florida. My thanks to Alan Gruber and the Archaeological Conservancy for research access to Stallings Island. Diana DiPaolo Loren and others at Harvard's Peabody Museum made collections and archives available for study on several occasions. My thanks as well to curators of collections that I examined at repositories spanning several states: Sharon Pekrul (SCIAA), Martha Zierden (Charleston Museum), Eugene Futato (University of Alabama), Steve Davis (University of North Carolina), and Gordon Blaker (Augusta Museum).

The list of folks who contributed time and energy to fieldwork and/or lab work is immense, but those with more than passing involvement deserve special thanks. These include, in no particular order, George Lewis, Kevin Eberhard, Keith Stephenson, Dan Elliott, Kristin Wilson, Melanie Cabak, James Bates, Wictoria Rudolphi, Tammy Forehand, Mark Brooks, Gifford Waters, Jamie Anderson Waters, Meggan Blessing, Asa Randall, Peter Hallman, Pat O'Day, Kara Bridgman, Beth Auten, Sharyn Jones O'Day, and Renee Walker. I have benefited enormously from the insights and encouragement of colleagues working independently on similar research, notably David Anderson, Dan Elliott, Jerald Ledbetter, Bill Stanyard, Ray Crook, Cheryl Claassen, Mike Russo, Becky Saunders, and Victor Thompson. I thank Jon Gibson for writing a book about Poverty Point that inspired me to approach this project with creativity and Tim Pauketat for blazing the trail that I like to follow through the theoretical morass of Americanist archaeology.

Portions of this book were adapted from a series of popular articles on Stallings culture I wrote for *Legacy*, the newsletter of the South Carolina Institute of Archaeology and Anthropology. My thanks to editor Nena Powell Rice for permission to use these passages. Comments on a draft of this book by Jerald Milanich, Jim Stoltman, and Joe Saunders were helpful in refining its content and style. I thank Meredith Morris Babb, John Byram, and the staff of the University Press of Florida for everything that a great press does and for their patience with my delays and pesky questions. My thanks to Mike Russo, Chris Judge, and Viva Fisher for assistance in acquiring illustrations and/or permission to use them. I am deeply grateful to Brad Sullivan for the artwork that adorns the cover of this book. Asa Randall photographed many of the artifacts illustrated herein and helped with a number of the line drawings. Both he and Meggan Blessing commented on an earlier draft and were always willing subjects in lengthy, convoluted discussions about Stallings culture. I am especially grateful to Meggan for appreciating my preoccupation with all of this.

Prologue

Stallings Island, 3793 B.P.

They left the island that day for the last time. No one spoke as they packed their belongings and loaded canoes for the journey downriver. The usually energetic waters of the surrounding rapids were equally subdued. After ten generations of reaping the bounty of the middle Savannah River, the People of the Shoals had to find a new way.

As their ancestors had done long ago, they would relocate and start anew. Mobility was in their blood, but the past few decades had witnessed a level of settlement permanence like nothing before. No one tried to explain how they came to be so sedentary, but most knew it was unnatural and detrimental. The shoals continued to supply them with the fish, turtles, and clams for daily fare, but increasingly the social demands of alliance were impinging on people's time and patience. The women had to work harder each year to collect enough food for ritual feasts, too often at the behest of their in-laws. Increasingly away on trading ventures, their husbands and sons were of little help. Some families had trouble finding prospective mates for their daughters. Two of the clans with whom they had traditionally intermarried had abandoned the area years ago. Feuding with one of the two remaining clans had grown intolerable.

Indeed there were plenty of reasons for leaving the island for good. The elders knew better than anyone that the main reason for leaving was the constant bickering among themselves.

When they first came to the middle Savannah region some three centuries before, the ancestors of the People of the Shoals were a tight-knit community. Legend held that they arose from the place where the progenitor, Mother Turtle, first poked her head up from the waters that once covered the earth. Children learned that this place lay to the west of the Great Mountains, though few in recent generations had the chance to travel that far. Like the middle Savannah, the homeland of the Ancients was a bountiful place, rich in fish, mussels, deer, hickory nuts, and acorns. For centuries the people thrived in harmony with nature. Eventually, as their numbers grew and resources dwindled, the balance was disrupted, and it became time to leave. The

People of the Shoals took some solace in knowing that their fate was that of their ancestors.

When the Ancients arrived in the Savannah River valley they encountered another people. These strangers were first seen on the island in the summer, living in small, scattered huts. The island apparently held great spiritual meaning to them, for it was the resting place of their ancestors. Despite its significance, the island was routinely abandoned in late summer as the community dispersed into the adjacent uplands to hunt deer and collect nuts. The People of the Hills, as they came to be known to the interlopers, preferred a mobile existence over life on the river.

Downstream from the island was a vast stretch of unoccupied river and land. A two-day canoe ride delivered them to a place where the river coursed like a snake. Among the winding bends and loops of channels were innumerable ponds and shallow swamps. The Ancients recognized this as a particularly rich environment, teeming with the resources on which they had come to depend, along with some, like the alligator, that were totally unfamiliar. The new land likewise offered abundant stone for making traditional spearpoints, knives, and other tools. This rock was different in color and texture from the rock that they were used to working, but it proved amenable to the heat-treating that was their custom. Missing from the area were other types of stone, the sorts used to prepare meals. The Ancients would need to develop alternatives to their stone-boiling method of cooking. The pottery that later became the hallmark of the People of the Shoals had its origins in the resourcefulness that a stone-poor land would encourage.

Another two-day canoe ride downstream delivered the people to the Edge of the World. Few among them had ever seen the ocean, but all had learned about it through story and song. To them the universe was a vast body of water, with the earth suspended over it by four cords, one at each of the four cardinal directions. Legend held that the Edge of the World was a place of mixed blessings. It offered vast supplies of fish, shellfish, and other water creatures; but it was devoid of stone, and any imbalance between people and nature brought a wrath of wind and rain like nothing ever seen in the land of rivers.

When the ancestors of the People of the Shoals arrived at the mouth of the Savannah, they found places where shellfish remains and other refuse had been piled up. They recognized this as human refuse, but not a single person was to be found. It would be days before someone spotted two canoes being paddled far offshore. No one tried to make contact with these strangers, for those able to venture so far from land might command malevolent power. The ancestors would meet these people in due time; for now, they settled on temporary camps a full day's ride upriver.

It was spring when the ancestors arrived in the lower Savannah. The ensuing months proved peaceful though busy as individuals pursued new resources and opportunities. The lack of oak and hickory trees in the immediate area worried many of the women, for the acorns and nuts they provided each fall were the staples of winter. The men began to comment, too, about the limited supply of deer and turkey. Clearly this stretch of the river had an endless supply of catfish, mud turtles, and water plants, even for the winter; but if they wanted to keep using traditional foods, forays into the hills were necessary. Many among them recalled the dense stands of oak and hickory trees of the middle Savannah, the place they first encountered in this new land, where the People of the Hills lived. They debated the need to confront these strangers, aware that long-term success in the area depended greatly on strong alliances with neighbors. The elders among them had much experience with diplomacy, for their territory in the homeland was surrounded by the territories of five other tribes. They decided to send a small contingent upriver to make friends with the People of the Hills.

Their good intentions proved difficult to realize. No one was seen on two consecutive trips in the early fall, and a small group of people fled from the river's edge when encountered on a third trip the following winter. They would later learn that the People of the Hills typically avoided strangers. The elders decided that further efforts to meet their neighbors would be postponed until the spring, when the island of their ancestors was again occupied. In the meantime they continued to make occasional hunting forays upriver. Anticipating future nut-gathering ventures, the hunters made mental maps of the best stands of oak and hickory.

Four more winters would pass before regular contact was established with the People of the Hills. Interactions at first were awkward, for these long-time residents lacked any sort of formal leaders or diplomats. As the newcomers learned, certain individuals among the People of the Hills were more inclined than others to enter into alliances. The more eager among them introduced their neighbors to some of the local traditions and special knowledge. They showed how a soft rock from nearby outcrops could be carved into flat stones and perforated with a stone drill to make cooking stones. The ancestors of the

People of the Shoals knew about this sort of material from their homeland over the mountains, but they had never seen it used for cooking. Many of them took samples back to their Coastal Plain camps, where they used the stones in earth ovens and with water-filled baskets and hide-lined pits in the traditional stone-boiling technique of cooking. Unlike most types of rock, this soft stone never broke when it was heated and cooled. Everyone marveled at its superior qualities, but some warned of the folly of becoming dependent on a raw material from such a great distance and under another people's control. Still, several households established strong ties with the People of the Hills and were rewarded with a constant supply of cooking stones.

As communication between the two groups improved, the ancestors of the People of the Shoals began to learn some things about their coastal neighbors. Long ago the People of the Hills had maintained regular contact with these far-away people. They traded a few items between them, mostly things of a symbolic or spiritual nature. The People of the Hills offered polished stone objects in exchange for marine shell beads and other ornaments. Occasionally the coastal people would ask for some deer meat and hides, for the local supply was relatively sparse. To entice trade, the coastal dwellers shared their folk knowledge about the healing power of shell beads. On trading trips down to the coast, the People of the Hills had observed small children wearing strings of beads. The spiritual power of the beads, they were told, would ward off the evil forces that often stole children's souls.

Contact between the two groups was irregular. There were periods of many months, sometimes several years, when the coastal people seemed to have vanished. When interactions were reestablished, the coastal folk would tell about great forces that swelled up from the ocean, bringing hard rain and powerful wind. Entire villages were destroyed, and many people drowned. The cause of destruction was uncertain, but they knew that those struck directly by such forces had to abandon their homeland for good. Some blamed the People of the Hills for their problems.

Nearly a full generation had elapsed since the People of the Hills had last been in touch with their coastal partners. The elders among them were not especially eager to seek out their former allies, although they would invite the opportunity to acquire more marine shell. Virtually all of the shell beads obtained in years past now lay buried with the dead on the island. They believed strongly in the healing and protective power of the beads, for on many occasions children stricken with illness survived by wearing strands of beads.

Those who did not survive took beads with them into the spirit world. Other media and practices of healing were used too, but nothing surpassed the beads in potency and effectiveness.

The People of the Hills began to ask their new partners about sources of marine shell. Not having established contact with the phantom coastal people, the ancestors of the People of the Shoals had nothing specific to offer. Still, some saw this as an opportunity to improve their diplomatic relations with the People of the Hills. As newcomers, they would have to establish lasting relations with neighbors for purposes of marriage. Indeed, there were far too few members of the immigrant group to satisfy demands for eligible partners. Competition for mates had already gotten hard, so anything that people could do to make themselves valuable to their neighbors could prove beneficial to brokering marriages. Several individuals invited the opportunity to make contact with the coastal people.

A contingent of three men and one of the elder women set off downriver one summer to find the People of the Coast. At the mouth of the great river they again located the piles of shell and food refuse observed on earlier ventures to the ocean. This time among the refuse they noticed pieces of a hard, earth-colored substance that looked a bit like rock, though not like anything they normally used. They also saw small pieces of the soft rock that they acquired from the People of the Hills.

Stretching out from the mouth of the great river was a vast landscape of marshes, islands, and open water. The explorers decided to paddle southward between the mainland and a series of long islands. The calm waters of this sheltered passage enabled quick travel. After only half a day they arrived at the head of the largest island yet seen, where smoke arose from several places just past a line of low, scrubby trees. Before long they were approached by a small party of men in canoes. Although they were unable to decipher what was being said to them, the explorers understood that they were to follow these men toward the place of the smoke.

Paddling their way along a small inlet amid marsh grasses and mudflats, the group arrived at an open area with an enormous ring of shell. As they left their canoes and climbed to the top of the shell heap, the explorers could see that this was a large village. Along the top of the ring of shell they counted no fewer than two dozen huts. Few people were seen in and among the huts, but from the high vantage point they noticed a large group of women and children collecting food in the marsh below.

Prologue 1. View of Fig Island shell ring complex from the air (photo courtesy of Christopher Judge).

The explorers were invited inside one of the huts and offered some water and smoked fish. Their attention was drawn to the containers lying about on the floor. The baskets were not all that different from their traditional wares, but the hard, earth-colored vessels were strange. This, they decided, must be the source of the unusual objects that they saw at the mouth of the river. Noticing their curiosity about the vessels, one of their hosts pulled several objects out of a basket and began placing them in one of the hard containers. They recognized one of the objects as a soft cooking stone, just like those they got from the People of the Hills; the others were round, not flat, and colored like the hard vessels. Excited to see something familiar, the elder woman reached into her traveling bag and extracted a soft cooking stone. Everyone seemed pleased about the shared experience.

Relations with the People of the Coast grew strong. In time the ancestors of the People of the Shoals would learn how to make the hard containers of their coastal neighbors, which came to be known to them as pottery. They also learned about making cooking stones from clay. These proved to be less effective than stones made from soft rock, but they were easy to make. The People of the Coast preferred clay stones over soft stones because access to the soft stones depended on alliances with the People of the Hills, distrusted by some.

With each passing generation, the ancestors of the People of the Shoals developed stronger ties with both their coastal and upriver neighbors. This was advantageous to the group, for they had many alliance partners to choose from. But it also caused problems, because individual families and clans tended to ally more with one group than with the other. This was especially troublesome when the ancestors of the People of the Shoals tried to do things together as a group, like collecting and drying fish from the great spring runs. Too often they found themselves bickering over the allocation of food. Some resented having to work so hard to see so much of the supply traded away to allies that were of no consequence to them personally.

Eventually the group agreed to split. Those who had nurtured good relations with the People of the Hills relocated permanently to the middle Savannah area. The move was not difficult, for they had spent an increasing amount of time each year at the place of the shoals. Not everyone was happy about it, however. Ever since encountering the newcomers, certain members of the People of the Hills discouraged too much interaction. They feared that marriages between them would erode traditional values and practices. They had already seen how more and more of the younger generation chose to stay near the river year-round instead of migrating into the adjoining hills for the cool season. With diminishing help from the young adults, the fall hunts and nut-collecting forays had become less productive.

Only the wisest elders of the People of the Hills predicted the peril that would befall those choosing to reside on the river permanently. And now, some 300 years later, as everyone abandoned the island forever, those predictions had come true. Since taking up permanent residence in the middle Savannah, the group had become a distinctive people, known to their coastal and upland neighbors as the People of the Shoals. Their dress, foodways, and architecture were intentionally distinct from those of others. Strict rules governing alliance and marriage prevented the spread of different ideas and practices, insulating the People of the Shoals from the sorts of cultural influences of their history. Certainly they interacted with others and upheld the custom of marrying outside one's lineage, but now the elders controlled dealings with "foreigners." Interactions and marriages were generally restricted to those residing on Brier Creek and the Ogeechee River to the west. These were communities that split off from the People of the Shoals soon after they took up permanent residence in the middle Savannah.

Times were good for many generations of the People of the Shoals. Food was plentiful, relations with neighbors peaceful, and most were satisfied with their options for alliance and marriage. But life had slowly grown more difficult. The strict rules governing interactions with others made it hard to be flexible in times of need. Alliances with the other river communities were supposed to solve occasional food shortages and other crises, but these proved too rigid in many cases. Factions within communities were in constant conflict over access to the best shellfish beds and fishing spots. Like the ancestors before them, they were never able to take full advantage of the spring shad and sturgeon runs due to lack of cooperation. Households had even resorted to hiding nut stores to prevent the inevitable mooching. Above all, they found it difficult simply to pick up and move away for short periods, as the People of the Hills had always done to alleviate disputes.

This time their breakup would be thorough and irreparable. The fabric of social life would hereafter be so different as to disrupt oral tradition. Their history would be altered in myth and song to fit their new circumstances. With no one willing or able to carry the traditions of the People of the Shoals, their life and times would dissolve. Little did they know as the island faded from sight and from memory that the history of their ancestors would someday be resurrected from the refuse that they left behind.

Stallings Island, June 3, 1999

We left the island this afternoon for the last time. Each day for the past three weeks we had traveled to and from the site in a 15-foot jon boat, taking three, sometimes four, trips to get everyone and everything there and back. Our mission was to locate and map the back-filled trench of a 1929 Harvard-sponsored dig and to collect samples for radiocarbon dating. The strategy called for a backhoe to remove the old fill. Unfortunately, an offer to barge over heavy equipment fell through, and the Army Reserve was reluctant to drop a backhoe by cargo helicopter for fear of clipping the power lines that spanned the island on three pylons. We faced the prospects of removing some 200 cubic meters of clay-rich fill by hand. I was grateful to have so many volunteers on this trip.

Locating the old trench was not easy. Seventy years of weathering and

Prologue 2. View of the University of Florida expedition to Stallings Island in 1999, facing southeast. Decades of looting at the site have left its surface pocked and eroded (photo by Kenneth Garrett, courtesy of National Geographic Society).

some three decades of intensive looting had obliterated the trench profile in virtually every place we looked. I had never seen looting as bad as this. The entire surface of the site was like a lunar landscape, pocked with holes ranging up to 5 m wide and more than 2 m deep. As we continued to clear the ground cover to facilitate mapping, the severity of looting grew more conspicuous. I remember thinking rashly on the third day that the site was completely destroyed; that the National Geographic Society, sponsors of the dig, would be disappointed; and that the Archaeological Conservancy, the new landowners, had acquired a worthless property.

It was the same feeling that I had the first time I saw a looted shell-midden site. Some ten years earlier I was told about a place in Burke County, Georgia, that was being looted. I had just completed a draft of my dissertation on early pottery and was eager to do some fieldwork.

When we arrived at the Midden Point site in January 1991, only a few square meters of a large shell midden remained. The looting was especially thorough in most places. Being so close to the quarries of so-called Coastal Plain chert, Midden Point was chock-full of spear points and other flaked stone tools. Strewn about on the surface were the animal bones, pottery sherds, and flake debris left behind by relic seekers. Beer cans and food wrappers were further testimony to the illicit activities.

Despite its damage, Midden Point provided important data. Our test excavations revealed a stratified sequence of shell, bone, and cultural debris 2 m deep, spanning three centuries of occupation. Good samples of pottery and stone and bone tools were collected from these intact layers, including a cache of five chert bifaces in a shallow pit. We likewise recovered a rich assemblage of animal bone, including evidence for an extinct species of fish heretofore unknown to science.

Little did I know that this experience at Midden Point would recur repeatedly over the ensuing decade as I responded to requests to salvage what we could from looted shell-midden sites. Each of seven field expeditions at four other sites in the middle Savannah region began with me bemoaning the severity of looting and limited potential for intact deposits. And each time I left in wonder at the wealth of information that can be gleaned from such badly damaged sites. Our expedition to Stallings Island this year was no exception.

We left the island after three weeks of difficult digging, having located dozens of undisturbed pit features and a stratified sequence of intact shell midden 3 m deep. I would need to rent a truck to get everything back to the University of Florida. It was a fitting end to a decade's worth of fieldwork.

1

Prelude to Prehistory

Stallings Island is a National Landmark in the middle Savannah River, some 13 km upstream from Augusta, Georgia. The site is the namesake for the oldest pottery in North America and those who made it, people of Stallings Culture. I refer to them as the People of the Shoals, for the stretch of river occupied by Stallings Island was rocky shallows before it was inundated by the dams and floodpools of the past century. The island today is but one of a few erosional remnants high enough to survive flooding. The highest portion of this 26-acre landform contains the so-called shell mound, the locus of intensive prehistoric habitation and resultant archaeological deposits.

Stallings Island is a famous site, known well to archaeologists and looters alike. No fewer than 12 excavations on the island have been conducted in the past 140 years. Several of the digs were reported in print; more of them went unreported. Until recently, illegal digging was rampant. The island is currently the property of the Archaeological Conservancy, an Albuquerque-based nonprofit organization that acquires and protects important archaeological sites in the United States. Professional investigations on the island are now under the careful watch of the Archaeological Conservancy, which is resolved to protect it from looting through surveillance and law enforcement. Our recent work proved it was a site well worth saving.

Views on Stallings Island and its people have changed with each passing investigation. Charles C. Jones, the nineteenth-century antiquarian, dug indiscriminately into the large shell-midden deposits seeking human skeletons and artifacts. As noted in the preface, his emphasis on burials led him to suggest that Stallings Island was a dedicated cemetery. Certainly Jones noticed the thousands of items of domestic refuse—pottery, animal bones, and cracked rock—strewn about the midden, even mixed with the pit fill of burials. But he never commented on this sort of evidence except to suggest that the island was used often. Jones instead surmised that the local "tribes" occupied adjacent upland sites to avoid occasional floods and came to the island primarily to inter and honor their deceased.

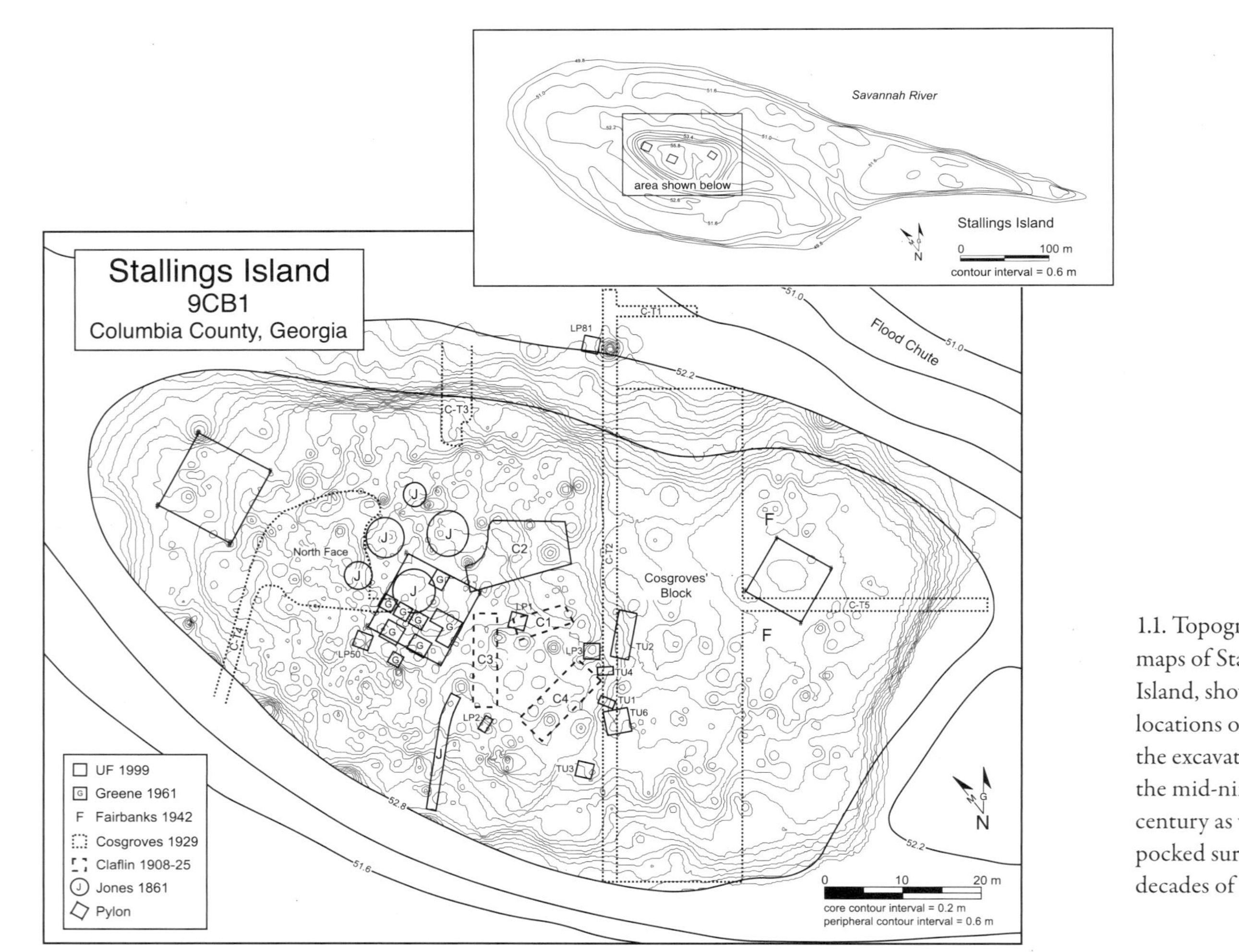

1.1. Topographic maps of Stallings Island, showing locations of most of the excavations since the mid-nineteenth century as well as the pocked surface from decades of looting.

1.2. View facing southeast of the 1929 excavation of Stallings Island sponsored by the Peabody Museum of Archaeology and Ethnology, Harvard University. (Photo by William H. Claflin Jr., *The Stalling's Island Mound, Columbia County, Georgia,* Papers of the Peabody Museum of American Archaeology and Ethnology, Harvard University, vol. 14, no. 1, 1931. Reprinted courtesy of the Peabody Museum, Harvard University.)

Jones's work inspired William Claflin, the son of a Massachusetts governor, to conduct his own excavations in the early decades of the last century. Claflin made several expeditions to the island and amassed an enormous collection of artifacts as well as several human skeletons. He understood the island's deposits as the work of mostly one people, the Stallings people, who not only buried their dead there but also lived among the dead. Claflin's early work was important in establishing that habitation took place, but his techniques of digging were insufficient to amass a convincing body of evidence.

Stratigraphic excavations continued at Stallings Island with the 1929 expedition headed by Charles and Harriet Cosgrove. Trained by the premier archaeologist of the American Southwest, Alfred V. Kidder, the Cosgroves appreciated the importance of careful excavation. They were the first to dig on a grid, sinking square test units oriented precisely on line. The Cosgroves were also the first to open a large block excavation and to recognize and excavate features other than burials. Agreeing with Claflin, they concluded that the site was indeed inhabited primarily by one "tribe": those who made the unusual pottery and left behind so much shell. They also recognized that below the deposits of this tribe were the remains of even earlier people.

Stallings Island was again dug into during the Great Depression. Charles H. Fairbanks, University of Chicago graduate and Works Progress Administration archaeologist, conducted limited excavations for the purpose of making a trait list. Fairbanks was trained in the tradition of culture history, a paradigm in American archaeology that emphasized the formal definition of artifact types and other traits that would allow the reconstruction of local and regional cultural sequences. About this same time another prominent archaeologist, James B. Griffin of the University of Michigan, published type descriptions for Stallings pottery based on a collection of sherds from a shell-ring site near the South Carolina coast. Now comparative studies could be conducted to determine the regional extent of Stallings Culture. Fairbanks took this a step further by adding flaked stone, ground stone, and bone tools to the inventory.

Growing interests in culture change guided the efforts of Florida archaeologist Ripley P. Bullen when he helped avocationalist H. Bruce Greene report limited excavations at Stallings Island in 1961. Greene dug through the site by layers, careful to keep the artifacts from the shell zone apart from the artifacts in the deeper, shell-free zone. Like others before him, Bullen reported that pottery was concentrated in the shell layers. But because Greene had emphasized the recovery of spearpoints and knives, Bullen directed his analysis toward the stratigraphic sequence of these artifact classes. He provided the first real numbers to demonstrate that point types in the lower zones were different from those of the upper zones. Fairbanks had combined these types in his trait list, perhaps unaware that his samples coincided with discrete layers.

The recognition of a marked change in culture history at Stallings Island set the stage for another round of excavation, this time by Donald Crusoe, then a graduate student at the University of Georgia. Like others in the 1960s, Crusoe approached the study of Stallings Culture from a regional perspective. His project was designed to collect data not only from Stallings Island but also from a series of shell-midden sites on the Georgia coast, where Stallings-like pottery was found.

When archaeologists like Crusoe first put some thought into the origins of Stallings Culture they were apparently struck by its unprecedented nature. Stallings was indeed innovative. It included the first shellfishing, the first pottery, and the first settled community life in the region. This new way of life stood in sharp contrast to the preceding era, causing some to speculate that Stallings was imported from far afield. The prominent southeastern archaeologist James A. Ford devoted much research to documenting similarities between Stallings Culture and the cultures of northern South America. He envisioned colonizing ventures from Colombia through the Caribbean and into Florida and eventually the coasts of South Carolina and Georgia. It was a romantic and exciting idea but considered by many archaeologists to be too fanciful and without supporting evidence.

Ford's timing was bad. When he published his ideas on Stallings origins in the 1960s, American archaeology was in the midst of a revolution. There were loud and strong urges for more scientific rigor in the field. Simple descriptions and reconstructions of prehistoric life were not enough. Explanation was the watchword, as archaeologists hurried to develop the methods and techniques of scientific inquiry. Out with the old went the concepts of migration and diffusion, and in with the new came an array of theories borrowed from the natural sciences. Ecological approaches to prehistory became especially popular.

The scientific revolution absorbed many American archaeologists, and the students of Stallings prehistory proved no exception. Stallings was now being viewed as an ecological phenomenon. Investigators began to look at environmental change as the impetus for shellfishing, at economic stress as the stimulus for pottery innovations, and at population growth as the cause for settled village life. Their focus was on local processes of change. They did not need to consider interactions among groups or long-distance influences to explain Stallings: the rise of Stallings Culture was a local ecological event.

This way of thinking has dominated hunter-gatherer archaeology worldwide since the late 1960s. It has many virtues and is indeed very scientific. But this ecological approach tends to overlook historical factors, such as group interactions and migrations, in favor of local environmental factors. We can certainly understand how historical events in the modern world redefine the identities and boundaries of cultures and ethnic groups. The breakup of the Soviet Union is a case in point. And anthropologists have been documenting similar historical circumstances among modern hunter-gatherers. They, like people everywhere, adjust their cultural practices to define their place in a complex web of global interactions.

I would not suggest that Stallings Culture arose from the sorts of geopolitical processes that we experience in the modern world, for that would be preposterous. But I do believe that group interactions, like the alliances and competitive relations described in the prologue, account for the rise of Stallings Culture, as well as its demise some 300 years later. Although my personal views on Stallings prehistory differ in many respects from those of my predecessors, I depend greatly on the foundation of knowledge that they built from careful excavation and analysis.

Recognizing Stallings Culture

The cornerstones of that foundation are the typological, chronological, and geographic parameters of Stallings Culture. Archaeologically, Stallings Culture sites are recognized by the presence of fiber-tempered pottery. This is a relatively distinctive trait that anyone can recognize from even the smallest fragments of pottery. Spanish moss or shredded palmetto fibers were intentionally added to the clay by Stallings potters for purposes not fully understood. These fibers were destroyed in the firing process, leaving behind tiny fissures or vesicles in the ceramic body. When a lot of fiber is used, the resulting pottery is very porous and light; when only a small bit of fiber is used, the pottery is solid and dense.

If we take fiber-tempered pottery as *the* defining trait of Stallings Culture, then Stallings Culture spanned nearly 2,000 years (ca. 5100–3150 years be-

1.3. Sherds of Stallings fiber-tempered pottery, showing classic drag-and-jab punctation designs.

fore present [B.P.]) and occupied an area that includes most of the Savannah River valley, coastal Georgia, and the southern half of the South Carolina coast. In fact, assemblages of fiber-tempered pottery are found even farther afield. Some are clearly different from Stallings, such as the Orange pottery of Florida and Wheeler pottery of the Midsouth. The relationships of others closer to the heartland of Stallings are not so obvious. For instance, fiber-tempered pottery from sites in the Oconee, Ocmulgee, and Chattahoochee river valleys of Georgia may be referred to as Stallings, but we know virtually nothing about the relationship of these sites to those of the Savannah River valley. Likewise, fiber-tempered pottery at sites in coastal North Carolina is sometimes called Stallings, yet there is a large gap between these locations and the heartland of Stallings. The point is that the mere use of fiber for tempering clay is not enough to define Stallings Culture adequately, especially if our goal is to trace its history in detail.

The decorations added to surfaces of fiber-tempered pottery help to identify different cultural traditions in the greater Savannah region. During the heyday of Stallings Culture in the middle Savannah, some 4,000 to 3,800 years ago, pots were decorated, usually with punctations. A linear design known today as "drag-and-jab" punctate was especially common. It was made by inserting a cut reed or other stylus into the wet clay at a low, oblique angle and then lifting, dragging, and inserting it again and again to form a continuous line of punctation. The angle of insertion, interval of punctation, orientation of the lines, and type of stylus used varied from pot to pot, ensuring that no two pots were exactly the same. Separate linear punctate, random punctate, incising, simple stamping, and plain wares were minority types during Classic Stallings times.

Long before the elaborate punctated pottery appeared, plain fiber-tempered pottery was typical in the Savannah River valley and often bore physical attributes that enable archaeologists to distinguish between early and late vessels, as we will see shortly below.

Fiber-tempered pottery from the coast of Georgia is a bit different from middle Savannah pottery. It consists of mostly plain ware throughout the period. Early plain pottery from the two locales is virtually indistinguishable, but the persistent popularity of plain wares on the coast stands in stark contrast to the pervasiveness of decorated wares later in the middle Savannah area. In addition, the decorated pottery from coastal Georgia sites, although a minority, is remarkably distinctive. Separate reed punctations and incising,

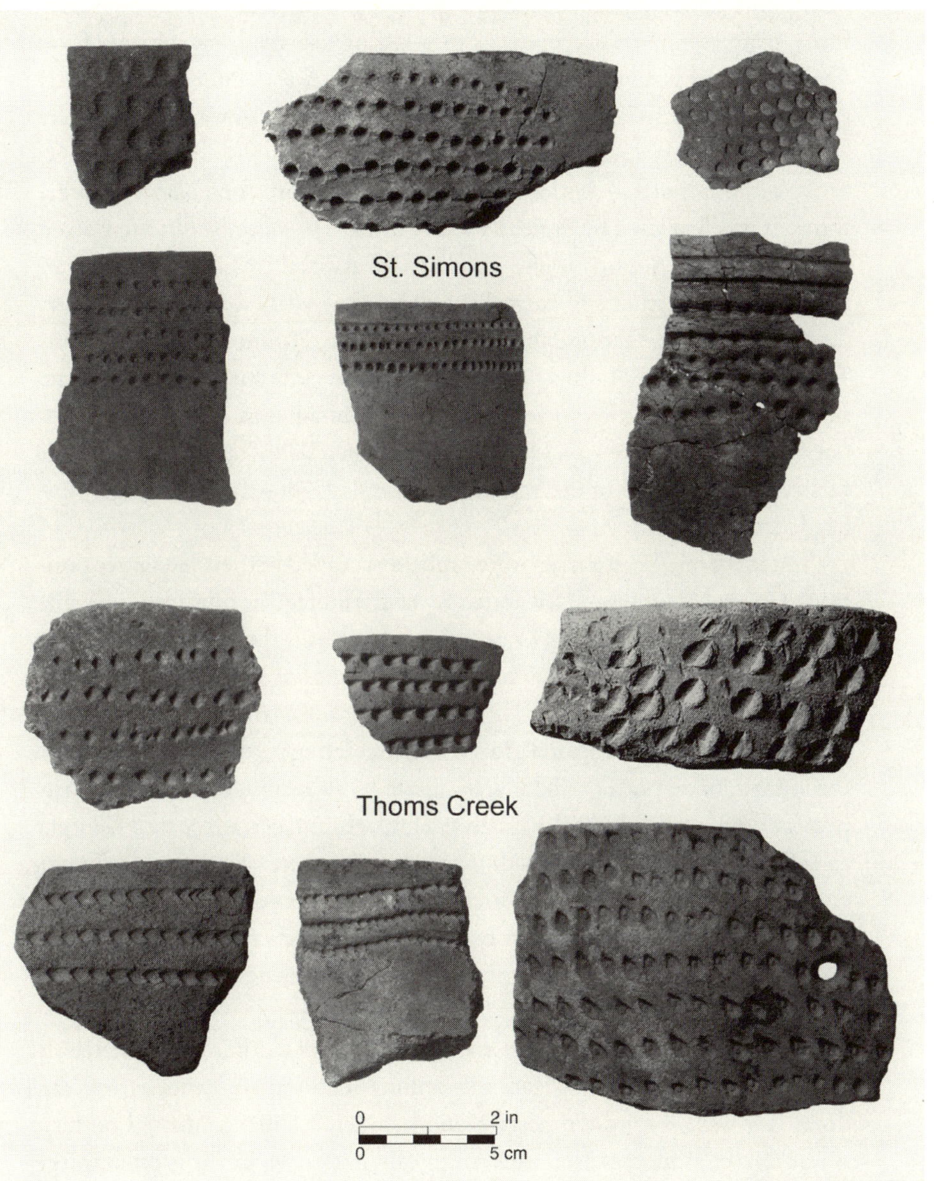

1.4. Sherds of St. Simons fiber-tempered pottery (top two rows) and Thoms Creek sand-tempered pottery (bottom two rows), showing types of decoration that characterize these wares.

shell point punctate, broad, shallow grooving, and linear punctations over incising are among the decorations that distinguish these assemblages from fiber-tempered pottery elsewhere. Taken together, the differences between coastal Georgia and Savannah River wares are sufficient to warrant a separate name for the coastal tradition.

St. Simons pottery is the accepted nomenclature for coastal Georgia wares. It was first used by Preston Holder in 1938 to describe fiber-tempered pottery from St. Simons Island and later formalized by Chester DePratter in a thorough synthesis of coastal sites. Over the years some archaeologists have expressed reservations about use of separate terminology for the coast. The founder of the Stallings nomenclature, James B. Griffin, felt that the similarities between the pottery from the Savannah and the Georgia coast outweighed the differences. He, and later Stephen Williams of Harvard University, advocated use of the Stallings terminology, but this went largely unheeded.

As it turns out, both parties were probably justified in their respective positions. Coastal Georgia and Savannah River assemblages are indistinguishable for the first several centuries of pottery-making, and there is no perceivable gap in the distribution of sites between the two areas. I am certain that we are looking at evidence for one large population at this time, no doubt subdivided into different residential groups but interacting regularly and sharing in the innovation of pottery-making. By about 4,000 years ago, when decorated pottery dominates middle Savannah assemblages and certain coastal Georgia assemblages, the repertoires of pottery design in the two areas are different enough to suggest that we are looking at distinct factions or ethnic groups. What is more, as we will see later on, coastal groups after this time used their pots for direct-heat cooking, an innovation that was never widely adopted among the People of the Shoals.

Pottery from the coast of South Carolina poses a different challenge to archaeologists trying to navigate the Stallings cultural landscape. There the dominant ware is sand-tempered or nontempered. Fiber-tempered pottery is not uncommon at coastal sites south of Charleston, but it is often intermingled with sand-tempered pottery bearing similar surface decorations. Separate reed punctate, shell point punctate, and drag-and-jab punctate are among the more common decorations along the south coast, with finger-pinched and simple stamped added to north coastal assemblages. As elsewhere, there is a trend from plain to decorated pottery on the South Carolina coast, although plain persists and may in fact rebound in popularity late in the sequence.

Diminished use of fiber and increased use of sand in the clay is another trend in the history of coastal pottery-making. Because this trend in temper appears to have preceded parallel developments in the middle Savannah area, it lends distinctiveness to the South Carolina coastal wares. By the time middle Savannah potters abandoned fiber in favor of sand for temper (ca. 3650 B.P.), the technologies in the two areas had grown markedly different in terms of wall thickness, vessel form, and lip design. Southward along the Georgia coastal zone fiber continued to be used for temper; sand was not added to clay throughout the period of early pot-making. The Savannah River delta was apparently a true boundary between South Carolina and Georgia populations.

Thoms Creek is the series name given to sand-tempered or untempered early pottery on the South Carolina coast and Coastal Plain. The namesake is actually a site near Columbia, South Carolina, some 275 km from the coast. Griffin was again responsible for the type descriptions; but Michael Trinkley is credited with the first synthetic treatment of Thoms Creek wares from the coast, and David Phelps contributed valuable data on assemblages from the interior. When David Anderson published a study of the distribution of pottery types in 1975, the full extent of Thoms Creek pottery became evident. It not only dominated the coastal zone but overlapped the distribution of Stallings wares throughout much of the Savannah River region. Trinkley added data to suggest that Thoms Creek was nearly as old as Stallings. Were the two pottery types made by the same people?

The relationship between Thoms Creek and Stallings pottery is not altogether clear. At an early stage they seem to share a broadly similar set of decorative forms, but later they diverge. Temper is the major difference, although virtually any assemblage of Stallings pottery includes sherds with both fiber and sand in the paste. These ambiguities decrease through time as Thoms Creek pottery from the coast becomes something markedly different from its counterparts in the interior.

The real challenge is discriminating among the various pottery types of sites in the interior. Two locales besides the middle Savannah include shell-midden sites that appear to have been occupied at roughly the same time. Those along Brier Creek, a major tributary of the Savannah River in Georgia, include mixtures of fiber- and sand-tempered sherds. Farther to the west, along the Ogeechee River, punctated pottery consists of mostly sand-tempered wares. Looking at decoration alone, we would be hard pressed to sort out the sherds from these various locales accurately. Besides the temper differences, however, the pottery from each locale is distinct in technological ways. This somewhat contradictory evidence suggests that potters from the three locales shared stylistic expressions, while barriers to interacting prevented across-the-board similarities in technology. It would be pointless, I think, to assert that one is Thoms Creek, the other Stallings, and the third something in between, as if these type names embody the secrets to cultural identity. I am more interested in understanding the histories of occupation and group interactions that led to these differences and similarities in material culture. In this spirit I regard the middle Savannah, Brier Creek, and Ogeechee River locales as all part of the greater Stallings Culture area, homeland to the People of the Shoals.

Dating Stallings Culture

When we look beyond the unusual temper to consider other attributes, we can see that Stallings pottery indeed provides a sound basis for culture history when found in good context. This all began with excavations at a site called Bilbo near the city of Savannah, Georgia. Antonio J. Waring Jr. was among a cadre of experienced and informed amateur archaeologists who became involved in the excavation of some of the area's most important sites. Waring dug into the Bilbo site in 1939 to find a deep, stratified sequence of shell, animal bone, and artifacts. Most of the pottery was fiber-tempered, and Waring was well-versed in the design repertoire of punctated and incised Stallings pottery. But dominating the Bilbo assemblage were sherds of plain fiber-tempered pottery, particularly in the lowest levels.

Waring's work at Bilbo provided the first solid evidence that the elaborate punctated pottery so well known from Stallings Island and elsewhere was preceded by an unassuming plain ware. Importantly, Waring also observed something about sherds in the lower levels that would later become an effective trait for discriminating truly early Stallings pottery from all other plain fiber-tempered pottery. Several of the rim sherds from the deepest levels at Bilbo had thickened or wedge-like lips, which lent them a T-shaped appearance when viewed in cross section. Because this lip form was absent among the plain rim sherds from higher levels at Bilbo, Waring speculated that it might be among the best attributes for identifying the beginnings of pottery-making in the region. My subsequent analysis of sherds from dozens of other sites bears this out. Plain fiber-tempered pottery fitted with thickened lips is the best marker for those I referred to earlier as the "ancestors" of the People of the Shoals.

The relative age of fiber-tempered pottery was well established by Waring from other excavations in the Savannah area. At both the Deptford and Refuge sites in the 1940s, Waring observed fiber-tempered pottery in strata beneath sand-tempered stamped wares now widely known as hallmarks of the Early and Middle Woodland periods.

The actual age of this early phase of Stallings prehistory would not be determined for years to come. The chief means of absolute dating in archaeology, radiocarbon dating, was not available until the 1950s, when a lab was established at the University of Michigan. Some of the first dates reported from the Michigan lab were run on samples of oyster shell from the Sapelo Shell Ring 1 on the Georgia coast. In 1950 Waring and Lewis Larson dug a trench into the side of the ring-shaped shell deposit and found plain fiber-tempered pottery throughout the fill. Shells from their trench were reported to be about 3,900 and 4,200 years old (*after* modern calibration; see the preface).

A few years later, Larson submitted a sample of oyster shell from another Georgia coastal site with plain fiber-tempered pottery. A calibrated age estimate of about of 4100 B.P. was returned on this sample from the Dulany site. A similar age estimate was obtained on a sample of charcoal from Stallings Island collected by Greene in 1961. Taken from the base of the shell deposit, the sample supposedly was associated with plain fiber-tempered pottery, a distinct minority at Stallings Island. Two other calibrated dates from Stallings Island placed the prepottery occupations at about 5,400 to 5,100 years ago.

Evidence was mounting for the beginnings of pottery at about 4200 to 4000 B.P. However, some hints of even earlier beginnings began to surface. In 1957 the Bilbo site was again opened up, this time by William Haag of Louisiana State University. Three radiocarbon samples that Haag collected produced calibrated age estimates in the range of 4300 to 3900 B.P.; but a fourth sample, from the base of the deposit, yielded an age of about 4650 B.P. These dates would go unreported until 1968, when Stephen Williams issued an annotated collection of Antonio Waring's papers.

Definitive evidence for the antiquity of Stallings pottery came a few years later from a Coastal Plain site in Allendale County, South Carolina. In 1964 James B. Stoltman, a graduate student of Williams, journeyed from Harvard University to the Rabbit Mount site on Groton Plantation. From this small shell-midden site Stoltman excavated a large assemblage of plain fiber-tempered pottery, soapstone cooking stones, and a variety of flaked stone tools. Nearly half of the plain fiber-tempered rim sherds were fitted with thickened or wedge-shaped lips. Decorated pottery was a distinct minority.

Two samples of charcoal collected from two separate places at the base of the Rabbit Mount shell deposit returned virtually identical age estimates, calibrated to a range of about 5300 to 5000 B.P. Pottery in the Savannah River valley was at least 800 years older than previously believed! This remarkable finding was soon published by Stoltman in the premier journal of American archaeology, *American Antiquity*, and later in the fine report of his dissertation research issued by the Peabody Museum. To this day, these dates from Rabbit Mount stand as the oldest reliable age estimates for fiber-tempered pottery in the Southeast.

Does the great antiquity for pottery at Rabbit Mount mean that this innovation arose first in the Coastal Plain of the Savannah River valley and not on the coast? The answer eludes us for now, although there is ample reason to suspect that pottery indeed originated among coastal dwellers a century or two before it was used at Rabbit Mount. Two factors render the coastal record of pottery's origins ambiguous. First, sites on the coast have been and continue to be subject to flooding from sea-level rise. About 7,000 years ago the rise in sea level following the last Ice Age slowed dramatically, but it has continued to creep upward ever since, occasionally interrupted by slight retreats that exposed formerly inundated land. Many of the sites occupied on the coast during early pottery times are now partially flooded; some are completely submerged. Any prepottery occupations within deposits below the pottery levels would be completely flooded, while those apart from sites with pottery levels were either buried by marsh mud or destroyed by transgressions of the sea.

A second factor is the radiocarbon dating of coastal deposits. The ages of many such deposits have been estimated from samples of marine shell, such as oyster or conch. The formula used to determine the age of a sample through the decay of radioactive carbon is based on a wood charcoal standard. Shellfish and organisms other than trees ingest and metabolize radioactive carbon in different ways, so the formula for estimating age has to be adjusted accordingly. Until recently, this was not done consistently, and many archaeologists were unaware of the problem. Michael Russo of the National Park Service has been instrumental in setting the record straight. In consultation with radiocarbon specialists and other colleagues, Russo has been able to correct many of the age estimates obtained from shell samples years ago. A correction of 400 radiocarbon years is added to any marine shell sample that was not previously adjusted. The difference after calibrating is even greater for radiocarbon dates for the fifth millennium before present. Thus, the assumed inception of pottery at about 4700 B.P. on the coast is more like 5350 B.P., a bit older than the oldest dates from Rabbit Mount.

What is more, Russo has discovered evidence for prepottery occupations on the northeast coast of Florida dating to as much as 6300 B.P. The food remains they left behind enabled Russo to determine that occupations this early were likely permanent. These remarkable new data are changing our outlook on coastal prehistory, suggesting that pottery indeed originated among people who had a long, established history of coastal dwelling.

Other work in recent years has thickened the plot. As the government implemented legislation requiring archaeological work in advance of federal construction projects, archaeologists began to look for sites in places never before surveyed. One such place was the floodpool of the Richard B. Russell Reservoir in the upper Savannah River valley. Excavations at several Late Archaic sites produced definitive evidence for occupations dating from about 4950 to 4000 B.P. that did not involve pottery. The oldest occurrence of pottery was a mere 3,700 years ago, more than a millennium later than the oldest pottery 200 km downriver.

The coexistence of groups with and without pottery is not very surprising; after all, it takes time for an innovation to spread from its source to outlying areas. But the protracted time of this process is a bit surprising, given the presumed advantages of pottery over traditional cooking methods. Moreover, recent research has shown that an early Stallings population shared territory in the middle Savannah with a group that resisted the adoption of pottery for up to 300 years. Deep, stratified sites like Stallings Island and Lake Spring have lulled us into thinking that once pottery was available locally everyone used it. The lower levels of these sites lack pottery, while the upper levels contain it throughout. This sort of stratigraphic evidence has been extrapolated to the greater region to suggest a sequence from prepottery to pottery times with no overlap of the two. Archaeologists refer to it as a unilineal sequence, where one culture replaces another thoroughly, through evolution, migration, or diffusion.

Again the change in our thinking about unilineal sequences came from work in places long ignored. The work of Jerald Ledbetter at the Mill Branch sites in Warren County, Georgia, has been especially enlightening. These remote, upland sites contained remarkable evidence for occupations by small groups lacking pottery at about 4350 B.P. Early Stallings groups had entered the adjoining Savannah River valley as early as 4600 B.P. Certainly these two distinct populations interacted in some fashion. My theory is that their persistent distinctiveness, including the reluctance of upland groups to adopt pottery, was a result of interactions between them, not isolation. As I implied in the story told earlier, one outcome of this history of interaction was the eventual abandonment of the middle Savannah by especially traditional factions even as ongoing interactions contributed to the formation of a new cultural identity—Classic Stallings culture, the People of the Shoals—that combined elements of the two ancestral cultures.

Radiocarbon dating has been the key to renewed perspectives on Stallings prehistory. Over 120 age estimates have been obtained on samples from about 20 sites in the past 15 years. This more than quadruples the number of estimates available over the previous three decades combined. Importantly, many of the new samples have been taken from small, unassuming sites, where the relationships between datable organic matter and human activity are fairly certain. Because they often contain evidence for only one occupation, small sites offer good time capsules for dating. Pit features with datable materials and diagnostic artifacts are the best bet. As long as we are certain that the organic matter was left by humans who left the artifacts—as opposed to, say, a later tree whose root system smoldered in the ground after a lightning fire—features like hearths and storage pits are the best contexts for dating. Large, complex sites such as Stallings Island contain hundreds or even thousands of features, but dating them is tricky because many have been affected by reoccupations over the millennia.

Sites lacking features and organic preservation have been especially hard to date. Remote, upland sites are problematic, for they generally do not contain the shellfish remains that act as a preservative for bone, charcoal, and other organic matter. The calcium in shell neutralizes acids in the soil, thus reducing the capacity for organic decomposition. Shell also reduces the percolation of water through soil, which washes away decomposed organic matter. Shal-

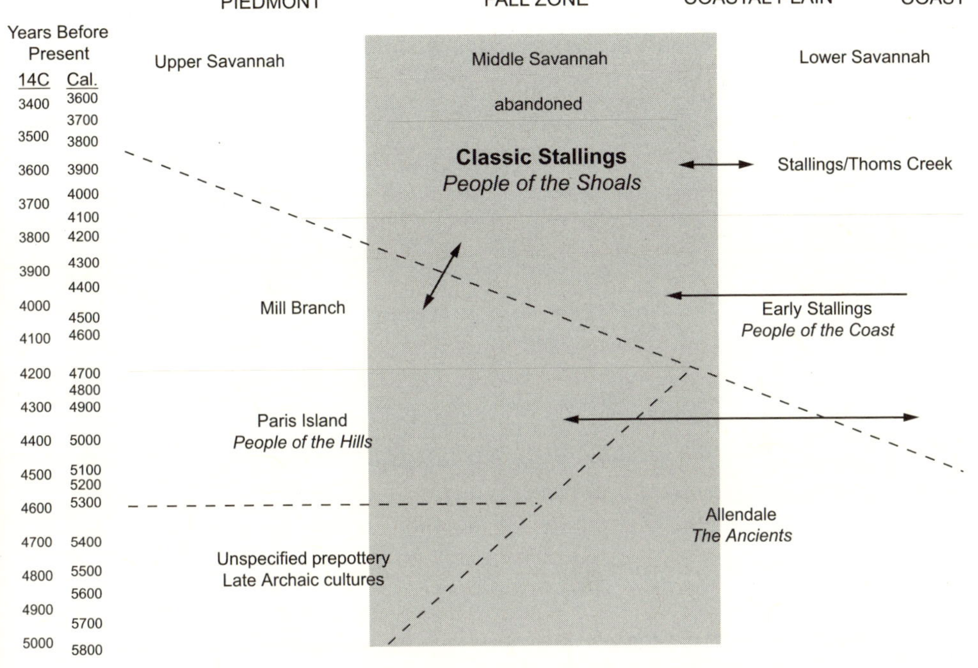

1.5. Chart of Late Archaic culture history of the Savannah River valley, based on radiocarbon age estimates from scores of contexts across dozens of sites. The vertical time scale provides both radiocarbon years and calendar years before present (B.P.). The 1,600 years of radiocarbon time represented here (3400–5000 B.P.) are nearly 2,200 calendar years (3600–5800 cal B.P.), due to fluctuations in the rate at which radioactive carbon is produced in the atmosphere. The consequence is that processes appear to develop much more rapidly in radiocarbon years than in actual years. Tree-ring chronologies have been used to calibrate radiocarbon years to calendar years. The software to calibrate age estimates has been made widely available, free of charge, by scientists at the University of Washington. The horizontal axis of this chart represents the spatial extent of the Savannah River Valley, with the Upper Savannah to the left and the Lower Savannah to the right. Corresponding physiographic provinces (Piedmont, Fall Zone, Coastal Plain, Coast) are listed at the top of this axis. Solid horizontal lines in the chart signify "events," such as the genesis of Mill Branch culture or the abandonment of the middle Savannah area. The dashed horizontal line signifies uncertain ancestry and processes of change. The dashed diagonal lines signify time-transgressive processes, such as the gradual movement of Early Stallings groups from the lower to middle Savannah. Single-ended arrow signifies population relocation; double-ended arrows represent alliances between groups of distinct identity.

low, sandy upland sites without shell generally do not offer the archaeologist much in the way of radiocarbon samples.

The advent of a new technique in radiocarbon dating has made it possible to date even the most problematic upland contexts. Accelerator mass spectrometry (AMS) is now used routinely to acquire age estimates directly from particles of organic matter as minute as a few milligrams. It is an expensive technique but well worth the cost when conventional dating is not possible.

As in conventional dating, AMS dates are useful only if the association between the dated organic matter and human activity is reasonably certain. Again, pit features offer good context, but few are preserved at upland sites. In lieu of features, I have sought out artifacts bearing traces of organic residue. Stallings pottery sherds sometimes have soot on exterior surfaces that formed when the vessel was used directly over a fire for cooking. This is actually a rare occurrence, because (as I will discuss later on in greater detail) Stallings pots in the middle Savannah area were not generally used over fire. Still, the occasional sooted sherd has been found and dated with the AMS technique. The results have helped to substantiate the conclusion that some upland sites were occupied during the time when river shell-midden sites were occupied.

The application of AMS dating of soot has been even more eye-opening in regard to the chronology of soapstone vessels. Archaeologists working in the Southeast generally believe that soapstone vessels predated the inception of pottery by a good long time. Ten years ago, before AMS dating of soot from soapstone vessel sherds, I would have agreed. Data are now mounting to show that pottery preceded soapstone vessels in many parts of the region. Clearly this was the case in the middle Savannah River valley, where the first soapstone vessels date to about 3650 B.P., after the heyday of Stallings Culture. Pottery also preceded soapstone vessels in Florida, in Coastal Plain Georgia and North Carolina, and perhaps throughout the Midsouth and lower Mississippi valley. This is curious, considering the great distances over which soapstone was traded from its source areas in the Piedmont province. Apparently the demand for soapstone was driven by factors other than the need to cook supper.

With the chronology and regional database now available for Stallings and pre-Stallings sites in the middle Savannah River valley, we can assemble a fairly detailed picture of the life and times of the People of the Shoals. As I

1.6. Sherds of soapstone vessels from northeast Florida (left) and northwest Georgia (right), both with soot on their surfaces that was sampled for radiometric dating.

have emphasized in the opening story, however, the history of these remarkable people cannot be understood apart from the goings-on in the greater Southeast. So I will range widely at times in sharing what I know today about the People of the Shoals. As we will see in the next chapter, the details of their beginnings take us far afield from the middle Savannah.

2

Stallings Beginnings

Origin stories are the lifeblood of any people. They teach us who we are, where we came from, how we got to be here. They are the stuff of mythical legends, full of heroes and heroines who, against all odds, triumphed over adversity to conquer new challenges. Life would be meaningless without a sense of beginnings, and origin tales about them would be boring if they were not so fantastical.

Like others, archaeologists have always been fascinated with origins. The beginnings of humanity, the advent of farming, and the first city-states are among the most popular topics of archaeological inquiry. Of course, archaeology, as a science, is supposedly guided by objectivity and empiricism, not by myth and fantasy. Knowledge claims about the origin of anything have to be backed by tangible evidence. Scholars must agree on what it is that they are seeing and assess its relevance and worth dispassionately and without prejudice.

But archaeologists are only human. Many claims about origins have depended more on wild imagination than on thoughtful data. Conversely, investigators are sometimes so wedded to conventional thinking that they have a hard time accepting new discoveries that lay bare the limits of our knowledge.

In American archaeology today, research into the origins of people in the New World has been brought center-stage by some tantalizing discoveries. Several sites in South America have produced evidence for human occupations as old as any in North America. This may not seem remarkable at first; but when we consider the accepted human route of entry into the New World, the new evidence becomes mind-boggling.

During the last Ice Age, when humans are believed to have first entered the Americas, sea levels were low enough to expose the now-submerged land in the Bering Sea linking Siberia to Alaska. The so-called Bering Land Bridge was a broad corridor that enabled vast herds of game to cross into new territory, followed, it appears, by the hunters that depended on them for food. The details of these crossings elude us, although the most popular theory is that these early immigrants soon made their way southward along an "ice-free" corridor in the Rockies to populate the rest of the Americas.

The Paleoindian Clovis culture is the oldest well-documented archaeological culture in North America, dating (in calibrated years) from about 13,700 to 12,600 B.P. Until recently, Clovis was widely regarded as the earliest human presence in the entire New World. It took direct associations with extinct Pleistocene animals and radiocarbon to make this claim; but for many decades Clovis had been ensconced in the culture history of the Americas as the first.

The fact that Clovis culture bore limited resemblance to its alleged ancestral stock in Siberia drew limited attention among archaeologists until evidence for something as old as or older than Clovis began surfacing. Even before the recent discoveries in South America, claims for pre-Clovis, as it came to be called, were issued from sites in Alaska, California, Texas, and Pennsylvania. Many of these claims faded away as critics undermined the contexts and dating of the finds or, worse, demonstrated that they were not of human origin.

The South American evidence is different. Clearly there were humans in the New World during or shortly after Clovis times but with a completely different culture. The elaborate fluted Clovis points are absent; nor is there evidence for an economy focused on game hunting. Coastal Peruvian sites show a markedly different lifestyle, revolving around the exploitation of sea birds and small fish. These data are renewing interest in possible maritime origins for America's first immigrants. They also cause us to ponder the relationship of Clovis to South American groups and whether other ocean routes of migration ought to be considered.

Two other bits of new evidence have led to one of the more remarkable claims of recent years. First, a few sites in the southeastern United States have begun to produce evidence for technologies that bear remarkable similarity to the flaked stone industries of Upper Paleolithic Europe. Second, the inadvertent discovery of a 9,000-year-old human skeleton in Washington state added to a small but significant series of individuals who do not fit well into the known range of biological variation among the presumed Asian ancestors of Paleoindians. These new findings, sketchy as they are, have led a handful of Paleoindian specialists to suggest that the immigrants who survived to beget Clovis arrived not from the west but from the east, passing from Europe into the New World in trans-Atlantic crossings.

I wonder what James A. Ford would have thought of all this. Just before his death in the mid-1960s, Ford made a case for trans-Caribbean colonizing ventures from South America to account for the southeastern origins of so-called Formative cultures at about 5750 B.P. His efforts were shunned by many of his contemporaries, but they were hardly as fantastical as the sorts of claims being made today. Ford did extensive research on the similarities between South American and Southeast cultures. His evidence consisted of a set of parallel traits in settlement patterning, lithic technology, ornaments, and fiber-tempered pottery. A site in Colombia called Puerto Hormiga was the oldest to have these various traits. Dating to over 5,700 years ago, Puerto Hormiga was a so-called shell ring, a donut-like accumulation of shellfish remains and other refuse presumably formed over many years of occupation in a circular compound of huts. Dozens of other shell rings are known from the coasts of Florida, Georgia, and South Carolina. Even the Gulf Coast has ring-like accumulations, although these tend to be later than those from the Atlantic Coast and lack the diagnostic fiber-tempered pottery.

In Ford's day the South American sites were clearly the oldest, but now the tables have turned. Recent work in the Timucuan Preserve north of Jacksonville has revealed evidence for one of the oldest shell-midden sites in the Southeast. Michael Russo of the National Park Service has been collecting data not only to demonstrate an age of about 6300 B.P. for this early occupation but also to show that it was a relatively permanent one. Pottery was not made and used yet, but all the conditions were in place for necessity to be the mother of invention: an intensive fishing economy, a sedentary lifestyle, and a lack of materials for traditional stone boiling.

Shell rings on the Georgia coast provide a glimpse into the emergence of pottery. Those on St. Simons Island contain assemblages of predominantly plain fiber-tempered ware. Oyster shell collected by Rochelle Marrinan from the base of one ring gave a radiocarbon age estimate of about 4200 B.P. This estimate was not adjusted to meet the charcoal standard for dating, so it would date to about 4600 B.P. when we add the 400-year correction factor, or about 5350 B.P. after calibration. With or without a correction for age, the St. Simons component remains among the oldest dated pottery assemblages from shell rings on the coast. Other rings on Sapelo Island to the north of St. Simons are probably just as old when radiocarbon corrections are considered, although age estimates as late as the mid-fourth millennium B.P. have recently been obtained by University of Kentucky graduate student Victor Thompson on one of the three rings he is investigating. Plain fiber-tempered pottery dominates the assemblages here, too. The remaining shell rings from Georgia to the mouth of the Santee River in South Carolina range in (calibrated) age from about 4350 to 3050 B.P. In general the oldest ones are to the south, the youngest to the north, with Sapelo Island now recognized as a late southern exception.

The function of shell rings has generated considerable debate over the years. South Carolina archaeologist James L. Michie regarded rings as ceremonial places. He had experience working some of the other shell-midden sites on the coast, notably Daws Island and Bass Pond, where assemblages included an array of stone and bone tools as well as pottery, shell, and animal bone. These sites had all the hallmarks of intensive habitations; but they were not rings, only amorphous accumulations of refuse. Because rings had comparatively little material culture aside from pottery, Michie suggested that they served limited functions. He also pointed out that the interior of rings lacked any traces of domestic activity and may have served as locations for special communal activities. The symmetrical configuration of rings was likewise curious, perhaps showing that rings figured into astronomical alignments or some such cosmological ritual.

Many of us would agree with Michie about the ceremonial importance of shell rings, but the evidence is scant. Excavations at rings have never been all that extensive or, with rare exception, designed to collect something other than stratigraphic data. The major exception is the work of Michael B. Trinkley. For his doctoral research in the late 1970s, Trinkley conducted test excavations at Stratton Place and Lighthouse Point, two shell rings near Charleston, South Carolina. His results provided convincing evidence that these sites were occupied year-round. Trinkley found that rings consist of several discrete activity areas. The ring itself formed through the accumulation of domestic refuse in and around houses arranged in a circular compound. Shellfish steaming pits at the base of the shell deposit showed that midden formed gradually from the use and infilling of these features. Eventually refuse from individual households converged into a contiguous ring. Thereafter, refuse accumulated on the outside edge of the ring. Use of the interior edge for food preparation was inferred from the presence of numerous roasting pits and hardened ash. Trinkley's work also confirmed that shell ring interiors are virtually devoid of cultural material.

Demonstrating that shell rings were permanent habitations does not preclude the sorts of ceremonialism that Michie envisioned; nor does it mean that other types of sites and settlement strategies were not being used by coastal populations. Stratton Place and Lighthouse Point are among the northern most and latest shell rings on record. Knowing how well they represent shell rings elsewhere awaits the development of comparative data. Ongoing projects at shell rings by Russo, his colleagues Rebecca Saunders and Greg Heide, and Victor Thompson are beginning to yield those very data.

There are also limits to our knowledge about early coastal settlement due to the problems of site preservation. We now have a sizable gap between the oldest shell-midden site on the south Atlantic coast—the prepottery Timucuan Preserve midden at 6300 B.P.—and the oldest shell rings with pottery—those of coastal Georgia, dating from 4700 B.P. but perhaps as old as 5350 B.P. We might be tempted to suggest that the coast was abandoned during this interval, although I think it safe to say that sea-level rise is the culprit in this case. During the interval in question, sea levels rose some 2–3 m. Occupations directly on the coast would be completely buried by marsh mud or at least flooded by water at high tide. Others were likely washed away due to minor fluctuations of sea level, which brought wave action and erosion. Severe storm surges over the years may have been a factor too.

Without a complete record of coastal settlement we simply do not have a clue about the groups that utilized the coast before about 4700 B.P., after pottery was well established. The early Timucuan Preserve settlement is truly remarkable. Its preservation is attributed to its sheltered location on a back barrier island with considerable topographic relief. Similar conditions elsewhere ought to have the potential for early settlements, but few besides Russo have made a concerted effort to find them. An exception is Rebecca Saunders of Louisiana State University, who has recently located and tested prepottery shell-midden sites on the Florida Gulf Coast dating as early as 7000 B.P. For now, the coastal record in Georgia and South Carolina remains silent on the prepottery period.

The Rabbit Mount shell-midden site in Allendale County, South Carolina, is the location of the oldest fiber-tempered pottery in the Savannah River valley. Its calibrated radiocarbon ages of about 5100 B.P. were obtained on charcoal from the base of the shell deposit at two separate locations of the site. We know a great deal about the artifact assemblages of Rabbit Mount because its excavator, James Stoltman, did an excellent job reporting his re-

2.1. Sherds of plain fiber-tempered pottery with the thickened and flanged lips characteristic of Early Stallings times.

sults. In addition, the site collection housed at the Peabody Museum at Harvard has been nicely curated and made available for further analysis.

The assemblage is dominated by a large collection of plain fiber-tempered pottery. Many of the rim sherds are fitted with thickened lips like those Waring observed at Bilbo site in Savannah, Georgia. A sizable assemblage of perforated soapstone slab fragments accompanies the pottery. Among the flaked stone tools are many large stemmed bifaces, a few drills, and various cutting and scraping tools. A polished stone axe fragment and a bannerstone are among the more unusual items. The hard igneous rock used to make these items, as well as the soapstone, came from sources no less than 100 km upriver in the Piedmont province.

Stoltman found a few postholes and other features at Rabbit Mount but not enough evidence to infer anything about community pattern or group size. Recovery techniques for food remains were insufficient to conclude much about diet or season of occupation. A single human interment was attributed to a later period of occupation.

One small aspect of the Rabbit Mount assemblage that drew little attention in the original site report is a series of narrow-bladed stemmed points made from heat-treated Coastal Plain chert. I had the chance to examine these items in 1989 when I was analyzing the pottery for my dissertation research. These points tended to occur at the base or slightly below the shell deposit.

A similar set of points is known from another small shell-midden site close to Rabbit Mount. The Fennel Hill site (aka Cox and Milberry Mound) was excavated in the 1960s by mostly avocational archaeologists. A report was never issued, but much of the collection was stored at the South Carolina Institute of Archaeology, where I saw the narrow-bladed stemmed points in 1989. One of the excavators confirmed that these came from the base of the shell deposit.

Local archaeologists and artifact collectors had known about these points for years. They are common throughout the Allendale County area and across much of the South Carolina Coastal Plain south of the Santee River. In his survey of private collections in South Carolina, Tommy Charles encountered numerous examples. Having no name for them, Charles listed them as "Type D" in his inventory. I believe that Waring also came across these points in collections from Burke County, Georgia. He called them Brier Creek points in recognition of the major watercourse in that county. Others have referred

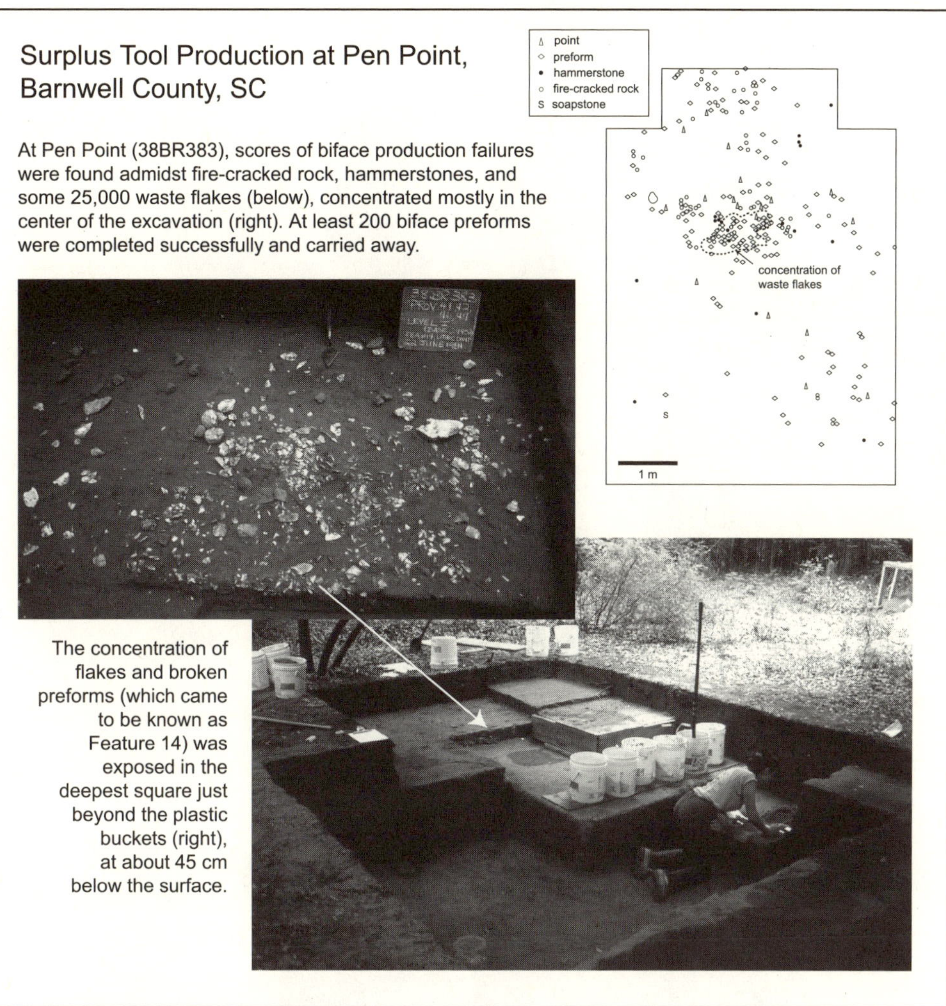

2.2. Photograph of block excavation at Pen Point site, with close-up photo (top left) and plan drawing (top right) of Feature 14, a cluster of flakes, preforms, and broken points indicative of surplus production.

to them as Kirk Stemmed variants, drawing on the established type name for an early Middle Archaic point defined by Joffre Coe from work in North Carolina.

Not until I aimlessly stumbled on a stratigraphic context for these points did we have a clue about what we were actually seeing. In 1984 I conducted

2.3. Allendale points from Feature 14, Pen Point site, Barnwell County, South Carolina.

limited test excavations at the Pen Point site in Barnwell County, South Carolina, hoping to collect data for a project on long-term changes in lithic technology during the Archaic period. The site was tested earlier by a crew under the direction of Glen T. Hanson, then director of the Savannah River Archaeological Research Program. Hanson recommended that I dig Pen Point because it had a stratified sequence going back to the Early Archaic period, some 9,000 years ago. Being young and eager, I jumped at the opportunity. Hanson helped me find two other willing subjects to dig.

As my crew and I dug down through the deposits of a block 33 m^2, we encountered the usual stuff. The plowzone contained a large assemblage of Middle and Late Woodland pottery and points. A smattering of Early Woodland and ceramic Late Archaic material was immediately below the plowzone, followed by a moderate amount of Late Archaic artifacts, but no pottery, from about 30–40 cm below the surface. The surprise came 5 cm deeper. I was away on other business on the day when the crew struck a dense deposit of flaked stone debris, biface preforms, and these curious stemmed points. I returned the next morning to find one of my team in the lab with two huge bags of flakes and a sly look on his face. "What do you want us to do with all this stuff?" was all he could say.

What they had intercepted and we eventually exposed completely was a discrete deposit of over 25,000 flakes, scores of biface preform fragments, and 14 narrow stemmed points. The entire assemblage was confined to an area of only a few square meters. Clusters of hammerstones and nodes of flaking debris appeared to be completely undisturbed from the time they were left there long ago. These must have been the by-products of a short-term but intensive episode of tool-making. I later calculated that over 200 finished products were made and transported away from this single event of flintknapping.

Aside from the wealth of technological information that the Pen Point deposit offered, its stratigraphic position was thoroughly enlightening. Below the lens of flaking debris was a small assemblage of Morrow Mountain points. Dating from about 8300 to 6800 B.P., Morrow Mountain points are a hallmark of the Middle Archaic period throughout much of the Southeast. With Morrow Mountain deposits below the layer of dense flaking debris, the associated narrow-bladed stemmed points were stratigraphically sandwiched between known Late Archaic and Middle Archaic horizons, roughly in the neighborhood of 6800 to 5750 B.P. Having no other name for them, I assigned them the provisional acronym MALA, standing for the transitional

2.4. Fragments of preforms of Allendale points from Feature 14, Pen Point site, Barnwell County, South Carolina.

status between Middle Archaic and Late Archaic times. For better or worse, the name caught on. Only recently, through the encouragement of John Whatley, so-called MALA points have been renamed "Allendale" in recognition of their geographic nexus.

Allendale points truly stand out as something different from other Middle and Late Archaic types in the region. They are generally stemmed at the base, a technique that enables the point to be attached to a slotted handle or shaft. Stemming is not at all unusual for the region. It can be traced back to the beginnings of the Middle Archaic period in the Carolina Piedmont tradition that included Kirk Stemmed and Stanly points. Stems on Allendale points, however, were usually formed by simply removing the corners of a squared-off base. Often one of the corners was notched and the other removed altogether, leaving a distinctive asymmetrical appearance. Occasional examples involve side-notching. Either way, the result was a short haft element. Damage evident along the margins of many of the haft elements suggests that the design was not terribly reliable.

The blades of Allendale points are distinctive, too. They have a lanceolate form, with parallel sides, an acute tip, and a thick, lenticular cross section. Numerous cases of impact fracture on tips attest to their function as projectiles. Other edge wear on several examples from Pen Point shows that they were drafted into use as knives, a function that may account for the haft damage. Clearly these tools were designed as "bullets" and used only secondarily as cutting tools.

Coastal Plain chert was the raw material of choice for Allendale points, and nearly all of it was heat treated. The nearest known quarry is about 25 km downriver from Pen Point. The flintknappers seem to have used only the highest-grade Coastal Plain chert that they could find. Many of the broken preforms and other pieces of good raw material were abandoned at the site. At first the high rate of failure and discard led me to think that the flintknappers were not quite used to working this raw material. I later realized after close examination of the many broken preforms that—rather than being dumbfounded—the flintknappers were maintaining exceptionally high standards. The quality of the work was far above the standards evident in other Middle Archaic tool traditions of the region.

By all appearances, the assemblage from Pen Point was telling us that interlopers arrived in the lower Savannah River valley some 6,000 to 5,000 years ago. The old archaeological term for this was a "site unit intrusion," which means that the new culture is so different from the indigenous archaeological cultures that it must have arrived from far away. I became preoccupied with finding the source of the people who made and used these points.

I began a search for possible foreign influences not in South America but closer to home. I was struck by similarities between these new finds and Benton Stemmed points of northern Alabama and Tennessee. Other similarities also became apparent; as I looked deeper into the archaeological record of Benton Culture I discovered plenty of reasons for at least some of these people to move out of their homeland in search of new opportunity.

As it turns out, the history of Benton Culture anticipated many of the same developments of Stallings Culture in the Savannah River valley. They, too, collected shellfish and established fixed settlements along the shoals of a major river, in this case the Tennessee River. Under these more-or-less stationary conditions their numbers grew, territorial competition ensued, and some factions appear to have migrated out. The 1984 excavations in Barnwell County brought into focus the possibility that some of these Midsouth immigrants chose the lower Savannah River valley as their new homeland.

Documenting this possible migration is not enough to explain the origins of Stallings Culture, for the chain of events it set off is of greater consequence. At about 5,700 years ago, when this new culture appeared in the lower Savannah valley, no one seems to have occupied the area that they chose to settle. In fact, the preceding millennia were generally quiet times in the lower Coastal Plain. After a stint of intensive use in the Early Archaic period, the lower Coastal Plain landscape changed from a mosaic of hardwood and pine forests to one dominated by pine. Records of fossil tree pollen show that southern pine surged in frequency after about 9500 B.P. Whereas this change in vegetation alone does not preclude human use of the Coastal Plain, the reduction in nut-bearing trees diminished the capacity to support white-tailed deer, squirrels, and turkeys and thus humans. Food-gathering efforts could certainly have shifted to resources of the river, if the people were prepared technologically and culturally to do so. Instead, Savannah River groups at this early time concentrated their efforts on the Piedmont province, which, as pollen studies show, was hardly affected by the climate changes that encouraged pine to flourish in the Coastal Plain. For millennia to come, until early Europeans arrived, the Piedmont was a vast forest of oaks, hickories, and other hardwood trees.

The situation on the coast at about 5700 B.P. is completely unknown. Given Russo's growing evidence for intensive coastal occupations in northeast Florida in the seventh millennium, it seems likely that the early shell rings of Georgia and South Carolina were preceded by coastal settlements that were long since buried or destroyed. In any case, the coast was most likely the hearth of early pottery.

Nothing in the archaeological record of the Coastal Plain interlopers suggests that they delivered fiber-tempered pottery or Stallings Culture from afar. Rather, the seeds of Stallings Culture were already in place when the population that made and used Allendale points arrived on the scene. As circumstances dictated, these newcomers established themselves between the two major populations of the region. Their interactions with these respective groups spawned the development of the distinctive Stallings Culture of the middle Savannah valley: the People of the Shoals. In a sense the Allendale people were the cultural brokers of change, mediating through intermarriage and alliance the indigenous cultural traditions that were separated by 200 km of sandy Coastal Plain. We will probably never know with any certainty how such interactions between the new arrivals and indigenous people got started, but they eventually involved the infusion of the two major cooking technologies of the region: soapstone cooking stones and fiber-tempered pottery.

Recently we have learned just how ancient soapstone cooking technology is in the upper Savannah River valley. At the Mims Point site in Edgefield County, South Carolina, several shallow pit features contained clusters of fire-cracked rock, quartz flakes, and biface preforms reminiscent of Morrow Mountain or Guilford points, two of the local Middle Archaic types. Although our excavations at Mims Points in the early 1990s were intended to collect data on classic Stallings Culture, we could not help but confront the Middle Archaic component, because Morrow Mountain points were everywhere. The few preforms found in these pit features anticipated the calibrated radiocarbon dating results: roughly 6600 to 6500 B.P. This is a bit late for the Morrow Mountain phase locally but not out of line with the subsequent Guilford phase, which, all seem to agree, is a tradition of tool-making that grew directly out of Morrow Mountain.

The few soapstone pieces mixed among the fragments of granite, gneiss, and other Piedmont rocks were the most exciting aspect of the pit features. These were simply lumps of soapstone (some 10 by 6 cm) that were lightly ground to achieve a smooth exterior surface and then pitted on either side.

The small, shallow pits were apparently added so that the stones could be lifted in and out of the cooking pit with tongs. Middle Archaic chefs seem to have discovered that soapstone was an excellent medium for absorbing and dissipating heat gradually without fracturing. Their efforts to modify the soapstone, albeit so slightly, reflected its lasting qualities, compared to other rock types. These features were earth ovens: subterranean cooking places where meat and vegetables could be steamed or dry roasted with fire-heated rocks.

From this moment of invention came a series of technological improvements that would lead eventually to the perforated soapstone slabs so numerous at Stallings Island and other sites in the middle Savannah. The sequence of developments has been nicely reconstructed by one of our loyal and insightful volunteers, Kevin Eberhard. On the heels of the prototype came a thick slab with biconical holes drilled only partially through either side. By 5700 B.P. holes were drilled through the stones, which now were ground down to a more uniform cross section. The ensuing few centuries saw the gradual development of the thin, perforated slab among Piedmont populations. At this point all edges and the flat surfaces of stones were thoroughly worked to achieve a uniform thickness of about one-half inch. Perforations were made with either cruciform stone drills, which created biconical holes, or hollow cane, which left a smooth, cylindrical hole. As with the prototype, perforations enabled the safe transfer of stones from the fire into the cooking feature.

Pottery was yet to be used by the local Piedmont communities, but I am certain that soapstone slabs at this time (i.e., 5700–5100 B.P.) were routinely used for so-called stone boiling in organic containers (baskets, skins, wooden bowls) or pits dug into impervious clay. We find a good example of this technology among the Chumash of California, who used similar soapstone cooking stones with baskets right on through the historic period. In the middle Savannah the technology would persist until about 3800 B.P., long after pottery was adopted.

Sites excavated in advance of the construction of the Richard B. Russell Reservoir in the upper Savannah River valley provided abundant data on the manufacture and use of perforated soapstone slabs near quarry sources. Dating from about 5000 to 4000 B.P., these sites contained the remains of intensive Late Archaic habitations along the river. Remarkably, not a single sherd of pottery was found at any of these sites, despite the fact it was being made and used routinely by groups less than 200 km down the river.

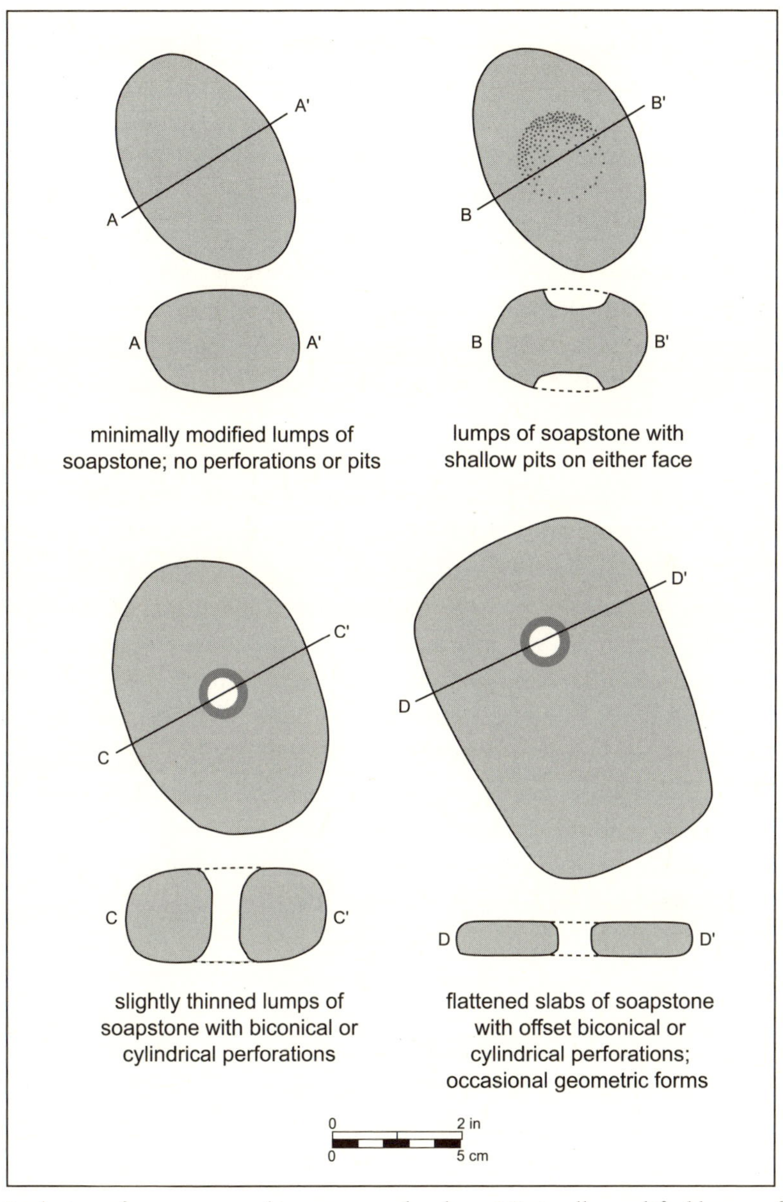

2.5. Evolution of soapstone cooking-stone technology. Minimally modified lumps of soapstone (top row), first without then with pits, are the oldest forms and have been found in earth ovens dating to over 6,000 years ago. Perforated lumps were slightly thinned to achieve greater surface area relative to mass (bottom left) and were most likely used with vessels for indirect "stone boiling." The evolved form (bottom right) is a slab that was thinned uniformly and perforated off-center to enable its transfer from fire to vessel with a tine or stick. These latest forms, occasionally geometric in plan and dating after ca. 5,000 years ago, maximized the surface area to mass ratio and thus quickened the rate by which heat could be absorbed and dissipated.

Among the upper Savannah sites, Paris Island in Elbert County, Georgia, is especially noteworthy for its large assemblage of soapstone. Over 14 kg were recovered in 109 m^2 of excavation. Based on the number of observable perforations on fragments, project archaeologist Dean Wood estimated that at least 78 slabs were represented. Another 387 slab fragments lacked traces of perforation, and some 1,200 miscellaneous pieces of soapstone apparently resulted from the on-site manufacture and use of slabs. None of the slab fragments was perforated more than once, which, it turns out, is a reliable measure of recycling behavior. A lack of conservation at Paris Island is not surprising, given that a quarry source for soapstone is a mere 3 km from the site.

In his report of excavations at Paris Island, Wood speculated that soapstone slab production was the work of part-time specialists. Dan Elliott also investigated this issue with data from the Oconee River valley of Georgia, where soapstone was also used to make perforated slabs, though more often to make vessels after 4200 B.P. Elliott concluded that production and exchange were organized by simple reciprocal relations among neighboring groups. Under these conditions, the dispersal of soapstone away from quarry sources assumes a smooth, gradual distribution of diminishing volume as items are passed "down-the-line" from one group to the next, with each successive group consuming a portion of the imported goods. The Oconee River data appear to fit this model pretty well.

Savannah River data on soapstone slabs do not quite fit the "down-the-line" pattern that we see in the Oconee. True, the volume of soapstone diminishes with distance from quarry sources. Sites in the Piedmont province and Fall Zone (where soapstone outcrops) typically have well over 100 g of soapstone per square meter of excavated midden, whereas Coastal Plain sites (which are 60 km or more from quarries) never contain more than 50 g per unit of excavation. When we count the number of perforations per slab, however, we find that recycling increases with distance from quarry. Middle Coastal Plain sites such as Rabbit Mount, Cox, and Theriault have an average of at least 1.26 perforations per slab, compared to no more than 1.07 for any of the sites near quarries. Recycling diminishes a lot of the evidence for slab use at Coastal Plain sites, much as our modern recycling of aluminum makes it difficult to calculate the actual rate of beer consumption from our garbage dumps alone.

When we factor recycling into the equation, the number of slabs per unit

2.6. Broken and recycled soapstone slabs. Each of the slabs broke along planes that intercepted a perforation; those on the bottom row broke again after being reperforated. The example at the top was ground along the fracture plane to achieve a uniform shape. All examples are from Stallings Island.

of excavation at certain Coastal Plain sites approaches levels seen at sites in close proximity to quarries. Rabbit Mount, for instance, yielded evidence for one slab for every 2 m^2 of excavation; at 1.4 slabs per 2 m^2, Paris Island yielded a density only slightly higher than Rabbit Mount. The difference, of course, is that Rabbit Mount did not contain evidence of manufacture like that seen at Paris Island. Being well over 120 km from the nearest source of soapstone, Rabbit Mount clearly was a recipient of imported material. The question remains: how did it get there?

The mineral composition of soapstone slabs from Rabbit Mount and other Coastal Plain sites provides some clues about the means by which soapstone was delivered from sources far away. Soapstone is basically talc, but it also contains a variety of other minerals that vary from source to source. Some soapstone is smooth and gray, some is grainy and speckled with black or dark green minerals, and some is consistent in color but porous. Slabs from sites near quarries tend to be made from the same type of soapstone, presumably the nearest source. This is the case with Paris Island and other "up-country" sites, but Rabbit Mount and other Coastal Plain sites have a plethora of soapstone. At least seven different types of soapstone are evident in a quick perusal of the Rabbit Mount assemblage. This diversity suggests that occupants of Rabbit Mount acquired soapstone through a variety of mechanisms. It follows that neither Paris Island nor any other site in the up-country was the sole source of soapstone in the Coastal Plain. This does not negate the possibility of part-time craft specialists, though it would suggest that many such individuals engaged in production for exchange, perhaps competing among themselves for alliances with their new low-country neighbors.

Soapstone arrived at Rabbit Mount in significant quantities at the same time that pottery was first adopted. While one would seem to have little to do with the other (other than both being involved in cooking, of course), when we consider the form and technology of these early pottery vessels it is abundantly clear that soapstone was used with pottery to advance the age-old technique of stone boiling.

Well over 200 fiber-tempered vessels are represented in the Rabbit Mount collection made by Stoltman. I spent the better part of a month in 1989 assembling the pieces in order to determine whatever I could about vessel size, shape, and use. What I found was that the vast majority of Rabbit Mount pots are wide-mouthed, shallow basins. They range from 32 to 45 cm wide and 16 to 18 cm tall. The bottoms are generally flat, the walls usually vertical. Wall profiles vary appreciably, as there seems to have been little effort to achieve uniform thickness. Few of the vessels are decorated, and about half are fitted with thickened or wedge-shaped lips, the telltale sign of an early fiber-tempered pottery component.

The literature on mechanical performance of pottery vessels provided all

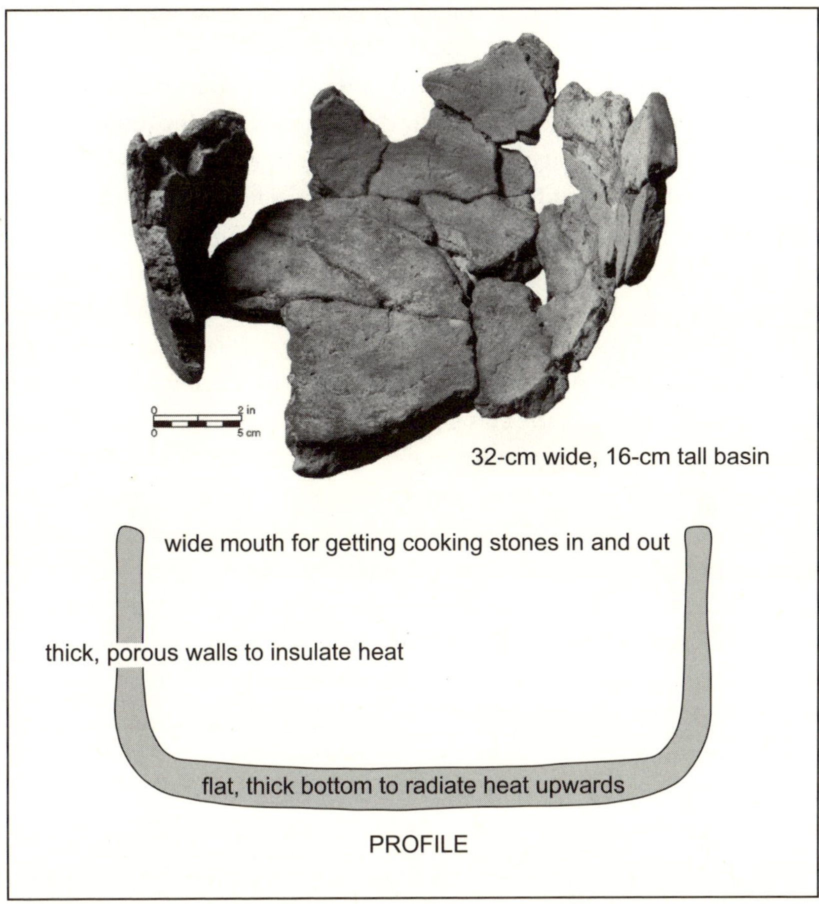

2.7. Partially reconstructed Early Stallings basin (top) and its cross-sectional profile, showing features that make basins conductive to "stone boiling."

the information that I needed to ascertain the function of these flat-bottomed basins. Properties like thermal conductivity, thermal shock resistance, and evaporative heat loss are all affected by the size, shape, and composition of vessels. An effective vessel for heating liquid contents directly over a heat source is a globular jar or pot with smooth, rounded wall profiles, an orifice that is small relative to the vessel volume, uniformly thin walls, and a sandy, nonporous ceramic body. Of course, the Rabbit Mount vessels have none of these qualities. In fact, they are just the opposite of an effective direct-heat cooking pot. The fiber-tempered composition is a poor conductor of heat.

Wide-mouthed forms allow too much heat loss. Irregular wall profiles encourage propagation of cracks from thermal shock.

Everything about the Rabbit Mount vessels that renders them worthless for direct-heat cooking makes them excellent containers for stone boiling. This cooking technique requires a container that is shallow and wide so that hot stones could be cycled in and out from a nearby fire. The flat bottom not only provides a surface conducive to retrieving stones but also radiates heat upward. Thick vessel walls help to conserve internal heat, as does a porous ceramic body, because air is a good insulator.

So the earliest pots were basically portable pits, similar in size and shape to the shallow cooking holes dug into the basal clay of many Piedmont and Fall Zone sites. Perhaps early pottery was simply an ingenious way of continuing a traditional cooking practice in areas lacking clay subsoil—namely, the Coastal Plain and coast. These basin-shaped vessels do indeed occur in the oldest coastal deposits, which are farthest removed from solid clay subsoil. Coastal dwellers clearly had access to abundant sources of clay in marshes and other wet locations, but clay typically did not occur in the high, dry spots that they chose for camping. Coastal locations were also the greatest distance from sources of soapstone or other raw materials for stone boiling. As we will see later, distance from suitable rock was likely a major incentive for the eventual innovation of direct-heat cooking with pottery.

Rabbit Mount stands as the oldest place in the Coastal Plain where the technologies of early pottery (from the low-country) and soapstone cooking stones (from the up-country) converged. From the base of the shell at this site, inconspicuous and apparently just beneath the oldest pottery, come the lanceolate stemmed points now known as Allendale.

Three other Coastal Plain locations provide evidence that people making and using Allendale points acquired soapstone cooking stones before pottery hit the scene. One is the Pen Point site itself, where the accumulation of lithic debris had a soapstone slab fragment nestled comfortably among thousands of flakes. Another is the G. S. Lewis–East site, only a few kilometers upriver from Pen Point. Large-scale excavations in 1984 revealed a dense assemblage of stemmed points, other flaked and ground stone tools, and 45 soapstone slab fragments but not a trace of early pottery. Neither Pen Point nor Lewis-East preserved much organic material, so radiocarbon dates are not available for these sites in particular and Allendale components in general. The only hope in this regard comes from a third Coastal Plain site with stemmed lanceolate points and soapstone slabs. At the Big Pine Tree site in Allendale County, South Carolina, Albert Goodyear discovered an organically enriched midden deposit chock-full of Allendale points and other Middle and Late Archaic types, but again no pottery. Soapstone slabs from this deposit may have come from later components; given the evidence from Pen Point and Lewis-East, however, they probably accompanied the Allendale points. Radiocarbon dating has been inconclusive, though suggestive of a calibrated age of about 5550 B.P. for the Allendale component.

Having arrived in the Coastal Plain of the Savannah River valley some 5,550 years ago, bearers of this foreign culture quickly set about building ties with up-country neighbors. I doubt that soapstone itself was all that important to these new arrivals, but they clearly needed to establish alliances with others to survive as a people. We see in soapstone exchange one dimension of these fledgling relationships. More than just a means of cooking supper, soapstone was symbolic of developing alliances, a tangible expression of social obligation and privilege. It was the beginning of a new tradition.

In the ensuing centuries, alliances with coastal groups enabled pottery to be added to the technological inventory of the direct descendants of these newcomers. For a long time, pottery and soapstone were used together by Coastal Plain groups in the age-old technique of stone boiling. But throughout these early centuries their up-country neighbors—suppliers of soapstone and stalwarts of traditional practice—never adopted pottery. Their resistance to innovation was matched by other cultural practices suggesting that relations with Coastal Plain neighbors were somewhat strained or at least occasionally contested. In fact, as Coastal Plain groups began to make increasing use of Fall Zone and lower Piedmont sites at about 4700 B.P., various factions began to assert themselves in a variety of ways, both physically and symbolically. The middle Savannah was becoming a multiethnic neighborhood, and the next several centuries were a time of rapid, unpredictable change.

3

A Multiethnic Neighborhood

Stratigraphy in archaeology is both a blessing and a curse. Borrowed from geology, stratigraphic principles form the cornerstone of culture history in American archaeology. The simple fact that layers at the bottom of an undisturbed body of sediment or rock are older than those at the top enables us to reconstruct relative chronologies for the things contained in these layers (strata). This geological principle, called superpositioning, is coupled with the concept of the index fossil to assign relative ages to specific sorts of objects. For instance, the trilobite fossils found only at the bottom of a stratified sequence must be older than the shark teeth found only at the top. We can then assign relative ages to similar trilobites and shark teeth found outside of stratigraphic contexts by cross-dating them with the original sequence.

The southeastern United States boasts a long and fruitful history of stratigraphic excavations in its many riverine, shell-midden, and cave deposits. None has been more influential than the 1950s digs directed by Joffre L. Coe of the University of North Carolina in Chapel Hill. At two sites in particular, Doerschuk and Gaston, Coe and his students identified deep stratigraphic sequences spanning at least 8,500 years. Coupled with work at a third, shallow site, Hardaway, Coe was able to define the major "index fossils" for the region. His 1964 publication *The Formative Cultures of the Carolina Piedmont* set out the type descriptions for more than ten projectile point types, including Hardaway Side-Notched, Kirk Corner-Notched, Palmer Corner-Notched, Kirk Stemmed, Stanly Stemmed, Morrow Mountain Stemmed, Guilford Stemmed, Savannah River Stemmed, and the Badin, Yadkin, and Caraway triangulars. Virtually all of these types and their relative sequence have withstood the test of time to survive as the core of the region's culture history.

The problem with the Carolina Piedmont sequence, and stratigraphic sequences in general, is that its index fossils—diagnostic artifacts, in this case—are often too perfect. Taken literally, the diagnostic point types appear to reflect episodic changes in style or technology, so that each period is represented by a single type, and types are mutually exclusive. Northeastern archaeologist Louis A. Brennan referred to this as the "Coe Axiom": one point type per period, each in sequence, one after the other, with no overlap, intermixing, or reversals. Ideally, that is exactly how diagnostic artifacts ought to behave.

Unfortunately, humans are not artifacts and do not always act in ways that make stratigraphy work as a measure of time. Undisturbed layers at a site are necessarily in sequence from early to late, but the artifacts they contain can often represent periods and cultural expression that go well beyond the time embodied by the layers of the site. A modern appointment book is a good analogy. Imagine taking a single page from a book and assuming that it accurately portrayed each day in the life of its owner. Unless that person had a totally invariant schedule (in which case an appointment book would not be needed!), we could potentially miscalculate the time and sequence of activities on other days if we generalized from that one day. That is precisely the problem with stratigraphic sequences: the unilineal arrangements they provide us are too often extrapolated through cross-dating to sites elsewhere without question.

Problems with the relative sequences of stratigraphic excavations often come to the fore when we apply independent means of dating, like radiocarbon dating. Initially, independent dates that contradict established stratigraphic sequences are dismissed as wrong. For instance, when the diagnostic types from distinct strata at a site are found to be coeval elsewhere, the dates are sometimes rejected as erroneous. In principle this is fine, because undisturbed stratigraphy does not lie. Still, stratigraphy at a single site, no matter how undisturbed, cannot possibly contain the complete regional histories of its constituent types.

This was the problem with Stallings Island. As critical as this site was to our recognition of cultural changes in the middle Savannah valley, it was a bit misleading. Its stratigraphic sequence accurately showed that Stallings Island was occupied first by people without pottery and then by the makers and users of Stallings pottery. Over the decades archaeologists have debated whether the pottery signified a wholesale introduction of a new culture or simply the addition of an innovation to the inventory of long-established residences. Either way, the sequence of events was unmistakable.

When radiocarbon dating began to be applied to Stallings components in the region, we learned quickly that pottery-using people and their neighbors without pottery coexisted for many centuries. This was immediately obvious when radiocarbon dating was applied to early Stallings components in the Coastal Plain and to prepottery components in the Piedmont. Calibrated age estimates showed that they overlapped by at least nine centuries, from about 5100 to 4200 B.P. More importantly, later work showed that these centuries entailed more than a long, gradual process of innovation diffusion. We know with great certainty now that the middle Savannah region in and around Stallings Island was utilized by two very distinctive groups from about 4700 to 4200 B.P. The stratigraphy of Stallings Island had long fooled us into seeing these groups as chronologically separate because it did not contain the earliest centuries of occupation by pottery-making groups. The once unilineal sequence is now a multiethnic neighborhood.

One of the ethnic groups is defined today as the Mill Branch phase, whose members I referred to earlier as the "People of the Hills." Due largely to the work of Jerald Ledbetter and Dan Elliott, Mill Branch is among the best-documented archaeological cultures of the region. Its calling card is the Savannah River Stemmed point, the long, broad-bladed biface type defined by Coe in 1964. Various other diagnostic traits, notably cruciform drills and winged bannerstones, set Mill Branch apart from its regional counterparts. Pottery, however, is conspicuously absent from Mill Branch assemblages, even the very latest ones. Throughout its 500-year history, Mill Branch Culture appears to be deliberately antithethical to Stallings Culture. Members of these respective groups most likely interacted in a variety of ways, but Mill Branch people seem to have actively asserted differences in the way they expressed themselves culturally. Understanding this dynamic relationship requires that we take a look at the roots of Mill Branch culture, an archaeological manifestation known today as the Paris Island phase.

Paris Island Culture

Rudiments of Mill Branch culture are evident in the Archaic history of the Piedmont. Its immediate ancestry is embodied in Paris Island culture, dating from ca. 5350–4700 B.P. We know about Paris Island culture primarily from excavations at the type site, Paris Island, and at Sara's Ridge, both under the direction of Dean Wood in advance of construction of the Richard B. Russell Reservoir on the upper Savannah River. I have introduced the Paris Island site in my discussion of soapstone cooking slabs in chapter 2. Both Sara's Ridge and Paris Island contained an abundance of these items, one of the hallmarks of Paris Island culture and their Mill Branch descendants.

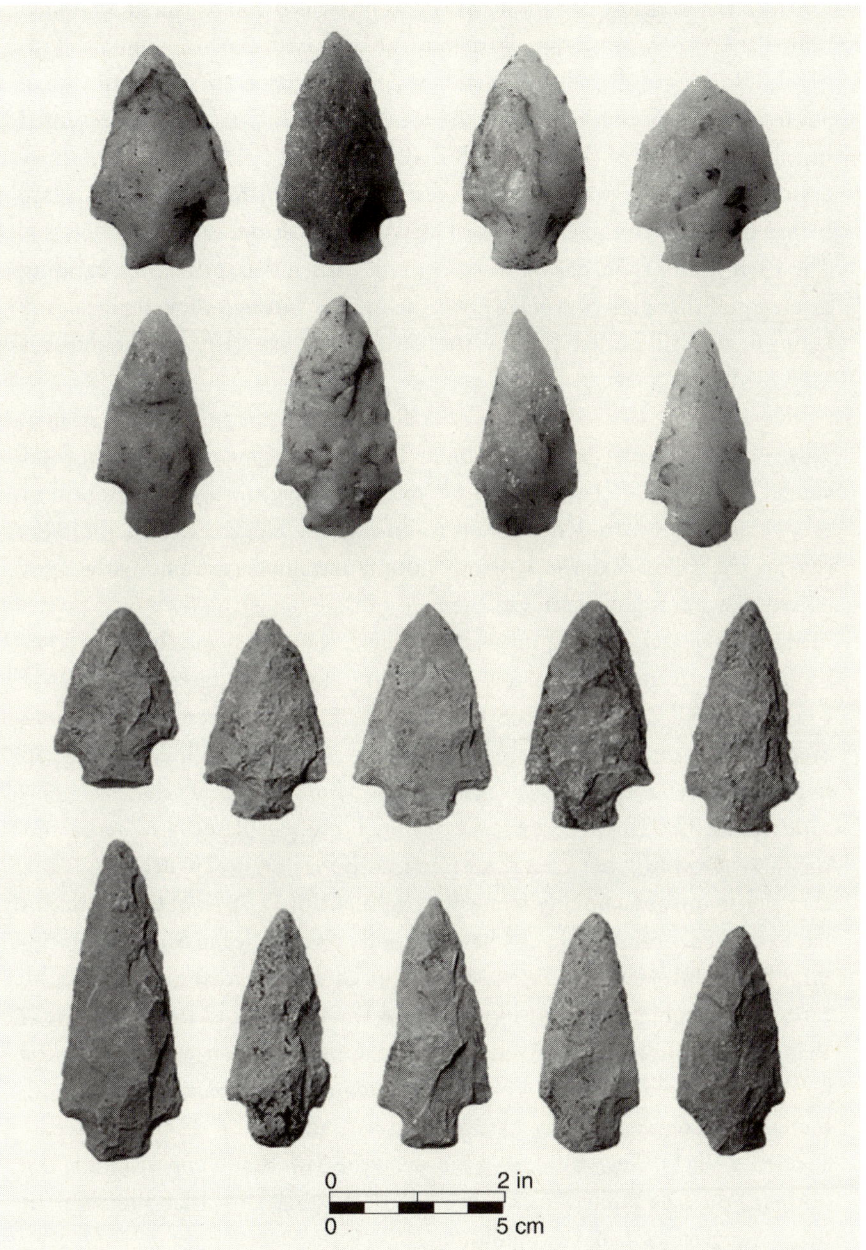

3.1. Paris Island and closely related biface types from the Moody site, Edgefield County, South Carolina. Top two rows made from quartz; bottom two rows made from metavolcanic materials.

The chief diagnostic of the Paris Island phase is the Paris Island Stemmed point. These are relatively small triangular blades with expanding stems, sloping shoulders, and slightly rounded bases. Similar forms are seen in the Small Savannah River Stemmed and Otarre types of North Carolina, the presumed lineal descendants of the Savannah River Stemmed point tradition. As successors to the larger point types, these diminutive northern counterparts are believed to date to the end of the Late Archaic period, ca. 3800–3150 B.P. The Paris Island type, dating a millennium earlier, defies the long-standing assumption that bifaces typically became smaller through time: its local successor in the Mill Branch phase is the classic, often very large Savannah River Stemmed type.

Regardless of the sequence of specific biface forms in North Carolina, Late Archaic forms in the Savannah River Piedmont clearly started off small. The most likely root for these relatively smallish origins is found in the widespread Morrow Mountain tradition. The tapered stemmed bifaces that are the hallmark of the Morrow Mountain tradition are among the most common types found at sites in the Piedmont. Paris Island Stemmed points made from quartz—a ubiquitous Piedmont raw material and the most common rock used to make Morrow Mountain points—bear great resemblance to these Middle Archaic predecessors. Indeed, if the stem of a Paris Island Stemmed was tapered, it would be a Morrow Mountain point. The long gap in time between the latest dates for Morrow Mountain points and the beginnings of the Paris Island phase makes it difficult to speculate on the actual historical relationships between these two traditions. It is noteworthy, however, that the soapstone cooking stones so prevalent in Paris Island assemblages have a precedent in Middle Archaic assemblages containing Morrow Mountain–like points (see chapter 2). Many more data are needed to chronicle the centuries bridging Morrow Mountain and Paris Island, but the point here is that the beginning of Late Archaic culture in the Piedmont was not marked by the genesis of large, broad-bladed and stemmed bifaces, as long believed, but by small stemmed forms that arguably evolved from local Middle Archaic ancestors. Big bifaces would soon follow in the Mill Branch phase, but at the outset of the Late Archaic came these relatively small Paris Island forms with deep historical roots in the Piedmont.

The Russell Reservoir excavations provide a glimpse into the lifestyle and community structure of Paris Island occupants of the upper Savannah River. At Sara's Ridge, Wood and colleagues excavated a 318 m^2 block to expose a

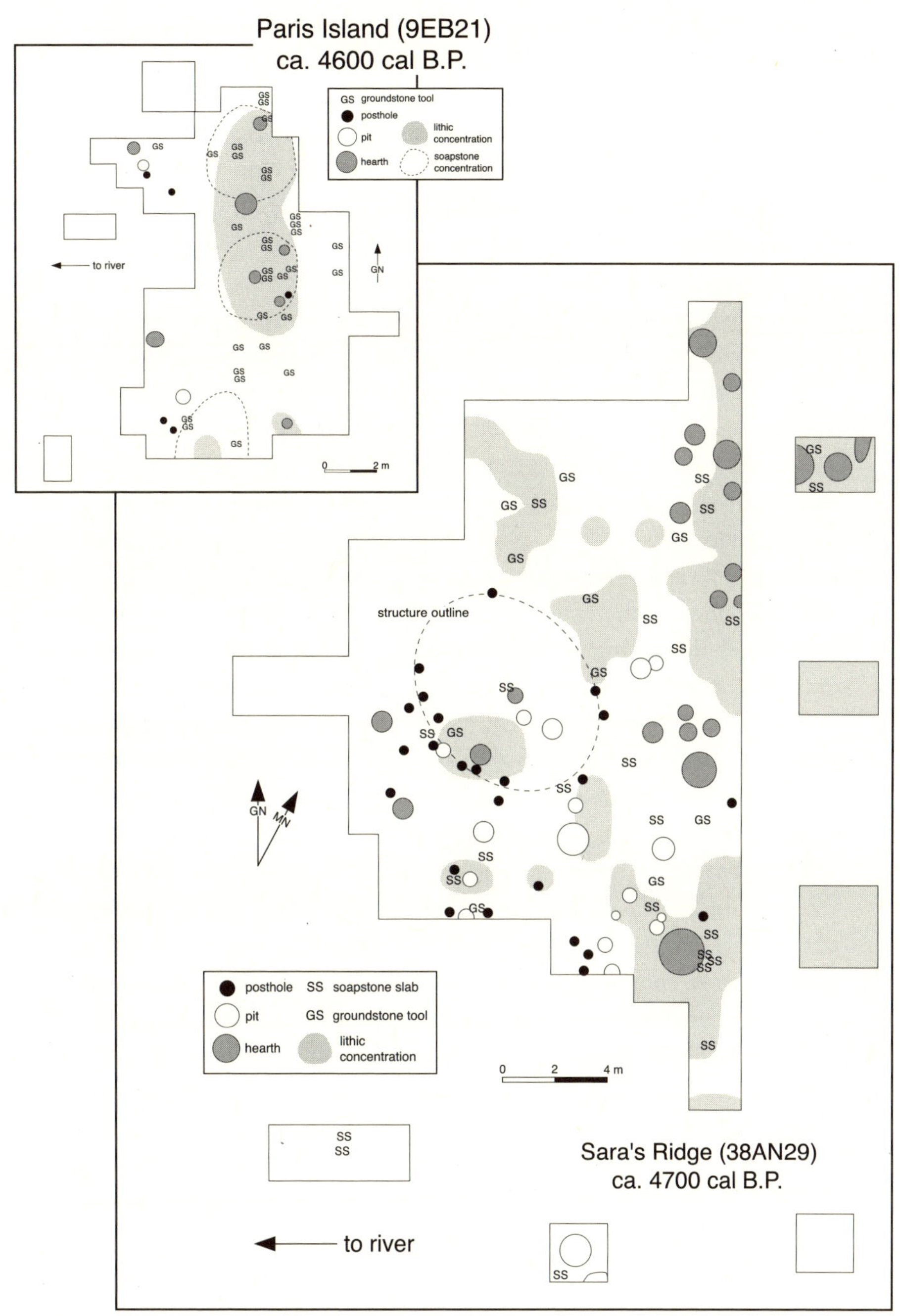

3.2. Plan drawings of excavations at Paris Island (top) and Sara's Ridge (bottom), showing features, concentrations of lithic artifacts, and an outline of a possible structure at Sara's Ridge (adapted from a report by Dean Wood and colleagues).

midden rich in cracked rock, debitage, and soapstone, bordering a nonmidden area with postholes, hearths, and pit features associated with at least one habitation structure. The midden ran parallel to the river channel for at least 25 m and was at least 8 m wide. Much of it may have accumulated through secondary refuse, although 18 formal hearths in this area attest to activities involving cracked rock and soapstone slabs. Groundstone items other than soapstone were not abundant.

The inferred structure at Sara's Ridge was situated on a levee paralleling the river, with midden forming on the back side of the levee. Postholes attest to some form of substantial architecture. From the incomplete pattern, Wood and colleagues postulate the presence of an oval structure some 7 m in maximum dimension. Two hearths and two shallow pits were internal to the structure, and several pits and hearths encircled the exterior to the south and east. Wood and his colleagues suggest that the shelter may have been open to the northwest.

A second series of postholes to the southeast of the first house may represent a second structure. If that is the case and the two were contemporaneous, interhousehold spacing would be roughly 12 m. Beyond this there is little to indicate that Sara's Ridge was the location of a structured, integrated community. Because of the position of the inferred structure(s) on a levee adjacent to the river it seems unlikely that additional structures would have been placed to the west. The arrangement of multiple structures, if present, would thus be linear rather than circular or arcuate.

Ethnobotanical evidence suggests that Sara's Ridge was most likely a warm-season settlement. Carbonized maypop and black gum seeds support a late summer occupation, and the lack of substantial groundstone and charred nutshell (when compared to other Late Archaic sites in the region) would appear to preclude a fall-winter occupation. Abundant debitage associated with the hearths, however, is interpreted by Wood and his colleagues as primary deposition, suggesting that core and biface reduction may have taken place around hearths for comfort during cold weather. Given the interior hearths in the shelter, a cold-weather occupation certainly seems plausible despite the lack of groundstone and substantial nutshell. In the end, archaeological evidence for the season of occupation at Sara's Ridge has proved to be ambiguous.

The second major Paris Island phase settlement with data on site structure is the type site, Paris Island, 29 km downriver from Sara's Ridge. A block

109 m^2 in area was excavated to expose most of a small midden, similar in content to the one at Sara's Ridge but with greater artifact density and abundant groundstone tools. Unfortunately, the area that would have held evidence for structures was largely destroyed by flood erosion. A few postholes, pits, and hearths west of the midden may signify the presence of one or two structures, although the evidence is ambiguous, as Wood and his colleagues note. Assuming that the location of the paired postholes reflects the presence of two structures, interhousehold spacing would have been roughly 10 m. The distribution of lithic debris duplicates this pattern if we accept that the concentration of debitage on the south edge of the Paris Island block reflects an activity area comparable in function to the larger cluster to the north. Three clusters (3 m in diameter) of soapstone slabs reflect patterned use of the midden area for cooking purposes at a use-area interval of 5–6 m.

Wood and colleagues argue that Paris Island was an intensive but short-term occupation. The seasons of occupation are uncertain, although greater frequencies of charred nutshell and groundstone tools compared to Sara's Ridge point to a likely fall-winter, if not year-round, occupation. Given the small size of the midden, perhaps no more than two structures would have occupied the site. It is noteworthy, however, that the area between the excavation block and the river's edge was sufficiently broad (over 30 m) to house a substantial community. The erosion noted earlier could have destroyed not only evidence for structures but their associated middens too.

Both Paris Island and Sara's Ridge produced evidence for relatively small-scale occupations along the channel of the upper Savannah River, and both appear to have been seasonal encampments. Given the lack of larger and more permanent settlement, we may be justifiably curious as to what Paris Island people did during the rest of the year and how they integrated themselves into collectives that were effectively reproduced for more than 20 generations.

The answer of course lies in the wider, regional distribution of sites of Paris Island age. Unlike the Russell Reservoir, the upland landforms paralleling the Savannah River have not been intensively investigated. Along with dozens of other biface types, Paris Island forms occasionally turn up in surface surveys and subsurface testing throughout the interriverine zone. But few sites in this zone have witnessed the large-scale excavations of the Russell Reservoir area. One exception is the Moody site of Edgefield County, South Carolina.

Located at the headwaters of Lloyd Creek, the Moody site was excavated by avocational archaeologists over a six-year period in the late 1970s and early 1980s. Although a complete report of their work has never been issued, plan maps and field notes were recorded and at least two presentations were given at annual meetings of the Archaeological Society of South Carolina. The group also donated a sizable collection of artifacts to the South Carolina Institute of Archaeology and Anthropology, where I pored through relatively well-provenienced bags in 1988 to discover a rich assemblage of Paris Island–aged material.

Among the thousands of artifacts dug from the shallow soil at Moody were scores of Paris Island points and perforated soapstone slabs, along with abundant debitage and cracked rock. Most impressive to me was the large number of bannerstones and bannerstone preforms. These drilled-stone artifacts have garnered a great deal of attention since the nineteenth century, when the term "bannerstone" was invoked to describe objects whose actual use remained mysterious. To some early investigators, bannerstones with large wings on either side of a central spine resembled double-bitted axes; hence they were referred to occasionally as "ceremonial axes." Later work in the Midsouth revealed drilled stones with spear points and antler hooks in human graves of Archaic age. The Depression-era archaeologist William S. Webb took special interest in these finds and devoted a great deal of thought to the design and use of Archaic spearthrowers with drilled stone weights. Often known as "atlatls," spearthrowers were used in various places worldwide, but only in eastern North America were they fitted with stone weights. Webb observed weights in direct association with other spearthrower parts in some Archaic graves in Kentucky, and thus his inference that so-called bannerstones were components of hunting technology seems unassailable. Trained in physics, Webb surmised that weights were added to enhance the momentum of forward motion when hurling a dart.

Reliable as Webb's observations may have been, certain bannerstones would appear to have confounded the mechanics of spearthrowing. A compendium of bannerstones published by Byron Knoblock in 1939 shows numerous examples whose size and elaborate shape go well beyond the technical specifications of atlatl weights. Among the more impressive are winged varieties with thinly tapered edges, recessed spines, and fine, raised details, such as spinal ridges. Borrowing a term from famed anthropologist Bronislaw Malinowski in his description of ornate exchange items among Trobriand

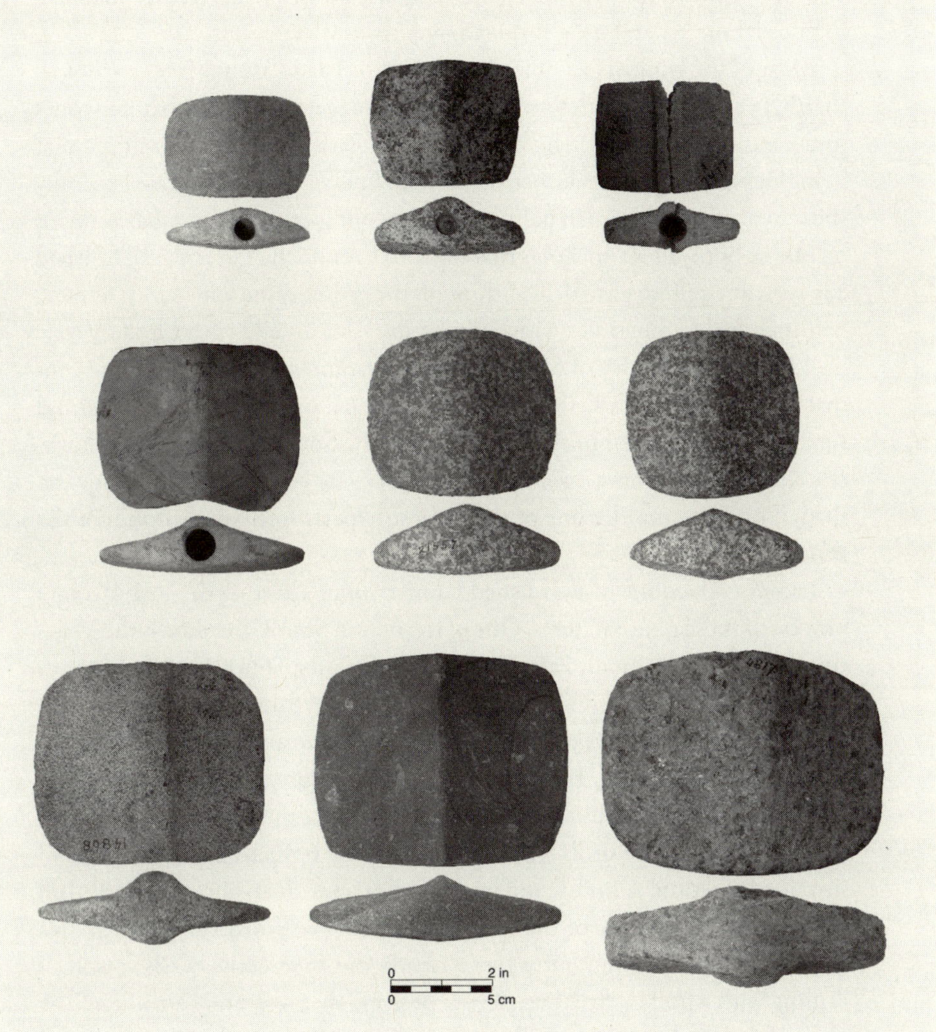

3.3. Plan and top views of Southern Ovate bannerstones and related types from the middle Savannah River valley. Those lacking holes are preforms; the example in the center of the top row shows a partially drilled hole (photo by Asa Randall; used with permission of the Peabody Museum, Harvard University).

Islanders, I like to refer to these fancy bannerstones as "hypertropic," meaning highly elaborated and usually quite large.

Most of the winged examples found in Paris Island assemblages are not all that hypertrophic, but they anticipate the exaggerated size of bannerstones in the ensuing centuries. The most common Paris Island form is a type that Knoblock dubbed the "Southern Ovate." In finished form, these are generally the size of an adult human palm, with a bisecting central spine that is raised on one or both sides and wings that taper to a rounded edge. Like all finished bannerstones, these were drilled through the center spine with a hole about a half-inch wide, sometimes with a tipped drill but usually with a hollow cane drill. The vast majority of Southern Ovates from Moody are finished items that broke along the drilled hole. One exceptional specimen is unfinished and square in outline, exemplifying a variant of the Southern Ovate, the Southern Rectangular. About twice the size of its ovate counterparts, this square-shaped preform may be one of the earliest hypertropic bannerstones in the region.

Larger collections of unfinished bannerstones attest to the manufacture process of these unusual items. One of the best in South Carolina is the Wiles collection from Calhoun Falls in Abbeville County, South Carolina. About one-fourth of the 30 bannerstones that I examined from this collection were preforms. Most were pecked to a near-complete size and shape, and one had a partially drilled hole. The pecking and drilling process was undoubtedly tedious, because the granitic materials used to make these items are very hard indeed. Hollow cane drills were likely turned by bows to achieve rapid and sustained rotation. A bit of sand would have served as an abrasive at the drill tip. The soft, pithy core of the cane would have been incapable of drilling a solid hole, but its tough outer tissue clearly did so effectively. The result of drilling with a hollow drill bit is a core of stone that resembles a golf tee. The taper of this tee-like drill core formed as the inner hollow of the cane widened from wear. Occasional examples of drill cores with complex shapes testify to the replacement of worn-out cane with fresh material.

The interpretive value of hollow cane drill cores far outstrips their small size and unassuming character. Dan Elliott recognized this in his excavations at the Lovers Lane site in Richmond County, Georgia, where he found five drill cores along with several bannerstone fragments of the Mill Branch variety. Small as these drill cores were, Elliott would not have recovered them without screening. In the absence of whole or broken preforms, cores may be

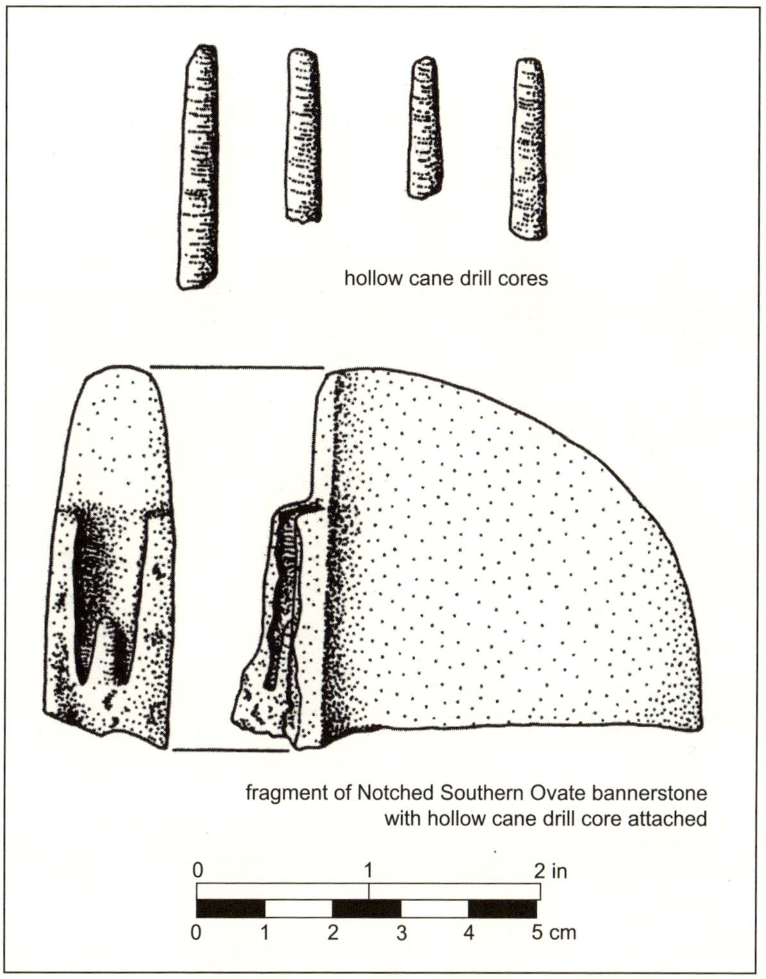

3.4. Drawings of hollow cane drill cores (top) and a preform fragment with the nipple of the drill core intact (bottom) (adapted from a drawing by Stephanie Brown).

the only evidence for bannerstone manufacture at a site. This was the case at Paris Island, where a single drill core was the only evidence of this technology. Cores are thus an important, if subtle, means of gauging the locations and scale of manufacture across the region.

Assemblages like those from Moody and the Calhoun Falls area attest to an intensive level of bannerstone production during Paris Island times. Interestingly, the small number of finished products in the middle Savannah area is

3.5. Mill Branch hafted bifaces from Stallings Island, Georgia (photo by Asa Randall; used with permission of the Peabody Museum, Harvard University).

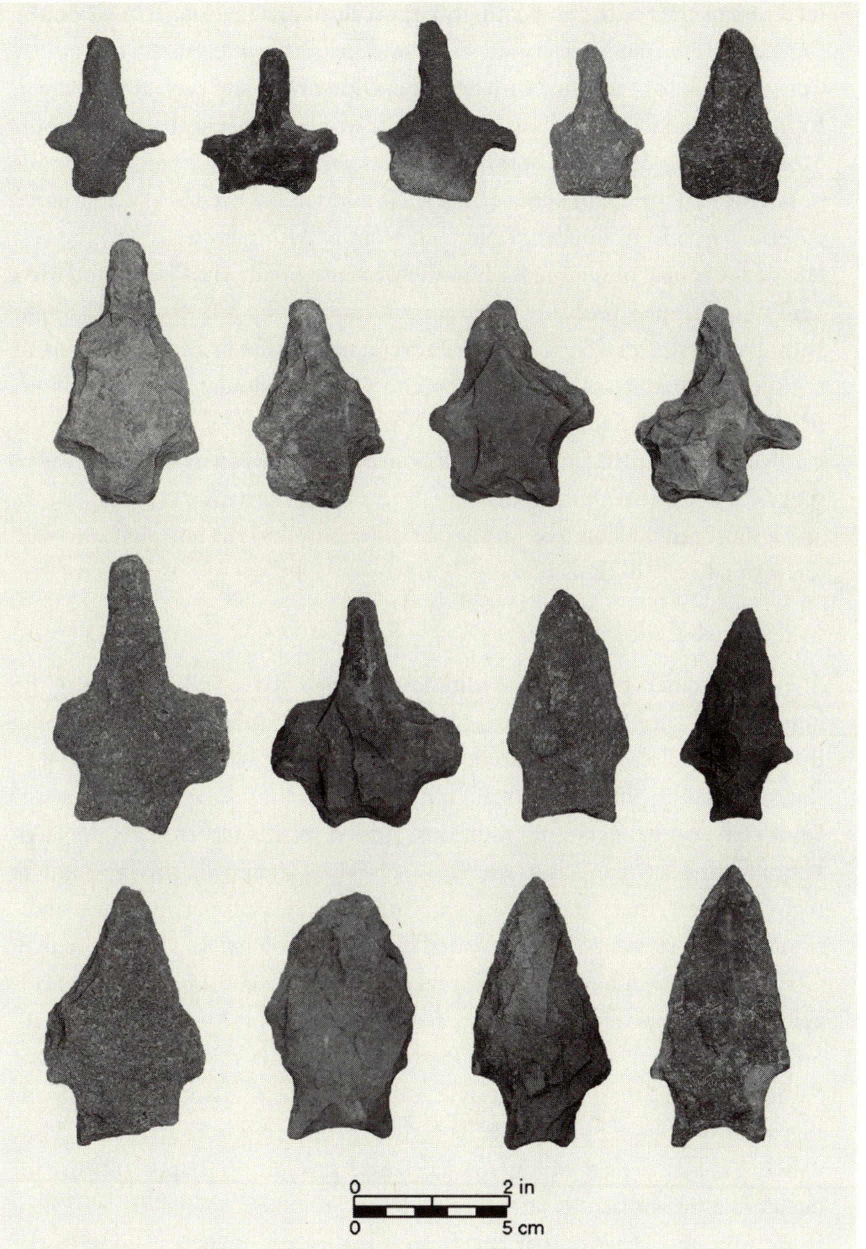

3.6. Mill Branch hafted bifaces from Stallings Island, Georgia, featuring examples of drills that were formed through advanced resharpening of blade margins (photo by Asa Randall; used with permission of the Peabody Museum, Harvard University).

incommensurate with the seemingly large scale of production. That is because some of the items manufactured in the middle to upper Savannah apparently were destined for exchange with neighbors downriver and even farther afield. Examples from Early Stallings sites include whole bannerstones from Rabbit Mount and Sapelo Island. Southern Ovates have also been found in mounds in northeast Florida, in some of the shell middens of the middle Tennessee River valley, and in northeast North Carolina. Although we cannot be certain of the source of remote finds to the west and north, the Florida and early Stallings examples probably came from locations like Moody and Calhoun Falls. Bannerstones were thus one of several media that linked the upper and middle Savannah to other locales far and wide. No doubt interactions with neighboring Early Stallings groups were most frequent and intensive; but the wildly divergent directions in which Southern Ovates seem to have traveled suggest that alliances with "outsiders" were varied, perhaps even competitive, and a source of tension that ultimately contributed to the emergence of new identities, like Mill Branch.

Mill Branch Culture

The Mill Branch phase of the middle Savannah River valley is among the best-defined Late Archaic phases of the region because it is both very specific in form and relatively well dated. Spanning the interval of 4700–4200 B.P., the Mill Branch phase follows directly from Paris Island ancestry in its soapstone slab and bannerstone traditions. Added to this repertoire is the large biface form known widely as the Savannah River Stemmed. This type and its regional counterparts across eastern North America are part of a vast tradition of broad-stemmed, broad-bladed biface technology. As promulgated by Coe, this tradition has been widely regarded as the root of Late Archaic culture; but, as we have seen, smaller stemmed bifaces predate Savannah River Stemmed forms in the Savannah Piedmont. Another misconception about Savannah River Stemmed points is that they are directly associated with Stallings fiber-tempered pottery. I believe that this bias traces to the limited but widely published work of Charles Fairbanks at Stallings Island. This site indeed contains thousands of Savannah River Stemmed points, but we know from more recent work that this form is earlier and unassociated with the equally numerous sherds of fiber-tempered pottery. Fairbanks conflated the prepottery and pottery assemblages into one trait list for "Stallings Island Culture." Coe no doubt drew on this work as well as on the report of 1929 excavations by Claflin when choosing to dub the broad-bladed bifaces of the Doerschuk site "Savannah River Stemmed," apparently undeterred by Fairbanks's asserted association with pottery. Archaeologists today agree that the hallmark bifaces of the Mill Branch phase are closely related to the Savannah River Stemmed type; but some prefer to use the term "Mill Branch point," in recognition of their specific culture-historical position in the Savannah sequence (neither early nor late, but rather intermediate between Paris Island and Classic Stallings culture).

One of the best glimpses into Mill Branch culture comes from a remote upland site 25 miles from Stallings Island. In advance of kaolin mining operations in Warren County, Georgia, Southeastern Archaeological Services of Athens conducted salvage excavations at two sites. Under the direction of Jerald Ledbetter, the excavations involved stripping large areas that were determined through shovel tests to contain potentially promising feature assemblages. One such area contained a dark stain 5 m wide with numerous artifacts. No such feature had ever been observed before at Archaic sites in the area. If not for the artifacts exposed at the surface, Ledbetter and his crew might have dismissed the stain as a natural feature, perhaps a tree throw. The feature instead proved to be the remains of a semisubterranean pit house, the first ever found and excavated in the region.

Ledbetter's excavation revealed that the pit house was relatively small, roughly 4 by 5 m in plan and approximately 35 cm deep. On the eastern margin of the floor was a small hearth within a larger earth oven. A small clay rim was observed around the edges of the earth oven. Postholes ringed the outer perimeter of the entire house pit. Some of the postholes slanted inward toward the center of the structure, suggesting that the roof support was a low, dome-shaped affair.

Small though it was, the pit house contained more than 7,000 artifacts. The inventory was dominated by metavolcanic flake debris, but many large Savannah River Stemmed points, soapstone cooking stones, winged bannerstone fragments, drill cores from manufacturing bannerstones, and numerous other ground and chipped stone tools were also well represented. Artifacts on the floor on the pithouse were concentrated around the hearth and along the inside of the walls. This pattern was observed throughout the fill overlying the floor, suggesting to Ledbetter that the house was used repeatedly in a consistent fashion. Charcoal samples taken directly from the hearth returned calibrated age estimates in the range of 4350–4200 B.P.

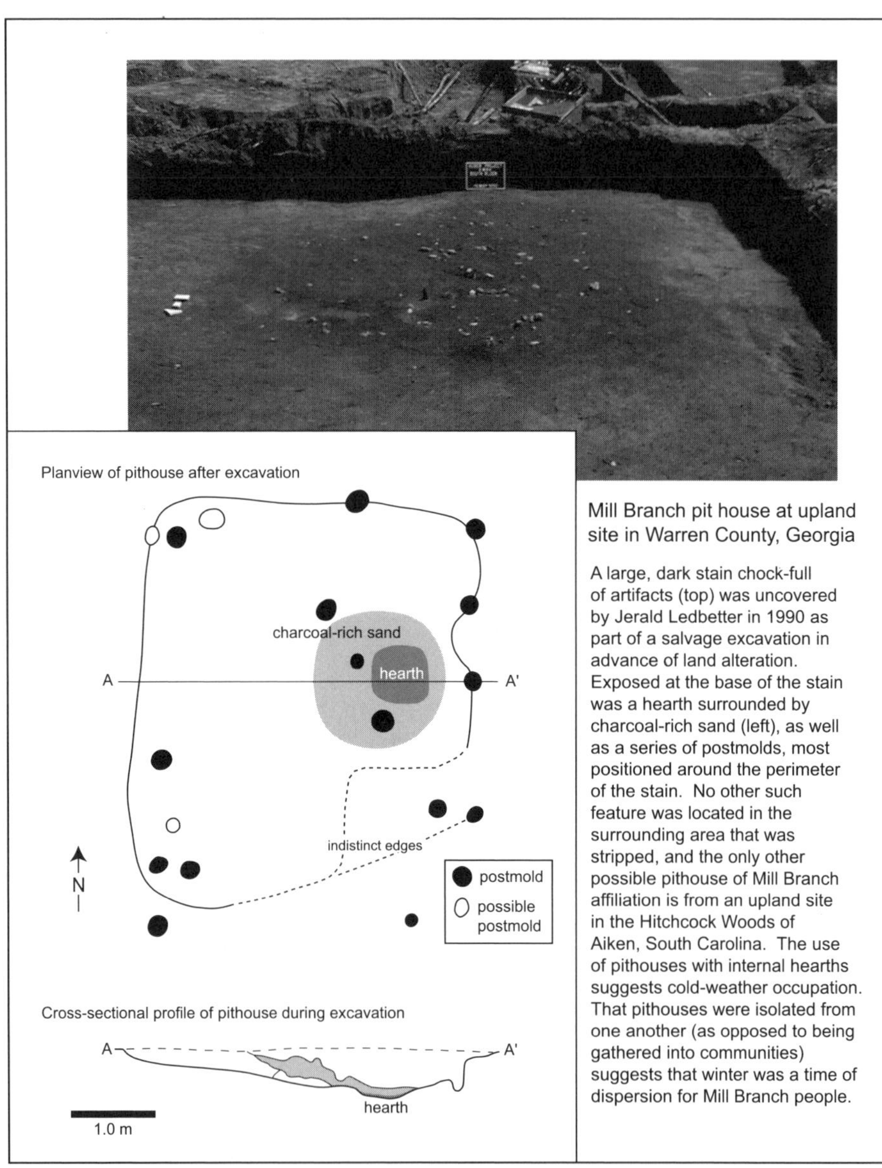

3.7. Photo, plan, and profile drawing of a Mill Branch pit house from an upland site in Warren County, Georgia (photo by the author; drawing adapted from report by Jerald Ledbetter).

The sheer quantity of ashy fill and heat-related artifacts (fire-cracked rock and cooking stones) suggests that the pit house was occupied during the cold months. Curiously, the pit house appears to have been an isolated structure. No comparable features were located in the surrounding 750 m^2 that Ledbetter and his crew investigated. A few isolated postholes were scattered across the area, but nothing to indicate the presence of a large resident population.

It is hard to know how common pithouse architecture may have been, because few other sites in remote, upland locales of the Middle Savannah have been investigated professionally. One possible counterpart in Aiken County, South Carolina, was thoroughly looted by two high school students in the early 1980s. One of the perpetrators later became deeply involved with volunteer excavation programs in the area and, of his own volition, made the collection available for analysis. The assemblage consists of an impressive array of Savannah River Stemmed points, cruciform drills, soapstone cooking stones, winged bannerstone fragments, hammerstones, and an usually large grooved axe. In all respects, the assemblage duplicates the Mill Branch type site assemblage. Our informant, the reformed looter, told us that many of the items came from an area roughly 5 m in diameter, perhaps a pit house. He also provided a sample of wood charcoal collected from a hearth preserved under the root system of a large hardwood tree. I submitted the sample for radiocarbon dating and received a calibrated age range of ca. 4300–4050 B.P. I have little doubt that this site represents the same sort of occupation that Ledbetter documented across the river, and the two are apparently contemporaneous.

Virtually all other knowledge about Mill Branch culture comes from sites along the Savannah River. Aside from the occurrence at Stallings Island already noted, Mill Branch occupations have been documented at Lovers Lane and Rae's Creek (on both the levee and terrace complex of the Georgia side of the river) and Ed Marshall (a shell-midden site opposite Stallings Island on the South Carolina side). Radiocarbon dates for these sites are consistently earlier than those few that we have from upland sites, but not by much. Both Ed Marshall and Stallings Island have provided several secure radiocarbon assays in the calibrated range of 4700 to 4600 B.P., the first century of the Mill Branch phase. The lack of later dates may constitute an error of sampling; but considering the new evidence from Stallings Island, we have reason to suspect that later upland sites reflect more than simply the last centuries of a long-standing pattern of seasonal transhumance.

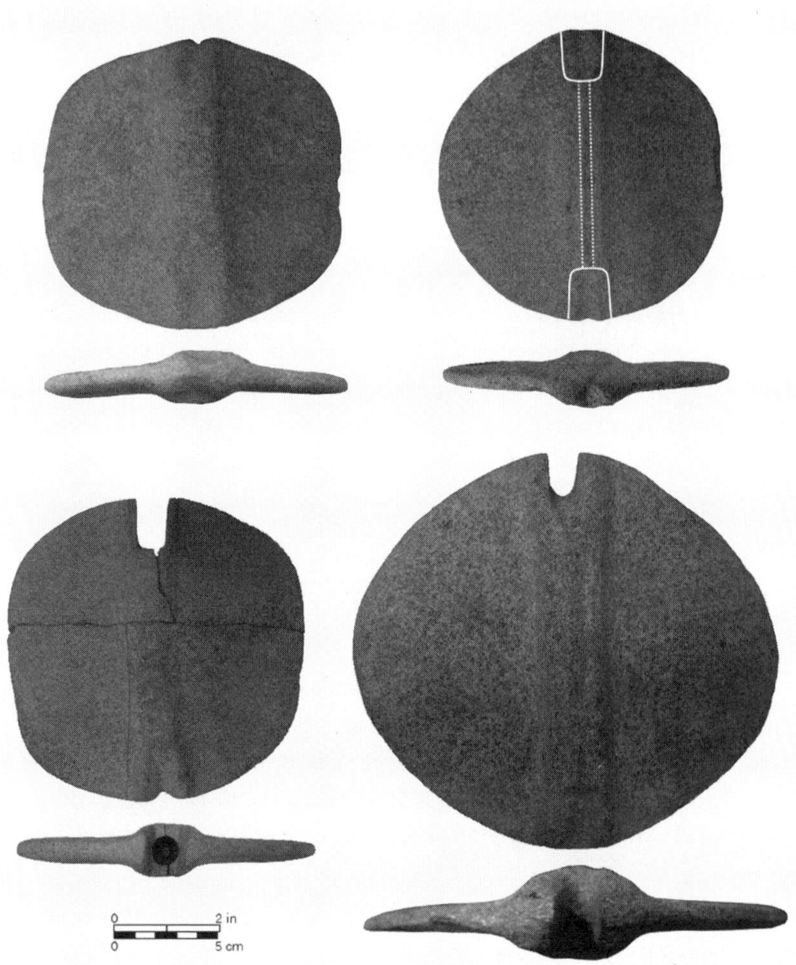

3.8. Plan and top views of Notched Southern Ovate bannerstone preforms from the middle Savannah River valley. The central spines have been roughed-out on four examples, but only the bottom two have one of the two notches cut out, and the drilled hole has been started only on the one on the bottom left. The solid white lines superimposed over the example in the upper right show what the outline would look like with both notches removed; the dashed lines down the middle represent the raised central spine of finished forms (photo by Asa Randall; used with permission of the Peabody Museum, Harvard University).

The Peabody-sponsored work at Stallings Island in 1929 produced hundreds of Savannah River Stemmed points and other diagnostic traits of Mill Branch culture. Later stratigraphic work showed that Mill Branch artifacts were concentrated in the lower half of the site, below the shell deposits that contained Stallings fiber-tempered pottery. Given the stratigraphic break between Mill Branch and Stallings, archaeologists tended to emphasize the differences between the two assemblages. Some suggested that Stallings immigrants from the coast completely replaced the resident Mill Branch population, bringing with them the practice of shellfishing as well as pottery.

Our recent work at Stallings Island has changed our perspective on preceramic use of the site. Like those before us, we observed Mill Branch artifacts in features and strata well below the upper stratum of Stallings affiliation, the shell stratum. But several of the deepest pit features also contained shell. Apparently occupants of the island collected and ate freshwater clams long before pottery was introduced. The comparatively limited amount of shell in these features, however, suggested that shellfish perhaps only supplemented a diet dominated by deer and nuts.

That was before we dug into the north slope of the island, which has an interesting history. Flood erosion had already washed out a considerable portion of the north slope by 1929, the year of the "big" dig. In that year the Peabody Museum crew trenched the eroded surface to reveal dense shell and refuse deposits nearly 3 m thick. They surmised that the shell and refuse had accumulated in an old flood chute. In other words, it was mother nature, not humans, that accounted for the thick deposit; thus further work in this part of the site was unjustified. Our interest in the north slope was piqued by looting activity. This area was the target of the most recent looting, some apparently occurring just prior to our fieldwork in 1999. One hole was especially impressive. In a spot only a few meters from the Peabody trench, a looter's pit some 3 m wide and 2 m deep penetrated dense shell and refuse similar to that observed by the Cosgroves in 1929. We took advantage of the exposure to open a 2 by 2 m unit adjacent to it. Even if the deposit proved to be redeposited, as the Peabody crew concluded, we could screen the fill and collect diagnostic artifacts for comparative purposes.

To our surprise, only the upper half-meter of the deposit was disturbed. Below that, for a depth of over 2 m, dense shell was interspersed with loamy soil in a tilted sequence of undisturbed midden. At the base of the deposit was a buried A horizon, an ancient surface. Two calibrated radiocarbon age

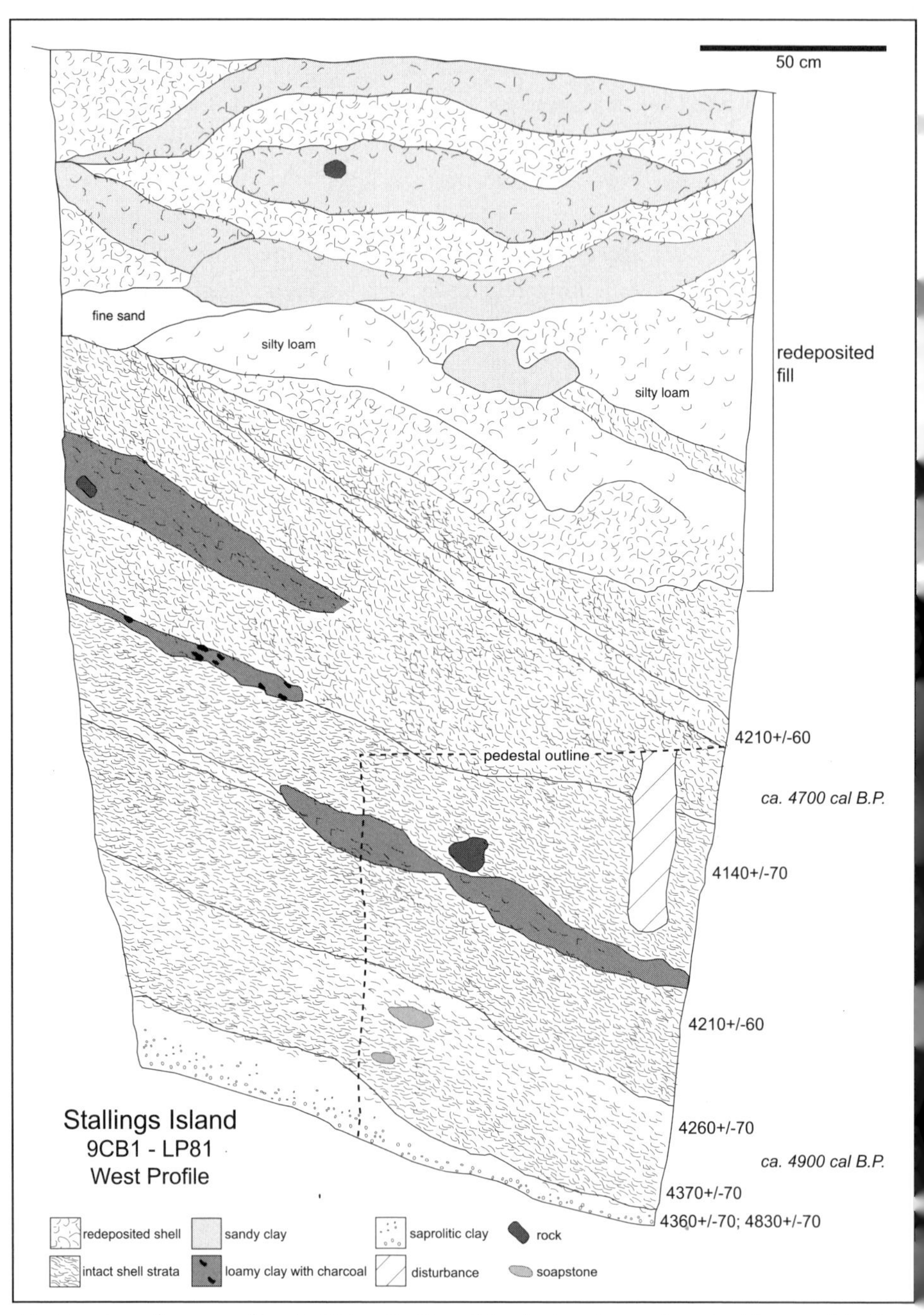

3.9. Drawing of west profile of LP81 at Stallings Island, showing undisturbed layers of shell in bottom half, with associated radiocarbon assays, overlain by redeposited fill.

estimates place the buried surface at 5000 to 4800 B.P., just prior to Mill Branch times. The bedded shell strata above the surface ranged in age from about 4800 to 4550 B.P. Throughout the fill were numerous soapstone cooking stones, fire-cracked rock, metavolcanic tools and flakes, and worked bone. Pottery was totally absent.

Mill Branch residents of Stallings Island apparently were just as fond of freshwater clams as were their successors, bearers of Stallings Culture. But rather than throw shells into pits adjacent to their dwellings, as Stallings people routinely did, Mill Branch residents tossed the refuse over the edge of the site. Granted, we have little evidence of Mill Branch domestic architecture at riverine sites like Stallings Island. But we have enough excavation to know that the large, shell-filled pits typical of Stallings occupations do not routinely occur at Mill Branch sites.

The Ed Marshall site provides our only glimpse of the type of housing used by Mill Branch people while living along the river. Ed Marshall is one of several shell-midden sites noted by Claflin in the 1931 Stallings Island report. It lies immediately across from Stallings Island on the South Carolina bank, on a level remnant only a few feet above current river levels. Our work there in the mid-1990s revealed a meter-thick deposit in a circular area about 40 m in diameter. At least one flood chute on the backside of the site cut through the shell midden as at Stallings Island, but at Ed Marshall the erosion was thorough. Even more damaging than recent floods were the prodigious efforts of looters. Dozens of large potholes pocked the surface of Ed Marshall, leaving only patchy remnants of intact shell stratigraphy. Happily, as at Stallings Island, looters stopped short of digging through the many pit features that penetrated below the shell. In these deeper sands resided cryptic clues of a Mill Branch occupation dating to about 4700–4500 B.P.

The typical Mill Branch feature at Ed Marshall was a shallow basin some 30–40 cm in diameter and about 25 cm deep. The fill of these features was typically very dark, chock-full of particulate charcoal and charred nutshell, along with examples of soapstone cooking stones, fire-cracked rock, and an occasional Savannah River Stemmed point. One such pit, Feature 25, was especially interesting, because of its abundance of charred acorn shell, the bones of waterfowl, and what appear to be the distal appendages of a juvenile canid, perhaps a young wolf. Against the usual backdrop of deer, turtle, and fish bone, the waterfowl and canid are strange enough; but more remarkable is the volume of acorns. No doubt acorns were a significant element in

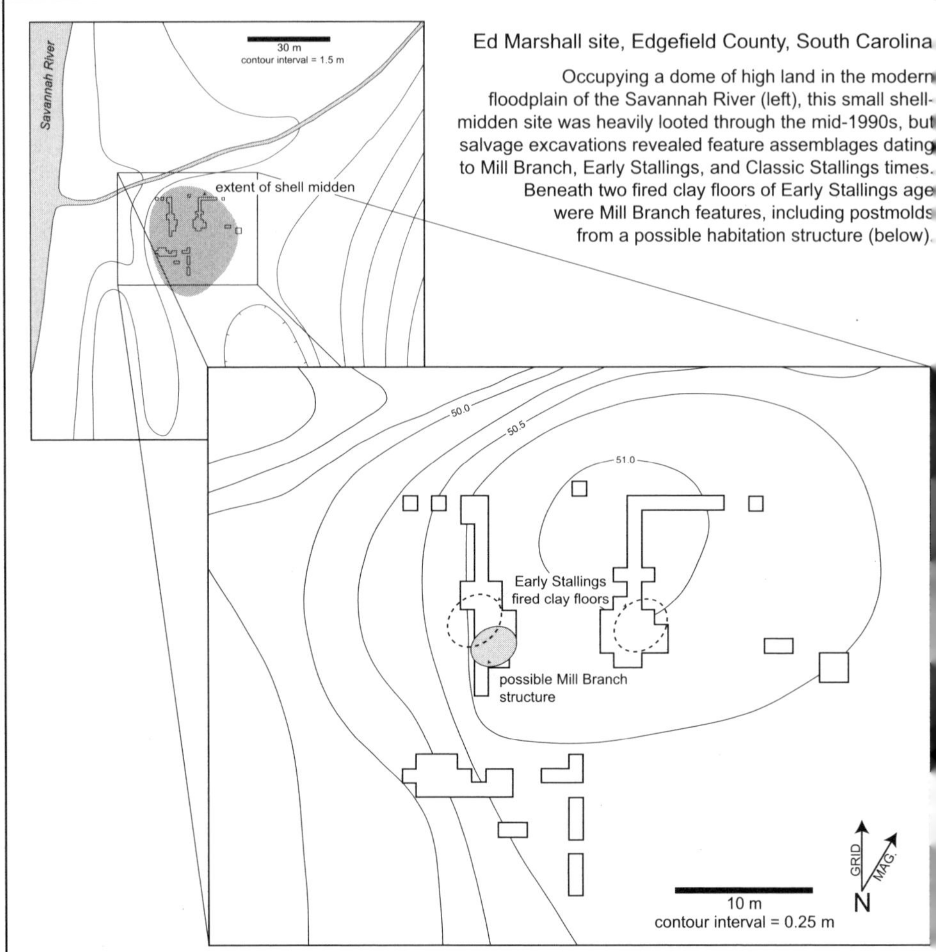

3.10. Topographic maps of Ed Marshall site (38ED5), showing locations of shell midden, excavation units dug in the mid-1990s, two fired clay floors, and a possible Mill Branch structure.

diets throughout the Archaic period, but their hulls are rarely preserved, even when charred, because they are so thin compared to hickory or walnut shell. The presence of so many acorns suggests that—like the Paris Island type site—Ed Marshall was a riverine locale with a major fall occupation.

Working among the looters' pits and mature trees of Ed Marshall, we were unable to open large areas down to the Mill Branch feature assemblage. In the largest contiguous area opened, however, we located several postholes in an

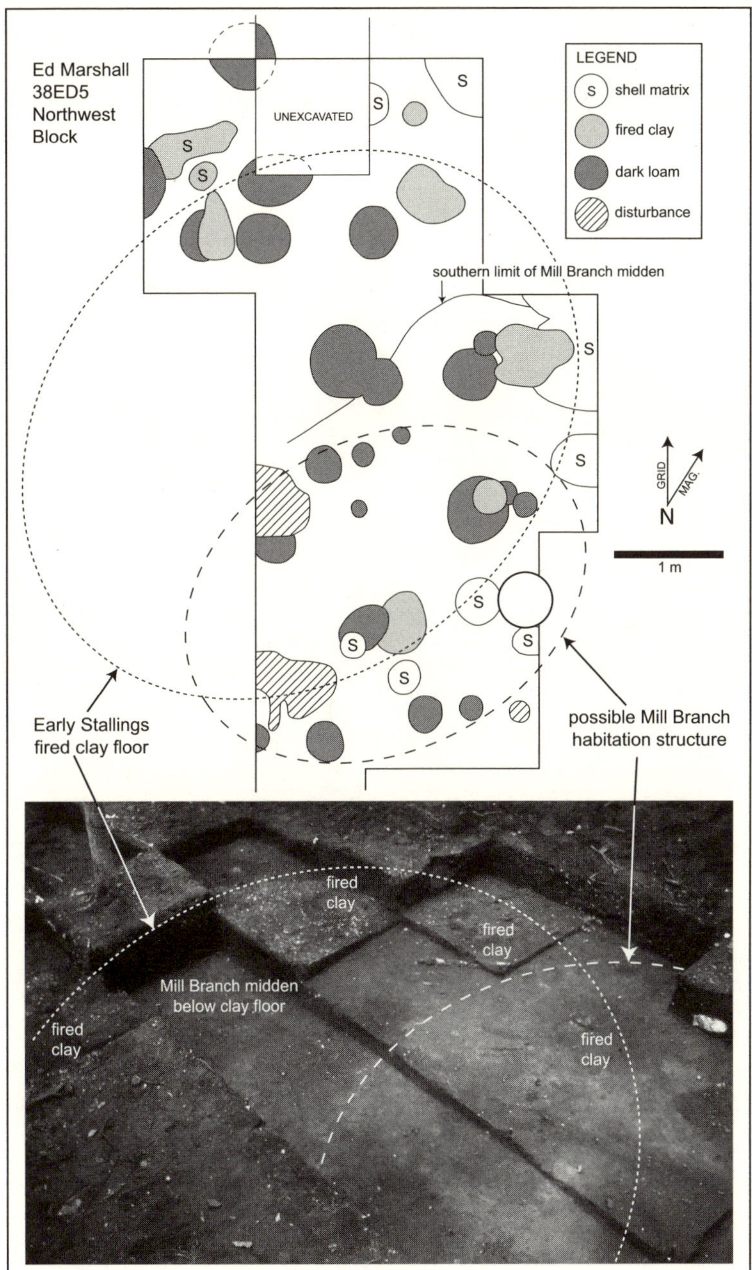

3.11. Clay platforms and dark stains in the subsoil at the Ed Marshall site provide subtle evidence for Archaic houses. In this small block excavation, about 20 m^2 in area, circular stains (20 cm in diameter) in the light subsoil formed an arc about 3 m wide; inside the arc were larger stains and outside it was a rich organic midden with Mill Branch artifacts. Overlying this presumed house floor to the north was a series of buried clay features in a second oval array about 4–5 m in maximum dimension.

arcuate pattern surrounded by shallow pit features. Incomplete though it was, the pattern of posts suggested a structure some 4 m in diameter, most likely oval or subrectangular in plan. We did not locate an internal hearth or any sort of thermal feature that might suggest cold-weather habitation, although Ed Marshall contained sufficient quantities of fire-cracked rock to attest to frequent thermal activities, like the type site and its Paris Island counterpart in the upper Savannah River. Another commonality between these sites and Ed Marshall is the small areal extent of the occupation. Even though Ed Marshall was not fully excavated, testing across most of the shell midden was extensive enough to indicate that the Mill Branch component was focused in the northwest corner of the site, an area too small to support more than a few structures.

Many other sites near Augusta attest to frequent, albeit usually small-scale, occupations of river-front locations by people of Mill Branch cultural affiliation. Coupling these data with evidence for interriverine occupations at places like the type site and Hitchcock Woods, we might be justified in thinking that Mill Branch settlement was structured by seasonal movements between riverine and upland sites. But the timing and seasonality of these presumed settlement moves do not square. Both upland and riverine sites provide strong evidence for fall and perhaps also winter occupation. Occupations at the river's edge during these seasons are certainly feasible, given typical weather patterns; most of the annual rainfall in the Savannah River valley these days comes in the late winter, spring, and summer. Occupation along the river may have be risky during the wet season, unless locations were selected for their relief. A low-lying site like Ed Marshall was especially vulnerable to seasonal flooding, but Stallings Island was high enough off the channel to provide secure lodging during all but the most severe floods. Thus year-round occupation of riverine locales during Mill Branch times may have been the norm, with minor adjustments in locations to sustain a reasonably productive domestic economy and to avoid the ravages of flooding.

This proposition is strengthened when we consider the timing of upland occupations and the temporary abandonment of Stallings Island. Both of the Mill Branch sites in the uplands date to the last 150 years of the phase (4350–4200 B.P.). Granted, two sites do not represent much of a sample. Considering, however, that no riverine occupation of Mill Branch affiliation dates later than 4450 B.P., a shift from a river-centric to an upland-oriented settlement pattern is clearly a plausible scenario.

The abandonment of Stallings Island is a key event in this scenario. Before radiocarbon dating was applied to a large suite of samples from Stallings Island, its stratigraphy was interpreted as a continuous sequence of events. Now that we have nearly two dozen radiocarbon dates to consult, it is clear that the island was largely ignored by local populations from about 4450 to 4200 B.P. This, of course, is the interval of upland occupations of Mill Branch culture. It is also the last few centuries of Early Stallings culture, which appeared in the lower Coastal Plain some 400 years before. Despite the seemingly total avoidance of Stallings Island during this 250-year interval, all was not quiet: other sites dating to this time attest to substantial Early Stallings occupations in the vicinity, two less than a kilometer from Stallings Island.

Stallings Island and other riverine sites of the middle Savannah were abandoned by Mill Branch residents just as Early Stallings groups began to infiltrate the area from their homeland downriver. These events are unlikely to be coincidental, given the long-standing interaction between Early Stallings groups and Piedmont indigenes. In fact, established alliances between these two groups no doubt enabled the relocation of Early Stallings people to the middle Savannah. Intermarriage may have been involved, along with a variety of other alliances predicated on trade. At the same time, some evidence would suggest that relations between the two groups were not universally agreeable. The abandonment of Stallings Island and vicinity by Mill Branch groups certainly suggests a bit of a problem. Equally curious is the elaboration of material culture among Mill Branch groups. Were some members of this Piedmont population bothered by the infiltration of interlopers?

The genesis of Mill Branch culture coincides with the earliest uses of middle Savannah sites by Early Stallings communities. These early forays may have been only seasonal and temporary, but they eventually grew to involve intensive and perhaps permanent use of sites like Ed Marshall. The response by at least some bearers of Mill Branch culture seems to have been emphatic. As a transformation of Paris Island practice and tradition, the emergence of Mill Branch culture coincides with the sustained presence of a "foreign" people in their traditional land. Elaborate bannerstones may have been a medium of interaction between these groups, perhaps a form of wealth for brokering marriages and other alliances. In systems-serving terms, such interactions may have underwritten insurance against failure, served as a means to alleviate conflict, or even diverted tendencies for competition into economically inconsequential directions. It is more likely that elaborate bannerstones signal efforts on the part of certain individuals or subgroups to assert identity in resistance to assimilation.

The abandonment of Stallings Island at 4450 B.P. may be another expression of this cultural movement. The final straw for descendants of Mill Branch culture was total abandonment of the area some two to three centuries later. Some members appear to have relocated to north-central Georgia, persisting for a few centuries more. Use of elaborate bannerstones and other practices of Mill Branch tradition ceased when they left the middle Savannah, however, signaling changes in practice that were spawned through interactions with "foreigners." The Mill Branch descendants would learn to deal with other people on the western fringe of traditional lands and, through these new dealings, conjure up new traditions and new ways of representing themselves.

Stallings Island would again be occupied at the time when Mill Branch disappears from the middle Savannah region. Known today as bearers of Classic Stallings culture, the new denizens of Stallings Island would leave an indelible and peculiar record of their existence. Their artifacts had a distinctive flair. Their pottery, for instance, was decorated elaborately with punctations and incisions. Carved bone pins sported a variety of concentric designs. Their clothing and hair designs were perhaps just as distinctive. There probably was no mistaking a Classic Stallings person.

All this attention to style and fashion suggests to me that Classic Stallings people, like their Paris Island and Mill Branch predecessors, were actively creating symbolic boundaries of inclusion as a means of self-identity and integration and boundaries of exclusion to distinguish themselves from their neighbors. In situations across the globe and through time, such actions arise in periods of stress and conflict, when rights and resources are being contested and individuals search for ways to define their place in a web of competing interests and claims. Inevitably, new cultural identities emerge from this process and come to dominate the landscape. For a few short centuries in the middle Savannah, the multiethnic landscape that led to such rapid transformations of culture would be dominated by a singular entity: Classic Stallings culture, the People of the Shoals.

4

Inventing Stallings Culture

There was a time in the 1970s when the origins of new cultural forms such as Classic Stallings culture were explained as consequences of environmental change or population-resource imbalances. These sorts of explanations were to some extent a response to the excesses of culture history of the 1950s and 1960s, when hypotheses for migrations and diffusion (such as those espoused by James Ford) were ridiculed by some as unscientific. Ironically, the alternatives inspired by theories of biological change became even more excessive, as they were predicated on processes of change that required specific cultures to exist in isolation from other cultures. Despite these excesses, some archaeologists still advocate the use of biological models to explain culture change.

Modern scientific understanding of biological change traces directly to the work of the nineteenth-century naturalist Charles Darwin. During a five-year worldwide voyage on the H.M.S. *Beagle*, Darwin observed things that most people of his time never even imagined. The diversity of plant and animal forms existing in remote places of the world was truly mind-boggling. On the Galapagos Islands off South America, for instance, Darwin documented species never before seen by Europeans. He also recorded variations among species more familiar to Europeans, like the common finch.

Variations in the size, beak form, and coloration of Galapagos finches were vast, and Darwin rightfully surmised that these differences arose as adaptations to particular niches, notably specializations in diet. He also correctly inferred that the ancestry of these species of finches could be traced to mainland South America, where a more generalized species of finch resided. Most importantly, Darwin recognized that mainland finches contained the rudiments of these island specializations: that diversity *within* species was the key to understanding diversity *among* species. At the time he did not have a sense of how completely new biological forms arose within species, a phenomenon known today as genetic mutation. But Darwin was pretty sure how new species arose.

Starting with an ancestral population (such as the mainland finches of South America), members spread out into new territory (such as the Galapagos Islands) and sought habitats that fulfilled their needs for food, water, shelter, and adequate mating opportunities. Slight variations among members of the ancestral populations, ultimately arising from mutations, enabled subgroups to fit into different niches. Given the process of natural selection outlined by Darwin, combined with the consequences of sample error known as genetic drift, these various descendent populations continued to evolve to become increasingly specialized. Given enough time isolated from one another, these evolving island populations became so distinct that they constituted different species. By definition, speciation took place when changes were so marked as to prevent members from descendant populations from interbreeding among themselves and producing fertile offspring. This, according to Darwin, was the origin of species.

As ingenious as he was, Darwin was no social scientist; and his theory of biological change was never intended to explain culture. Nonetheless, generations of social scientists since Darwin's time have turned to natural selection theory to account for the vast diversity of cultural phenomena worldwide. This is unfortunate, because cultures are not biological species, and human innovations are not genetic mutations. Although all cultures contain the seeds of their transformation in the diversity of their members, they rarely undergo major change apart from interactions with similarly constituted cultures. The point here is that—unlike the diversity of biological forms—cultural diversity arises from interactions, not isolation.

As is clear from my exposition to this point, I regard culture change as an active process of asserting identity in the context of competing or alternative identities. It assumes consciousness on the part of cultural beings—deliberate motives, agendas, and aspirations. Processes of biological change do not, as the invisible hand of adaptation sorts through diversity to select out those whose particular cultural practices fit particular environmental circumstances. Humans in this case are passive pawns in the "survival of the fittest."

As in the genesis of Mill Branch, Paris Island, or Allendale cultures, Stallings Culture was anything but passive. Its elaborate material culture was matched by an equally elaborate subsistence economy involving storage, the capture of large fish, and ceremonial feasting. Its community organization was highly structured around principles of circularity and internal differentiation. And its run was relatively short-lived. Despite a long gestation period, the apogee of Stallings Culture—the Classic Stallings phase—lasted only a few centuries in the middle Savannah region.

In this chapter we take a close look at Classic Stallings culture as it was manifested in settlements of the middle Savannah River valley. Stallings Island is, of course, a key site in this regard; but unassuming settlements such as Mims Point and Ed Marshall on the river and a handful of even smaller sites in the adjacent uplands are equally informative. We start off with the most conspicuous aspect of Classic Stallings culture: the famed punctated pottery that is the hallmark of this 300-year phase.

I have introduced Stallings fiber-tempered pottery in chapter 1 as the calling card of Stallings culture and considered its technological origins as a container for stone boiling in chapter 2. Here I want to consider the unique technological and stylistic dimensions of Stallings pottery as a measure of the cultural circumscription of the People of the Shoals. Several things make fiber-tempered pottery from the middle Savannah distinct from its counterparts elsewhere. Most obvious are the punctated and incised surface treatments, which distinguish Classic Stallings pottery not only from related wares but also from its plainware antecedents. At first blush the repertoire of decorations from middle Savannah sites appears no different from those in coastal Georgia or South Carolina. Yet subtle differences in the use of punctation styluses or in the way they are applied to form linear patterns set the middle Savannah apart from its neighbors. Even more distinguishing is an even subtler difference: the orientation of punctations to the right or left—a reflection, I believe, of the handedness of potters. These sorts of data may be the most revealing measure of the social organizational principles that circumscribed the People of the Shoals as a distinct people.

Beyond style are matters of technology and function. We have already seen how Stallings pottery started off as container technology for indirect-heat cooking (stone boiling). After about 4200 B.P. in the middle Savannah, and a bit earlier on the coast, vessels evolved to include shapes and pastes conducive to direct-heat cooking. Whereas the telltale evidence for direct-heat cooking (i.e., soot adhering to vessel walls) is apparent in assemblages from the coast, vessels from the middle Savannah are never sooted. We know this to be accurate, not merely a symptom of poor preservation.

I have long argued that the persistence of indirect-heat cooking among middle Savannah groups was a consequence of traditional practice, that Classic Stallings folks deliberately resisted the innovation of direct-heat cooking to preserve traditional stone boiling in the context of interethnic relations with Piedmont neighbors. This may have been the case, but recent work with the enormous Stallings Island collection housed at the Peabody Museum brings to light another possibility. Among the thousands of sherds of Stallings pottery in this collection are scores of rims from carinated bowls, a form with only trace occurrences at other sites in the region. Through analogy with similar forms of Mississippian age (after A.D. 900), these carinated bowls were likely serving vessels, not cooking vessels. As such they were probably often used in highly social contexts, such as ceremonial feasting. It is perhaps not terribly surprising that Stallings Island has so many carinated vessels, given its central role in greater Stallings society. They represent more than simply "guest ware," however, when we consider the time and labor demands that feasting may have placed on daily domestic activities. In ethnographic cases worldwide we know that such events and the ethos surrounding them can be the driving force of the economy. It is reasonable to suggest that in the carinated bowls of Stallings Island we find the seeds of this society's later economic transformation and demise.

Classic Stallings Pottery: The Hands of Punctation

Native American potters throughout prehistory in the American Southeast pressed into the wet clay of their prefired vessels all manner of decorative expressions, using carved paddles, cord-wrapped sticks, and styluses for punctation and incising. These methods resulted in tremendous variation: individual styluses varied not merely in form but in orientation, in the spacing, direction, and depth of punctations or incisions, and in the location of decoration. The options appear almost infinite. I once remarked that the range of variations in punctated Stallings pottery is so great that no two vessels had exactly the same decorations. This holds true to a certain extent, but clearly the range of options available to Stallings potters was not unlimited. It was bounded by traditional practice and by the allowance for individual creative expression, which, in all societies, has its limits.

Although the Classic Stallings punctations seem infinitely diverse, they are based on a pervasive set of decorative motifs. Linear punctations in the "drag-and-jab" variety are the most prevalent; among the many styluses used to create these designs, a subtriangular pointed variety was the most common. To execute a series of lines with an individual hand-held stylus, a potter typically inserted a carved stick at a low angle, pressed it into wet clay, dragged it a short distance, pressed it in again at a low angle, and repeated this motion until a complete line was achieved. Lines were most often oriented parallel to

4.1. This close-up view of drag-and-jab punctate design on a Classic Stallings sherd shows the intricate arrangement of individual punctations in curving lines of the vessel surface (photo by the author; used with permission of the Peabody Museum, Harvard University).

the rim but were occasionally perpendicular, oblique, or set in curvilinear or rectilinear fashion. No matter what the orientation, the method of drag-and-jab punctation required considerable dexterity. Like cursive writing, in order to be executed neatly and consistently drag-and-jab punctation demanded a delicate, controlled touch, the sort of fine motor skill that most people can execute only with their dominant hand. This technical constraint proved to have analytical value in our efforts to reconstruct Classic Stallings social organization. If we could determine the handedness of potters—that is, whether a potter was right-handed, left-handed, or ambidextrous—we could potentially infer patterns of descent and co-residence.

Understanding how we can infer social organization from pottery requires an excursion to the Puebloan Southwest. In the mid-1960s, when archaeologists were actively experimenting with the methods of their trade, certain Southwest specialists proposed that patterned variation in the way pottery was decorated revealed patterns of residency among potters. Like most potters in modern Pueblo societies, those of the ancient past were assumed to be women. Although any assumption about the gender of ancient craftspeople is questionable, cross-culturally over 90 percent of potters in nonmarket, non-Western economies are women (including those of Pueblo societies). We also know from ethnographic observation that in traditional Pueblo societies women remained in the villages of their birth, even after marriage to men from other villages. In anthropological lingo this is known as matrilocal postmarital residence, and the long-term consequence of this practice is residential continuity among blood-related women.

To see whether matrilocality was followed in ancient Pueblo times, archaeologists William Longacre and James Hill formulated the following testable hypothesis: if matrilocal postmarital residence was routinely practiced, variations in the way pottery was made and decorated would be greater between rather than within villages. If, instead, women left their natal communities to join their husbands' villages after marriage (patrilocal postmarital residence), then variation in pottery would be greater within rather than between villages. In addition to assuming that potters were usually or exclusively women, Hill and Longacre also had to assume that fledgling potters learned the craft from their mothers and thus carried forward the manner in which pottery was made, decorated, and used across generations of descended women. Their analyses generally supported the hypothesis of matrilocality and gave archaeologists hope that even lowly potsherds encoded meaningful information about social organization.

I never intended to search for social organization in the pottery of Stallings people, for lack of relevant comparisons. Contemporary Puebloans provided a direct historical link to the ancient past for Longacre and Hill, but no such homologue existed for Stallings culture. Under these circumstances I normally look for cross-cultural generalization as a basis for formulating hypotheses about the past, but in this case generalizations were suspect. Anthropologists used to believe that all societies with hunting economies followed patrilocal postmarital residence because it kept related men together and thus enhanced the success rate of cooperative hunting. We know now that postmarital residence patterns vary wildly among hunter-gatherer societies, and

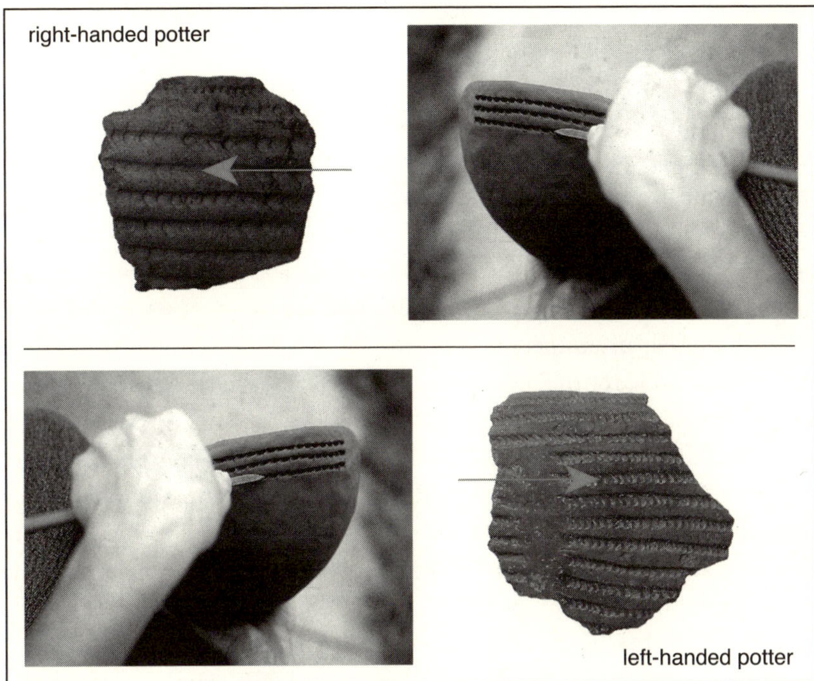

4.2. Lines of punctation oriented to the right (top) and left (bottom) correspond with the dominant hand of the potter if the vessel is held in an upright position when decorated. If indeed this was the manner in which vessels were decorated, then the handedness of potters can be inferred from the orientation of punctations on rim sherds, such as those shown here (photos by the author).

there is little to recommend the idea that any given pattern is determined simply by the sort of economy that people followed. I therefore had no basis for predicting the particular postmarital practices of Stallings communities.

Having no preconceptions or particular hypotheses in mind, we stumbled onto evidence for matrilocality from the punctations of Stallings pottery. It all began when a research assistant noticed that the low-angle punctations on drag-and-jab sherds from two sites in Georgia were almost always oriented to the right. I had assigned Kristin Wilson the task of analyzing a variety of technological and stylistic attributes for a large collection of pottery from the Chew Mill and Strange sites on the Ogeechee River. Frankie Snow of South Georgia College had salvaged the collection from looting at these sites and made it available to me for analysis. These were among the first sherds I had seen from Ogeechee shell middens, an understudied cluster of Stallings-related sites some 80 km south of Stallings Island. Although surface treatments on Ogeechee sherds were very similar to those from Stallings Island and other middle Savannah sites, the technology of this ware was much different. Ogeechee sherds were thicker, sandier, and denser than typical Stallings ware; many, in fact, lacked the diagnostic fiber and more closely fit the technological parameters of Thoms Creek pottery. Moreover, as Wilson recognized, few of the Ogeechee sherds had left-oriented punctations, a trait not uncommon in middle Savannah assemblages.

With the help of another research assistant, Wictoria Rudolphi of Sweden, we began to code for the orientation of punctations in sherd samples from 27 sites in the region, mostly from the middle Savannah, the Ogeechee River, and the intervening Brier Creek (a tributary of the Savannah). In our regionwide sample of 598 punctated vessels, the orientation of punctation could be reliably coded for 504 vessels. Of these, 89.7 percent were right-oriented, and 10.3 percent left-oriented. It is probably no coincidence that these figures match the proportions of right- and left-handed people worldwide. Because these figures duplicate global trends, I felt confident that our method for determining orientation was sound. We simply oriented rim sherds upright and coded as to whether the motion of punctation went from right to left or vice versa. If potters routinely decorated vessels with their dominant hand and held the vessel upright and not upside down, then the proportion of southpaw potters during Classic Stallings times matched the cross-cultural proportion of lefties today. If they routinely decorated vessels in an inverted position, causing a mirror image of handedness when turned over, then nearly 90 percent of the Stallings potter population was sinistral. This is an unlikely proposition, given that the highest proportion of left-handed people ever recorded in a population was 22 percent among the Kwakiutl Indians of the Northwest Coast, a complex hunter-gatherer society.

That the Stallings population matched worldwide averages for left-handedness is interesting but not terribly revealing about social organization. As Rudolphi continued to pore through collections, however, she began to see extremely high rates for sinistrality from sites in the middle Savannah. Drag-and-jab sherds from Stallings Island, Mims Point, and Ed Marshall had punctations oriented to the left at rates of 19 to 22 percent. Given the lesser rates of left-oriented punctations on sherds from the Ogeechee sites (9–11 percent), the high proportion of lefties from the middle Savannah suggested

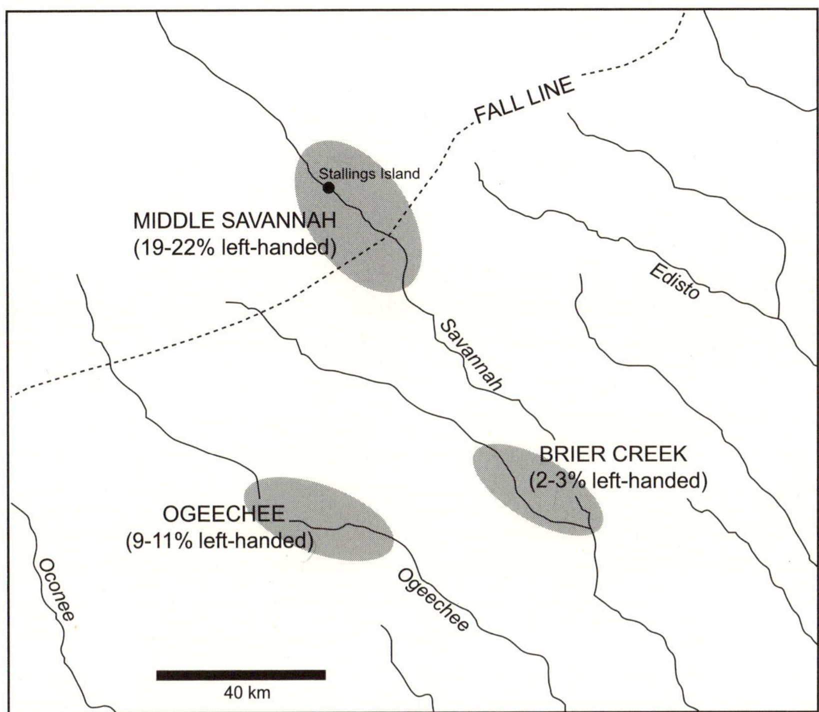

4.3. Locations of three major Classic Stallings communities with distinctive proportions of drag-and-jab punctated vessels with designs believed to have been executed by left-handed potters.

that the contrast between locales was nonrandom. Moreover, the intervening Brier Creek drainage yielded left-oriented specimens at rates of only 2–3 percent. It appeared that we had three distinct patterns to explain.

I was inclined at first to dismiss the differences among assemblages as sample error. But as Rudolphi completed the analysis of each assemblage it became clear that proportions of left-oriented sherds remained roughly the same within each locale. For example, after establishing that Stallings Island had a high fraction of lefties, she observed similarly high fractions in independent analyses of the Mims Point and Ed Marshall assemblages. This pattern of intersite regularity held across all three locales, although the number of sites in each locale is admittedly small and in need of bolstering. Nonetheless, an appropriate statistical test was employed to verify that minute differences *within* each locale were simply random and that differences *between* the locales were unlikely to be the result of chance but instead were indicative of some nonrandom process. The next step was to explain this nonrandom process in human terms.

Handedness is determined by a combination of genetics and cultural environment. The scientific literature on handedness and laterality is vast, with some authors on either side of the nature-nurture debate and many agreeing that both matter. Much of the evidence for environmental or cultural influences on handedness is compelling. Many studies have documented the strong social pressures for right-handedness among peoples worldwide. In some settings the pressure to conform is deliberate, as when the left arm is bound to the body to force use of the right hand. Sometimes the pressures are indirect, as when technology handicaps the sinistral. For example, the majority of chainsaw accidents in the United States are by southpaws trying to start and use a tool made exclusively for righties. This may be the closest that culture comes to Darwinian natural selection—assuming, that is, that left-handed chainsaw users are eliminated from the breeding population before they reproduce at rates equal to or higher than those of right-handed people. It also implies a genetic propensity for handedness, almost certainly a hereditary factor, if not well understood. In the absence of cultural pressures to conform, rates of left-handedness climb to just over 20 percent, as in the Kwakiutl and Stallings cases. They do not go higher, which suggests that the genetic component is subject to some sort of selective pressure, even if it is not directly related to the actual expression of handedness.

Regardless of the genetic propensity for handedness, the relative frequency of left-handed individuals in any population is affected by family arrangements and residential patterns. Offspring with at least one left-handed parent are as much as nine times more likely to be left-handed than are offspring with right-handed parents. Maternal influence appears to be a particularly strong factor. It follows that residential practices that keep related females together through multiple generations would have the long-term consequence of creating nonrandom distributions of left-handed individuals among residential units, all else being equal. If women indeed were the makers and users of Stallings pottery—an assumption I am willing to accept—then the handedness data allow us to infer a matrilocal postmarital residence pattern among Classic Stallings riverine communities.

Given the minority frequency of left-handedness in any population, unilocal postmarital residence practices over the long run would produce an effect in material culture analogous to genetic drift in founder populations. Importantly, the effect would be apparent only in the material culture specific to the gender experiencing generational continuity in postmarital residence, in this case women's pottery. About 15 generations of potters are represented in the span of Classic Stallings times. Observed variations in proportions of left-oriented vessels can be accounted for by differences of merely one or two left-handed potters in the founding populations of each settlement locale. Whereas these differences may appear insignificant, over the course of 15 generations these respective communities of potters became not only numerically distinct in their proportion of left-oriented vessels but technologically distinct in the preparation of ceramic paste and vessel walls. Potters of all three locales shared a repertoire of surface decorations, suggesting that alliances such as marriage enabled the spread of stylistic elements. But the technology of manufacture and techniques of stylistic application still varied consistently enough to enable modern observers to discriminate among locales.

If the geographical patterns that we perceive in orientation of punctations indeed reflect matrilocal postmarital residence among Stallings riverine communities, then a reciprocal pattern ought to be evident in the geographic distribution of men's technology. That is, a pattern of mate recruitment that effectively reallocated young adult men through marriage to the communities of their spouses should serve to randomize the distributions of male-specific material attributes, whatever those may be. While we cannot assume that all flaked stone tools were made and used by men, the apparent increased diversity in hafted biface form and raw material selection marking the onset of Classic Stallings times may very well point in this direction.

The upshot of all this is that Classic Stallings communities were circumscribed around groups of related women. The material evidence of women and their activities may indeed be the dominant aspect of the Stallings archaeological record. Besides the pottery, the record is rife with the remains of shellfish and fish, which are the product of activities that women participate in or even dominate in cultures across the globe. Fire-cracked rock, groundstone, and soapstone slabs, all tied to plant-processing and other cooking activities, might also be largely the purview of women. So pervasive is the gender bias that I once called Classic Stallings culture a "culture of women." Ironically, feminist criticism of archaeological research on hunter-gatherer societies through the 1980s centered on the pervasive male bias of hunting technology, notably stone tools. Classic Stallings culture is perhaps the opposite effect, involving our archaeological recognition of the social structures that ensured that related women lived together throughout their lives.

Serving Up Stallings Culture

It is hard to reconcile the idea that Stallings communities were made up of related women with the large amount of variation in decorative expression. Again, a shared set of stylistic conventions links the various communities together. Nonetheless, no two decorated pots are identical, even those from the same assemblage. Could Stallings potters recognize the works of others? In cases across the globe, non-Western potters add personal touches (if not outright signatures) to their products, which are recognized by others in the community and beyond. If stylistic expressions were simply passive and subconscious, we would expect a great deal of conformity among potters if they resided together, with one generation learning the craft from another and subconsciously following the routines that they were taught. Most anthropologists would agree, however, that style is actively manipulated by craftspeople to project an identity or sentiment, especially in contexts that are highly social and potentially contested or competitive. It certainly looks as if Stallings potters were striving to be seen and recognized, but by whom? Certainly not just by their kindred.

A theory of style promulgated by the archaeologist Martin Wobst helps us to realize why Stallings potters projected themselves so emphatically. Wobst was interested in understanding style as information. He recognized that information transmission, or signaling, took place at different scales of social distance. If the people around an artisan are familiar with that individual's identity and social status, there is little need to use symbols of identity that are highly visible and conspicuous. As the social distance between the observer and observed increases, however, the encoded messages get louder and clearer. It follows that decoration of Stallings pottery, being loud and clear, was not intended to remind sisters and mothers and daughters and spouses of who the potter was. Instead it was intended to project identities across co-resident groups—mothers-in-law, daughters-in-law, and sisters-in-law, the affinal relations that come with marriage.

This leads us to the proposition that highly punctated Stallings wares were intended for use in social contexts involving nonresident guests from other

4.4. Rim sherds from carinated vessels from Stallings Island, Georgia (photo by the author; used with permission of the Peabody Museum, Harvard University).

communities. If so, then intercommunity visiting during Classic Stallings times must have been the number one pastime. Considering that little, if any, of the Early Stallings pottery was decorated, the burgeoning in decoration that occurred at about 3,800 years ago signals a major change in the social landscape. Like the hypertropic bannerstones of Mill Branch, elaborate Stallings pottery was an emphatic way of establishing social boundaries and the rules of engagement.

All Classic Stallings assemblages in the middle Savannah contain examples of especially elaborate decoration, such as geometric designs, use of multiple styluses, and zoned punctation motifs. Much of it is also very well executed, so I suspect that intercommunity use of vessels was common. No site matches the artistic elaboration of Stallings Island, however; nor do any other assemblages have more than a trace of one particular form that (based on analogs) was almost certainly used in highly social contexts of food serving. That form is the carinated bowl.

We have known about carinated vessels at Stallings Island since the publication of the Peabody report in 1931. Claflin shows several examples in photographic plates in the report and briefly describes these "ridged" shouldered vessels in his discussion of Stallings pottery. But he provides no insight on their prevalence at Stallings Island or on their uniqueness in the region. Not until I visited the Peabody Museum a few years ago to examine the Claflin collection did I appreciate the significance of these forms. In the week that I spent there I examined about three-fourths of the 1,200 rim sherds in the collection. Of 913 vessel lots that I identified, 130 had carinated rim profiles. This amounts to over 14 percent of the vessel assemblage.

As is true with Stallings pottery in general, surface treatments on vessels with carinated rims are diverse. Although the majority involve some form of decoration, nearly one-quarter are plain, and another third are merely simple stamped. The balance consists of 20 percent drag-and-jab punctate, 4 percent separate linear punctate, 8 percent incised, and 10 percent with multiple treatments, usually a combination of simple stamping and punctation or incising. The prevalence of simple stamped surface treatments is not duplicated in other assemblages of Classic Stallings times and would seem to suggest that the typology established for relative dating of Stallings pottery does not apply to carinated forms.

The formal and technological properties of carinated bowls from Stallings Island are consistent with those of serving vessels used during late prehistoric times. In his study of Barnett phase (northwest Georgia) Mississippian vessel function, David Hally argues convincingly that this form was used primarily to prepare and serve large quantities of liquid-based foods in highly social contexts. The low, flat profile of the form and its wide orifice provide good access to contents while remaining stable and spill resistant. Carinated bowls in Hally's Barnett phase sample fall into two size classes: small bowls with orifice diameters in the range of 15 to 25 cm and large bowls with orifice diameters ranging from 28 to 42 cm.

Carinated bowls from Stallings Island do not cluster neatly into distinct size classes, although the entire range conforms moderately well to that of the Barnett phase. With a few exceptional outliers at either end, the frequency distribution of orifice diameters for Stallings Island specimens is unimodal, with an average of about 33 cm. Some are as large as 50 cm in diameter, a few as small as 18 cm. If these forms served primarily a serving function, as Hally and others have suggested, the larger specimens must reflect the biggest parties. Of course, more guests could be served with more vessels, so larger size is not the only way to feed more mouths.

Chapter 6 considers the extent to which carinated vessels were used for special occasions, such as ceremonial feasting. For now I reiterate that this form is largely restricted to Stallings Island and, to a much lesser extent, Lake Spring. A few examples have been documented at remote upland sites and riverine sites in the upper Savannah. Most of these coincide with large shell-midden sites with multiple human interments, raising the possibility that their use was associated with mortuary practices (perhaps feasts for the dead, which are known for any number of non-Western societies in the western hemisphere). It is also worth noting that the lack of evidence for direct-heat cooking among the garden-variety Classic Stallings vessels points to the likelihood that most were used for serving, not cooking or storage. The typical form is a bowl with a direct rim, some 30 cm wide and 14–15 cm tall. The generic form could have served any manner of functions, and we know from the adhering soot on some coastal counterparts that they were at least occasionally used over fire. I always believed that Classic Stallings bowls from the middle Savannah, which lack soot but match the features of coastal cooking vessels, were used in the traditional fashion of indirect-heat cooking. Now I am convinced that serving was the chief function, and the telltale stylistic elaboration of their surfaces points to social settings with nonresident guests.

Will the Circle Be Unbroken?

All indications are that Classic Stallings culture was purposefully designed, like cultures worldwide, to serve the dual purposes of including some and excluding others. The organizational rules of marriage and residence hint at a society turned inward, with figurative ramparts erected to preserve the autonomy and unique identity of discrete riverine communities. At the same time, the elaboration of Stallings pottery and emphasis on serving ware hints at a society designed to interact with "outsiders." The balance between alterity and self-identity, between exclusion and inclusion, was no doubt structured by explicit social rules but also by symbolic cues, many perhaps not consciously held. I believe that one of the more powerful cues was the physical arrangement of households in circles.

Good evidence for Classic Stallings houses, let alone community patterns, has been hard to find. The frustration that this has caused archaeologists is evident in William Claflin's report on the Peabody's Stallings Island expedition. He was confident that the concentration of firepits and storage pits at the top of the "mound" marked the location of a cluster of houses, but none of the telltale postholes or house floors were ever found. Adding to the frustration was the seemingly random arrangement of pits and fireplaces. Although they were indeed concentrated at the top of a mound-like midden deposit, occupations took place over such a protracted period and by such a variety of groups that deciphering community patterning was nearly impossible. Stallings Island was simply too complicated to be read so literally.

This is why Mims Point is such an important site. Located only a kilometer north of Stallings Island, Mims Point is the closest thing we have to a snapshot of a Classic Stallings community. It includes part of a community of several households arranged in a circle some 30 m in diameter. Each household had a series of pit features for food storage and processing. The largest pit—presumably for storage and later trash disposal—was located to the right of a doorway facing a small central "plaza," some 12–15 m in diameter. Shallow hearths were placed primarily on the back side of each house. At only 3.5–5 m in diameter the houses themselves were modest in size and construction but substantial enough to withstand cold and wet weather.

I wish that the evidence were this apparent, but the residues of houses and community patterning at Mims Point are actually a bit cryptic. Even so, the weight of circumstantial evidence and nonrandom patterning among fea-

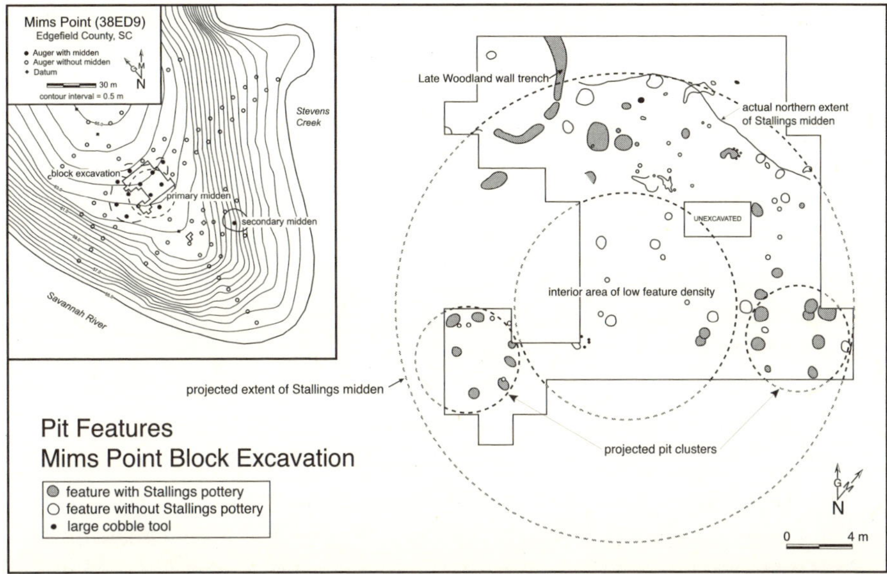

4.5. Topographic map, plan drawing, and photograph of block excavation at Mims Point (38ED9), Edgefield County, South Carolina. Clusters of pit features in the southwest and southeast corners of the block were likely associated with habitation structures arranged in a circle around an open "plaza" about 15 m in diameter. With a view to the west from the southeast corner of the block excavation, the photograph features in its foreground one of the two pit clusters (photo by author).

tures are convincing proof, I believe, of a formalized plan for Classic Stallings living—something that was uniquely Stallings. It took three field expeditions to amass the evidence.

Mims Point has been on the archaeological map since the 1931 publication of Claflin's Stallings Island report. He described it as a shell deposit covering about one-half an acre. Today it sits at the southern tip of the Sumter National Forest, with an elevated position on a ridge nose formed by the confluence of Stevens Creek and the Savannah River. It has all the makings of a good place to live. Still, in its wooded condition today, the location's traces of prehistoric shellfishing and habitation are inconspicuous. Working for the National Forest in the early 1980s, Dan Elliott had the chance to test Mims Point. He called on volunteers to help; and Glen Hanson, my old boss, and one of the local stalwarts, George Lewis, obliged. I don't remember why I did not tag along but remember them telling me upon their return that the site was largely destroyed and had little research potential. Elliott knew otherwise.

About eight years later I received a call from Forest Service archaeologist Robert Morgan. Looters had hit Mims Point, and Bob suggested that we do some work there before more was destroyed. He offered a partnership with the Forest Service and its Passports in Time program, which enabled interested members of the public to help with the fieldwork. With the institutional support of the Savannah River Archaeological Research Program (SRARP) and the South Carolina Institute of Archaeology and Anthropology (SCIAA) and a half-paid, half-volunteer crew that included Elliott, in January 1992 we began what eventually became a three-season project.

The first field effort produced mixed results. The crew opened 68 m^2 of the site to expose a variety of features from at least three distinct components. A portion of a Late Woodland wall trench was the most surprising feature, and it fooled us by containing several Classic Stallings sherds along with a handful of cord-marked and incised sherds dating to ca. 1250 B.P. Also surprising was the vast number of Middle Archaic spearpoints, notably Morrow Mountains and Guilford-like points. One of three human interments also dated to this earlier period; at least one of the other two was a Stallings burial.

Sherds of Classic Stallings pottery were found throughout the plowzone that covered the basal clay and feature assemblage, but few good Stallings features were found that first year. We did, however, succeed in delimiting the extent of the buried midden and its features by coring most of the ridge nose at a grid interval of 10 m. Midden on top of the ridge, where Elliott and now our group had dug, was restricted to a roughly circular area some 30 m wide. Our collective efforts to this point had concentrated on the north edge of this circular deposit.

In the second year we moved a bit southward and eastward, encountering more Middle and Late Archaic features, including some nice hearths and possible postholes. I was happy to see such well-preserved features but was disappointed that so few dated unequivocally to the Classic Stallings era. We continued to find the telltale punctated sherds throughout the midden; and the lack of plain fiber-tempered sherds and Mill Branch points gave us hope that we could isolate a distinctive Classic Stallings feature assemblage, Late Woodland and Middle Archaic features notwithstanding.

The third year was at last gratifying. Opening the largest area yet, we came across two pit clusters with combinations of deep storage pits, shallow basins, and hearths, along with some scattered postholes. All the sizable features contained drag-and-jab pottery and abundant, well-preserved faunal remains. A few of the largest features also provided a wealth of artifacts, including the usual bifaces, debitage, and soapstone slabs as well as axe fragments, bone fishhooks, and socketed antler points. One feature in particular, Feature 51, contained so many interesting and unusual artifacts that I could not get the crew to quit at the end of the day because they had more to remove. Naturally I let them continue.

We did not uncover and excavate the entire Classic Stallings feature assemblage at Mims Point. Nonetheless, we uncovered enough in the 364 m^2 that we opened to see the nonrandom patterning of Stallings features. Pits of diverse size and shape were associated with hearths in clusters along the inside perimeter of the midden. Except for one pit cluster and a hearth in the northeast quadrant, the interior core of the midden was relatively devoid of pit features, giving the impression of a central clean area some 15–16 m in diameter.

Pit clusters along the inside perimeter of the midden included at least one large storage pit. Nearly 1 m wide, these meter-deep pits were sunk into residual clay and later used as receptacles for refuse, like Feature 51, which was filled with abundant diagnostic artifacts and well-preserved organic remains. In the two best-documented clusters, storage pits occupied positions to the right of an orientation facing the center. I suspect that each of these feature clusters was the location of a domestic structure, with an associated storage pit to the right of an opening that faced inward. Occasional postholes and negative spaces among pit clusters are suggestive although admittedly inconclusive evidence for actual structures. House floors were compromised by historic-era plowing, and post construction must have been shallow, if at all routinely practiced. Nevertheless, the proxy evidence for structures afforded by the pit clusters suggests about eight domestic spaces on the order of 30 m^2 each, spaced along the inside perimeter of the midden about 6–8 m apart.

It is not at all surprising that Classic Stallings communities would have arranged themselves in circular or arcuate fashion. After all, the cultural roots of their pottery technology and penchant for shellfish are traceable to coastal populations, as noted in chapter 2. These People of the Coast constructed and occupied shell rings throughout their history. Their donut-shaped accumulations of shell ranged from tens to hundreds of meters in diameter. Researchers over the past few decades have observed enough cooking features and associated food refuse to know that the shell rings formed through subsistence activities, presumably associated with households arrayed in a circle around an open, public space. Direct evidence for household architecture is missing, but it is almost certain that people actually resided at shell rings at least seasonally, if not year-round.

Mims Point is not a shell ring (and would be among the smallest ever recorded if it were). Its affinity to coastal shell rings is simply in the circular plan. Whereas this sort of community plan is widespread later in southeastern prehistory, and is actually common worldwide, it was unique for the time and place of Classic Stallings culture. If it indeed signifies Classic Stallings culture like its counterpart in pottery, then circular village arrangements must have been pervasive. So far only one other small site in the middle Savannah, Ed Marshall, offers testimony to circular community structure, albeit faint testimony. Like Stallings Island, Ed Marshall has multiple Late Archaic components and was subject to intense looting and flood damage in recent years. We dug enough of this quarter-acre floodplain site to know that Classic Stallings sherds are concentrated in a ring-like fashion, 30 m wide. I wish that we had the feature evidence to corroborate the Mims Point pattern.

Stallings Island has no shortage of features and no shortage of shell either. It is the largest accumulation in the middle Savannah and, as we have seen, the locus of some unique activities. Could Stallings Island be the interior equivalent to large coastal shell rings? This proposition grows increasingly likely as we continue to delve into the internal configuration of this complex riverine site. Consider, for instance, the thick accumulations of shell around the perimeter of the "mound" at Stallings Island. Claflin knew that what his predecessors called a mound was actually a natural dome of clay left by the erosive currents of the Savannah River. The 3- to 4-foot midden atop this dome of clay was surrounded on all sides by thicker accumulations of shell and refuse. Claflin reckoned that "the occupants of the mound threw their refuse over the sides, thus surrounding their house site with vast masses of these food shells." As noted earlier, Claflin also recognized that pits, hearths, and other evidence for habitation were concentrated at the top of the clay dome.

Given the spatial relationship between habitation space and the secondary refuse strewn about the perimeter of this space, it follows that—if Stallings Island was a flat landform—long-term occupations would have resulted in a circular or oval ridge of shell and refuse around a central village area. As tantalizing as this may sound, two points of deviation from a coastal shell-ring pattern are immediately noteworthy. First, domestic activities at Stallings Island appear to have been concentrated at the center and top of the landform and would have been impossible to stage on the surrounding side slopes, whereas the center portions of coastal shell rings were usually devoid of archaeological residues and the rings themselves were apparently the locus of domestic activities. Second, as noted in chapter 3, our 1999 expedition to Stallings Island showed that much of the shell accumulation on the north side of the deposit is prepottery in age. As Claflin warned, floods had ravaged the sides of the "mound," and thus most of the Classic Stallings side-slope midden presumably was scoured away in the early twentieth century. Nonetheless, the differences between Stallings Island and coastal shell rings show that interior Stallings communities were not simply displaced coastal groups carrying on unchanged, while the similarities are strong enough to suggest that "life in the round" was a shared tradition.

When we added to this mix the substantial evidence for a circular village at Mims Point and possibly at Ed Marshall, we had ample reason to expect a circular village at Stallings Island. The question remained: how could one tease out a circular village from the seemingly random array of features and complex midden on Stallings Island? After all, the digging had been done. Claflin and the Cosgroves found no structures.

Undeterred, my graduate students and I aimed to decipher Stallings Island through a two-pronged approach: a bit more fieldwork and a lot of collections research. Our 1999 expedition to Stallings Island was designed expressly to locate the Cosgroves' Trench 2, which bisected the entire mound-like deposit, and find datable organic material so that we could establish an internal chronology for the site. Although Claflin and his colleagues were convinced that the majority of the deposit was the work of one people, later investigators documented substantial prepottery uses of the island, including pit features and burials. It was thus critical to discriminate among the various components before trying to interpret site structure or community patterning. Which features belonged to each group?

Our frustration in locating the trench was immediately offset by the discovery of pit features at the top of the clay substrate. Some of these features had been dug and backfilled by the Cosgroves. The plan map published by Claflin showed the location and size of all the pits excavated by the Cosgroves, so relocating some of the features enabled us to relate our finds to the published feature plan spatially. In addition, we located features either overlooked or ignored by the 1929 team, giving us the opportunity to extract pit contents for modern analyses of fauna, plant remains, and artifacts. What we found in these unexcavated pits did not surprise me, given our work at Mims Point. Pits independently dated by radiocarbon to the calibrated interval of ca. 4200–3800 B.P. consistently contained drag-and-jab Stallings pottery; those lacking pottery consistently dated to much earlier occupations, mostly in the range of 5300–4600 B.P.

We have the trash-removal practices of Classic Stallings people to thank for the strong tendency of their features to contain diagnostic artifacts. The pits they dug for storage and cooking purposes usually became receptacles for trash. This gave us hope that if we could identity all the pits at Stallings Island containing drag-and-jab and related decorated pottery sherds, we could possibly infer community patterning. Unfortunately, Claflin did not publish a table or appendix with the contents of the 110 pits dug by the Cosgroves, and they indeed dug out the heart of the site. The few pits we encountered and dug in our limited work would hardly suffice.

Luckily, the Cosgroves recorded some field notes about pit contents. Peabody Museum curator Diana Loren surprised me with these notes on my first visit to see the collection in 2001. The notes include systematic descriptions of the location, diameter, depth into basal clay, and general content and condition of all 110 pits that the Cosgroves mapped and dug. Clearly indicated

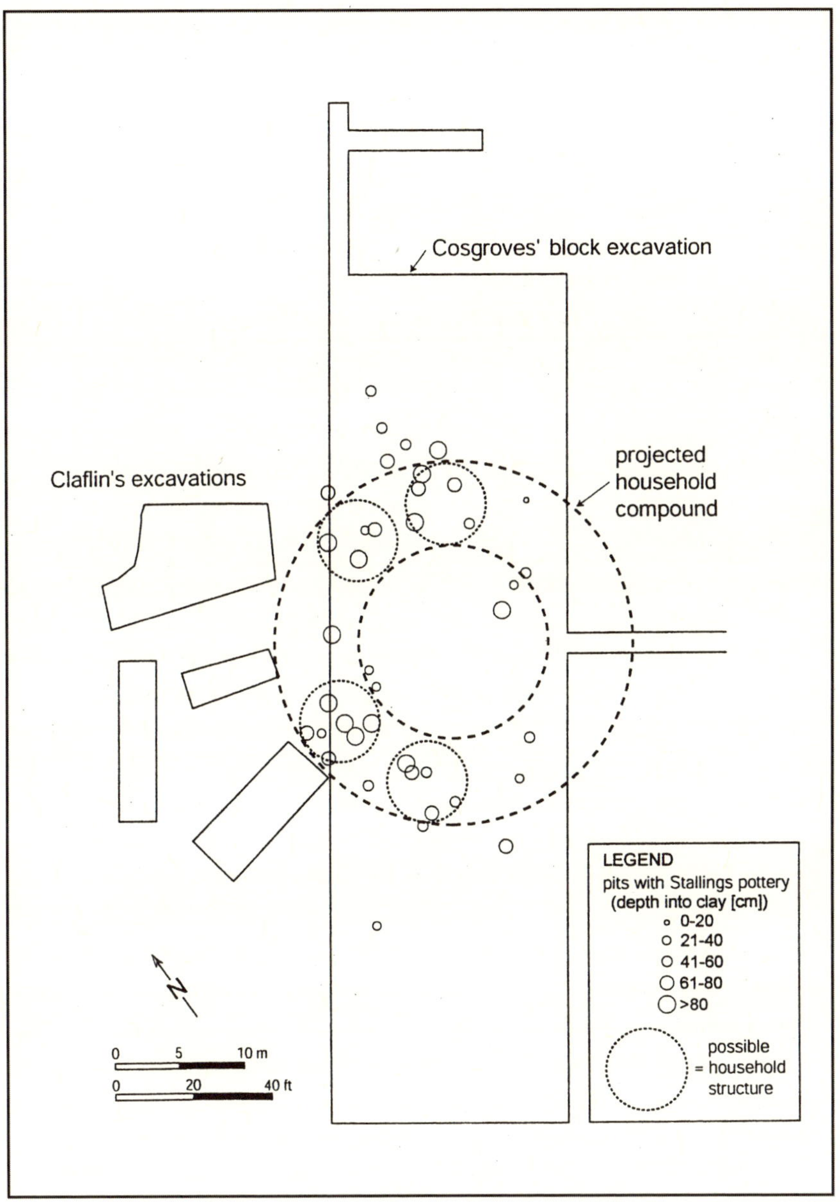

4.6. Plan drawing of the Cosgroves' block excavation at Stallings Island, showing only those pit features with Stallings pottery and a projected circular compound with four possible households. Each of the pit clusters of the possible households includes a combination of shallow and deep pits. Pits located outside of the block were mapped and excavated in 1999 by the University of Florida expedition.

are pits containing sherds of the "typical" Stallings ware. Decoration on pottery from pits is described initially as "parallel line stick marked" or "striated and stick marked" and thereafter simply as "typical." Of the 57 pits with diagnostic artifacts in the Cosgroves' block excavation, 38 contained Classic Stallings pottery. Several of the remaining pits contained telltale evidence of later Mississippian occupations, while most of those without pottery but with soapstone slabs are most likely prepottery in age.

These newfound data on pit content were entered into a digital database on the locations of all pits in the Cosgroves' block to search for spatial regularities. Remarkably, pits with Stallings pottery assumed a semicircular arc in the west-central part of the block. Extrapolation of this arc to an entire circle gave a maximum diameter of 30–35 m. Moreover, pits with Stallings pottery tended to be clustered in groups of three to six, with clusters spaced 5–10 m apart. The similarity to Mims Point geometry and spacing was uncanny.

Four household clusters and a possible fifth each contain from four to seven pits with Classic Stallings pottery. Each of the four definitive clusters has a diverse set of pits, with at least one 90 cm or more deep into the basal clay. In fact, the diversity of pits by cluster is some of the best evidence that the clusters are meaningful. If the spatial clusters that we imposed on the feature plan were simply random, then we might expect a random distribution of attributes (such as depth into clay or maximum diameter) among them. Why would we expect each of the four clusters to have both small and large pits, shallow and deep pits, if their placement was randomly independent of their form? They clearly are not random, at least according to the same sort of statistical tests that I applied to the handedness data. What is more, the deepest pit in three of the four clusters lies to the right of an aspect facing to the center, just as at Mims Point. The fourth sits on the left side of a presumptive inward-facing door.

The Cosgroves did not expose the household remains of an entire community, but they came close. Extrapolating what they did expose to an entire compound, we arrive at a circle not much bigger than that seen at Mims Point and Ed Marshall, capable of accommodating eight or nine households. Other coeval compounds may have existed at Stallings Island at any one time. But if so, they were not to the north and south of the Cosgroves' features; nor were they likely to have occupied the areas to the west dug by Claflin. The Stallings Island community does not seem to have been any larger than its counterparts at Mims Point and Ed Marshall.

The biggest difference between Stallings Island and all other circular villages, including coastal shell rings, is not the living population but the dead. Stallings Island is the only location with a population of human interments placed in the center of a circular compound. This central space contains 32 burials, and another 12 are located in and around the houses encircling the plaza. Not all of these individuals are Classic Stallings age, but I suspect most are. The Stallings Island burials are discussed further in chapter 6 (which considers the social significance of being buried so centrally). Here we need to consider more closely the household economy and larger community organization that ensured (or perhaps impinged upon) biological well-being.

Now that we have determined the structure and size of Classic Stallings co-resident groups, how big was its population at any given time? Three villages, if occupied simultaneously, with each housing 35–40 individuals, would give us a total local population of 105–120 people. Most likely we are missing some coeval villages, perhaps at locations like Lake Spring, Kiokee Creek, and German Island. Still, local communities were perhaps never very large; and collectively the Classic Stallings people were perhaps no more than 500, even counting Brier Creek and the Ogeechee River sites. This is a small population by any human standard, to be sure, but it is not the size but the formality that is of interest here. Part of that formality was deeply inscribed in redundant, perhaps permanent land-use practices with occasionally intensive episodes of activity that brought much of the regional population together. Stallings Island may have had greater cultural significance than the size of its relatively small resident population would bespeak.

Everyday Culture?

Stallings Island was a special place, where the essential elements of Classic Stallings culture met with the tradition of Piedmont indigenes. People were clearly buried there long before Stallings Culture emerged. The site already held great historical and cultural significance for those whose ancestors, stipulated or real, resided there in death. Rituals conducted at Stallings Island most likely commemorated that past while reproducing the new cultural order. Both the burials and the large number of carinated vessels point to the uniqueness of the island, a place where unusual things happened. Feasting with or for the dead may have been among the passion plays of the time, actions that united past with present in a shared though not necessarily unified sensibility about this place.

But unlike a cathedral, synagogue, or mosque, Stallings Island was also a home, a place where the routines of daily living outnumbered the mystical moments of ritual activity. Thus, before we consider the political economy that ensured the reproduction of Classic Stallings culture, let us examine the domestic economy that ensured human survival. Classic Stallings culture may not have looked all that different from the cultures of those who came before and after, who made livings finding, capturing, and processing natural foods in the area. Greater than the difference between what others and Stallings people collected and ate was the unprecedented permanence of life on the river. No matter how rich the biome, finding sufficient food and fuel to consume in any environment can be hard when a group decides to stay put.

5

Living Off the Land

When the seventeenth-century philosopher Thomas Hobbes described the life of "primitive man" as "solitary, poor, nasty, brutish, and short," he needed no statistics to make his case. To him, people who had to scour the landscape in an unrelenting search for food were truly impoverished. Lacking the ability to grow their own food, such "primitives" were considered slaves to nature, unable to establish permanent settlements and thence the finer things in life—"no culture of the earth; . . . no account of time; no arts; no letters; no society."

Some three hundred years after Hobbes penned these influential words, anthropologists began collecting some hard data on hunter-gatherer populations. The results proved surprising. Far from being impoverished, the food economies of hunter-gatherers were exceptionally good. Their diets were ample and well balanced. It took only about 20 hours a week per adult to collect enough food to meet or exceed international nutritional standards for an average-sized family. This leisurely schedule left plenty of time for family life and socializing. Theirs was a close-knit society, providing economic security and social harmony for all. So rich were hunter-gatherers in these basic human needs that anthropologist Marshall Sahlins dubbed them the "original affluent society."

Additional scientific study verified that the key to "affluence" in hunter-gatherer economies is mobility. Whereas economic systems based on non-portable processes or facilities tie people to particular places, an economy of foraging works best when people can move at will. Over the long haul, it takes less energy to move people than it does to move resources. This is true simply because the food available at any given location will eventually be depleted, requiring foragers to travel greater round-trip distances each day to feed their families. Relocating camp before resources are depleted locally not only avoids the diminishing returns of staying put but also is ecologically sound behavior, and thus sustainable.

So Hobbes had it all wrong. Mobility was not the bane of "primitive man": it was his greatest asset. It follows that under conditions of restricted mobility hunter-gatherer economies change. Several recent studies document just how damaging such restrictions can be. Unable to relocate at will, hunter-gatherers are forced to diversify their strategies to include new resources and technologies. The solutions are not always healthy ones, as some populations experience increased social strife, disease, and nutritional stress, even widespread starvation. This is the usual plight of groups impacted by the expansion of nation-states. Exiled to reservations or otherwise stripped of autonomy, hunter-gatherers of the modern world suffer greatly. Had Hobbes witnessed such conditions, he might not have denigrated the "primitive" lifestyle.

As extreme as modern impacts have been, it would be wrong to glorify the prehistoric past as a world without economic or social stress. Prehistory is rife with examples of hunter-gatherers who, for one reason or another, relinquished the mobile lifestyle for a more settled existence. In many cases this process was the prelude to more complex societies built upon economies of food production that necessitated permanent settlement. In other cases, reduced mobility proved detrimental, perhaps for the same reasons witnessed today.

The fourth-millennium B.P. Stallings Culture was an experiment in settled living that eventually failed. After establishing relatively permanent settlement in the middle Savannah River valley at about 4000 B.P., communities of Classic Stallings affiliation disbanded some three centuries later and returned to the mobile lifestyle of their ancestors. Clues to the rise and fall of this hunter-gatherer society are encoded in a variety of archaeological evidence for foodways, including the technology of subsistence as well as remains of plants and animals that they ate. Here I want to focus on these clues to understand how and why a hunter-gatherer society with a Coastal Plain heritage was affected by its relocation to and permanent settlement of the middle Savannah region.

Primary Forest Efficiency?

Without delving into the minute traces of Stallings subsistence, we are struck immediately by its innovations and novel dietary practices. After all, Stallings pottery is the oldest durable container technology in the region. If such an innovation signaled an improvement over existing technologies, then the Stallings economy would appear to have been on the rise. This certainly is the logic of Westerners, who have come to depend on technological innovations to solve life's problems. We live in an era when every newfangled gizmo is marketed as an improvement over existing choices, a time-saving or labor-saving device that enhances the quality of life through greater efficiency and economy.

This underlying Western logic was routinely perpetuated in archaeological literature of the mid-twentieth century. Joseph Caldwell's highly influential work *Trend and Tradition in the Prehistory of the Eastern United States* (1958) exemplifies this dominant theme. Caldwell described the sweep of prehistory in the Eastern Woodlands as a gradually accumulated repertoire of applied knowledge that enabled Native American peoples to make increasingly efficient use of natural resources. Pottery was directly implicated in Caldwell's model of Primary Forest Efficiency because it could be used to maximize the dietary potential of mast resources such as acorns and nuts. Caldwell particularly had in mind the pottery of north Georgia cultures of the Early Woodland period, whose dense village middens included abundant quantities of hickory nuts, walnuts, and especially acorns. Caldwell was very familiar with ethnohistoric descriptions of mast processing. The tannic acid of acorns had to be removed before consumption, and the real dietary value of nuts such as hickory resided not in the meat per se but in the oil that could be extracted from it. Removing tannins and extracting nut oil required both water and containers to hold water. The added requirement of heating water gave pottery an advantage over inorganic containers, especially if pots could be used directly over fire. Thus, to Caldwell, pottery was an innovation whose application in mast processing was a huge improvement over existing technologies. If he had known in 1958 that fiber-tempered pottery was over 1,000 years older than Early Woodland wares, he might have placed the establishment of Primary Forest Efficiency at the onset of Stallings Culture.

Native populations in the Southeast utilized mast resources long before Stallings communities and their Early Woodland descendants applied pottery to their processing. Typically, fragments of nut shell or acorn parts are scarce at prepottery sites, especially at open-air locations with acidic soil. Resistance to decay is enhanced when nutshell is charred, but even this does little to preserve the thin hulls of acorns when soil conditions are inhospitable to organic matter. With such limited direct evidence for mast use, changes in the economy of nuts and acorns must be gauged by changes in associated technologies. This is clearly the case for Stallings Culture.

Indirect though it is, the evidence for mast use during Stallings time is formidable. Nowhere is this evidence more strongly expressed than at the

Victor Mills site in Columbia County, Georgia. This is a surprisingly small site, situated on a side-slope of the bluffs overlooking the Savannah River, no more than a kilometer as the crow flies from Stallings Island. It was recorded by Claflin as Site 7, "a small shell bed less than a tenth of an acre in area." The shell deposit is indeed very small for a Stallings site, but this aspect of the site pales in comparison to the large pit assemblage associated with it. Rather than being a typical habitation site, Victor Mills appears to have been a nut storage and processing location, whose unimpressive shell midden was incidental to a more specialized function.

Victor Mills came to our attention in 1993 when George Lewis learned that its owner intended to sell the property for residential development. Early the following year, with permission of the developer, we conducted two short field expeditions to salvage what we could before houses went in. As usual, we started with the shell deposit, knowing that its neutralizing chemistry provided the best preservation regime to collect organic matter for dating and dietary reconstruction. Looters had compromised this deposit, although they apparently gave up after digging only a bit. We soon learned why they quit. The shell deposit was very shallow and patchy and contained virtually no "flashy" artifacts, such as whole spear points or decorated pottery. But it did contain the diagnostic sherds of Early Stallings times (sherds with plain surface treatments and lips that were either thickened or flanged), along with perforated soapstone slabs, broken bifaces, flake debris, and fire-cracked rock. Overall this is not the sort of deposit that attracts looters, but it quickly got us excited because it appeared to be a single-component deposit of Early Stallings times. Later radiometric dates would confirm a calibrated age of ca. 4450 B.P.

As work on the small midden progressed, one of the regular volunteers, Kevin Eberhard, suggested that we dig outside the midden. It never really dawned on me to do such a thing: like the drunk who looks for his keys under the street lamp because the lighting is good, I had always aimed for the shell because the preservation was good. Eberhard had a point, however; the small shell midden at Victor Mills was on a slope, not a location conducive to sustained human activity, especially not habitation. If we were to find good evidence for the function of Victor Mills, we needed to seek flatter, higher ground.

We began a trenching operation up the slope toward the ridge top. As the gradient of the slope diminished, we started to encounter large dark stains

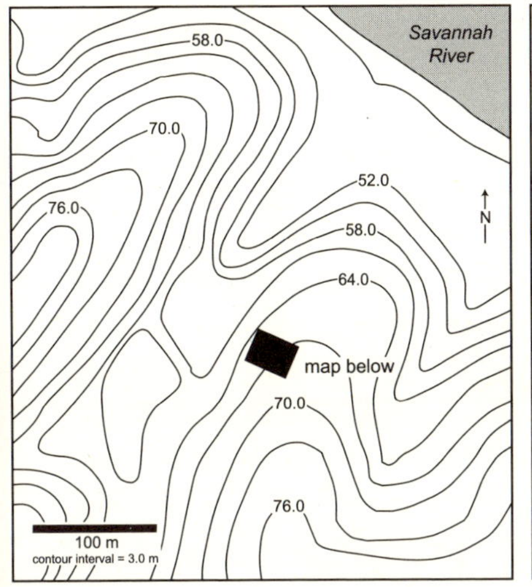

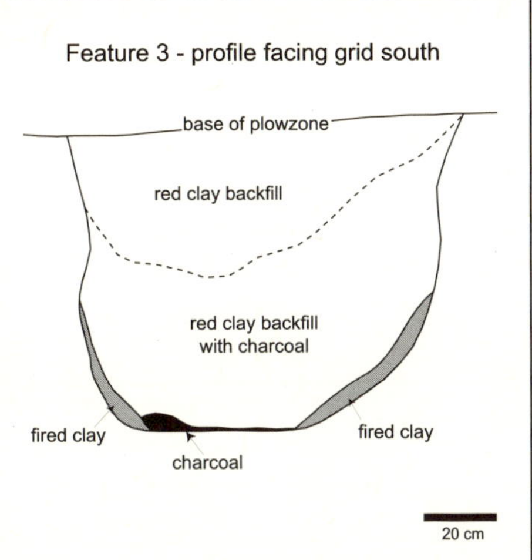

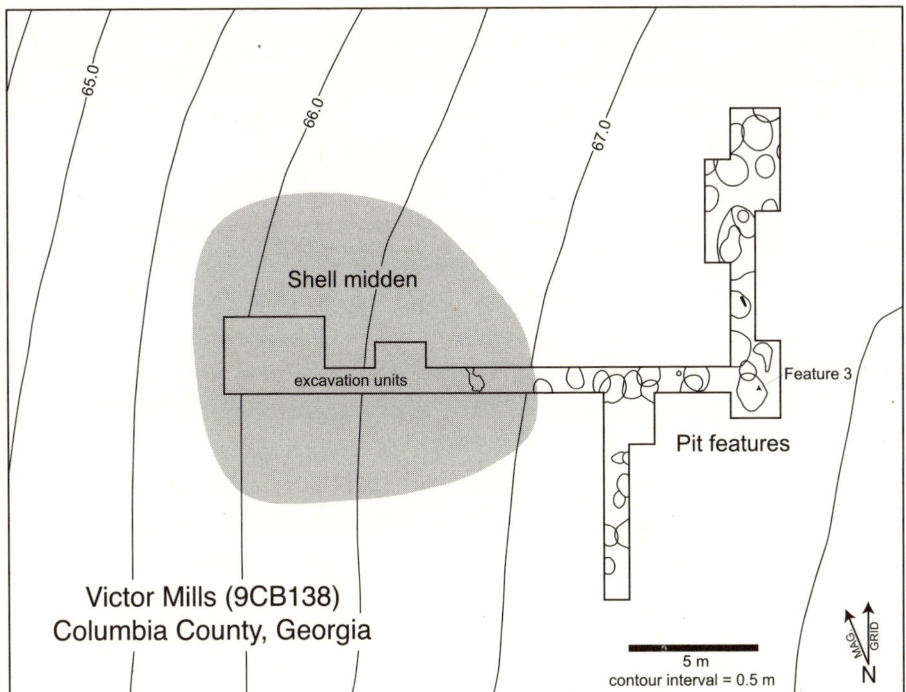

5.1. Topographic map (top left), plan map of excavations and pit features (bottom), and profile of a pit feature (top right) from the Victor Mills site (9CB138), Columbia County, Georgia. Up the hill from a small, shallow shell midden is a cluster of large pits called "silos" that are believed to have been used to store nuts. The profile of one such pit, Feature 3, shows that its bottom was fired hard, perhaps to seal out moisture and pests in the underlying orange clay. At first I was not impressed, for I had been seduced by too many tree throws and other natural disturbances to allow these to fool me. After more area was opened it became clear that these stains were legitimate pit features. We encountered pits everywhere we trenched, both up the slope and to either side along the top of the ridge. We recorded over two dozen such features in the 65 m^2 that we stripped, most ranging from 75 to 100 cm in diameter and some up to 110 cm deep. Each contained an organic fill with particles of charcoal and occasional nutshell that stood in sharp contrast to the background clay matrix. A cross section of one that we dug completely revealed a layer of burned clay and charcoal at its base and lower sides, overlain with two layers of organic fill with soapstone slabs, plain fiber-tempered pottery, and fire-cracked rock. Another pit nearby contained a massive slab of granitic rock with pecked surfaces, apparently a large nutting stone.

The amount of charred nutshell in each of the pits that we tested was small, owing in part to the lack of clamshell for better preservation. Still, in flotation samples that we collected hickory was consistently present, along with minor traces of acorn, walnut, and fruit seeds. Graduate student Beth Auten identified and counted the botanical remains from this and other Stallings contexts for her M.A. thesis at the University of Florida. Her research was focused on the use of mast, and she was particularly interested in documenting any changes in the use of these resources over the course of Stallings prehistory. The Victor Mills pit assemblage seemingly marked a dramatic increase in the intensity of nut collecting. If each of these pits was used to store nuts, then the volume of procurement and use was unprecedented for the middle Savannah area.

Calculating the scale of these activities is a bit tricky, because excavations at Victor Mills were incomplete. We exposed some two dozen pits in about one-fifth of an area of 180 m^2. Extrapolating from these figures, I estimate a minimum of 120 pits with an average volume of 550 liters each. By any standards, the 1,800 or more bushels that these pits could have held would be a lot of nuts. Of course, we know the pits were not used all at once, for many of them intercepted one another. But if only 10 percent of them were used in any given season, the volume involved would have to represent the stores of more than one household.

Here, then, was evidence for a process that likely involved not only cooperative labor but long-term investments in facilities and resources. Importantly, the Victor Mills assemblage is early in the history of Stallings Culture. Dating to about 4,450 years ago, these pit activities took place at the very time when Coastal Plain populations were beginning to expand into the territories of their Piedmont neighbors, members of Mill Branch Culture. We know this from the larger regional record of Early Stallings sites, but even Victor Mills offered proof of Coastal Plain connections. Among the many broken bifaces were a handful of worn specimens made from Allendale chert. A matching set of small chert flakes attests to maintenance of these nonlocal tools. The vast majority of chipped stone at Victor Mills is local vein quartz, exposures of which occur at the top of the ridge that it occupies. The evidence suggests that groups residing in the Coastal Plain made the journey up the river to harvest mast resources in the vicinity of Stallings Island, bringing with them tool kits made from their local chert. After arriving at Victor Mills to collect and store nuts, they quickly exhausted their chert tools and replaced them with temporary, expedient forms made from the local quartz. Anticipating return to Coastal Plain homes once the stores were made, these work parties had no need to gear-up with quartz, because it was inferior to their chert. Instead, quartz tools made at Victor Mills were abandoned there.

With nuts stashed away in pits far from home, Early Stallings residents of the Coastal Plain had to make return trips to Victor Mills to retrieve the stores as needed. Rather than transport the entire harvest back for processing at home, they chose to bring with them the requisite pottery and other tools for processing at the site of storage. Some materials for processing, notably the soapstone slabs and granitic anvils, were likely collected from sources near Victor Mills. Very few of the waste by-products from processing nuts for oil were deposited at Victor Mills, suggesting that nut shells were not routinely charred. Although they make a great fuel, nut shells may not have been drafted into such use because of the limited time spent there. The small shell midden at Victor Mills attests to short stays as well. The freshwater clams and other food remains of the midden must have been the convenience foods of a people who would spend no more time in the middle Savannah than they had to.

The use of middle Savannah resources by folks inhabiting the Coastal Plain raises two related questions: why couldn't they find equivalent resources in their home territory, and, if mast resources figured so prominently in their daily fare, why didn't they relocate to the middle Savannah to take full advantage of them? The answer to this first question is that the Coastal Plain during

Early Stallings times apparently did not support much hardwood vegetation. Southern pine began to encroach on hardwood forests as early as 9000 B.P. in the Coastal Plain of South Carolina and came to dominate the province over the ensuing millennia. Certainly hickory, walnut, and oak could be found scattered about, and even dense stands may have persisted in oases of moist, organic soils such as river and swamp margins and perhaps Carolina bays. Compared to forests of the Piedmont and Fall Zone, however, Coastal Plain forests were bereft of mast-bearing trees. No doubt the squirrels, deer, and turkeys that depend on mast at least partly for their subsistence were likewise relatively sparse in the Coastal Plain.

The answer to the second question is that Early Stallings groups eventually decided to relocate to the middle Savannah permanently. Victor Mills may in fact date to the precise time when certain communities made this move. Middle Savannah sites with Early Stallings components dating from ca. 4450–4200 B.P. attest to increasingly permanent settlement. At Ed Marshall, for instance, at least one and perhaps two Early Stallings structures are evident in prepared clay floors and associated postholes. Rae's Creek in Augusta and a site at the mouth of Uchee Creek are two additional examples of possible habitation sites dating to this interval. Remarkably, Stallings Island was largely ignored by Early Stallings groups. As discussed in chapter 3, their Mill Branch counterparts abandoned this and other river sites at about 4450 B.P., just when Early Stallings groups asserted themselves in the local area. Combined with the apparently clandestine use of Victor Mills and its subterranean stores, the avoidance of Stallings Island—a known Mill Branch sacred site—may signal contentious relations between the two groups. Either way, Early Stallings groups prevailed in making the middle Savannah their exclusive home for two to three centuries, as Mill Branch people sought refuge in the adjacent uplands and river valleys.

The move to permanent use of the middle Savannah by Early Stallings groups changed the way in which nuts were exploited. Communal efforts to collect and store nuts among Early Stallings groups were abandoned. By the time they began residing in the middle Savannah, Early Stallings groups opted for household-based storage. This carried forward into Classic Stallings times, with isolated storage features adjacent to domestic structures. Now able to take a more autonomous approach to nut collecting, Stallings households relinquished interdependencies for more immediate control. They continued to store nuts in deep, subterranean features (as opposed to

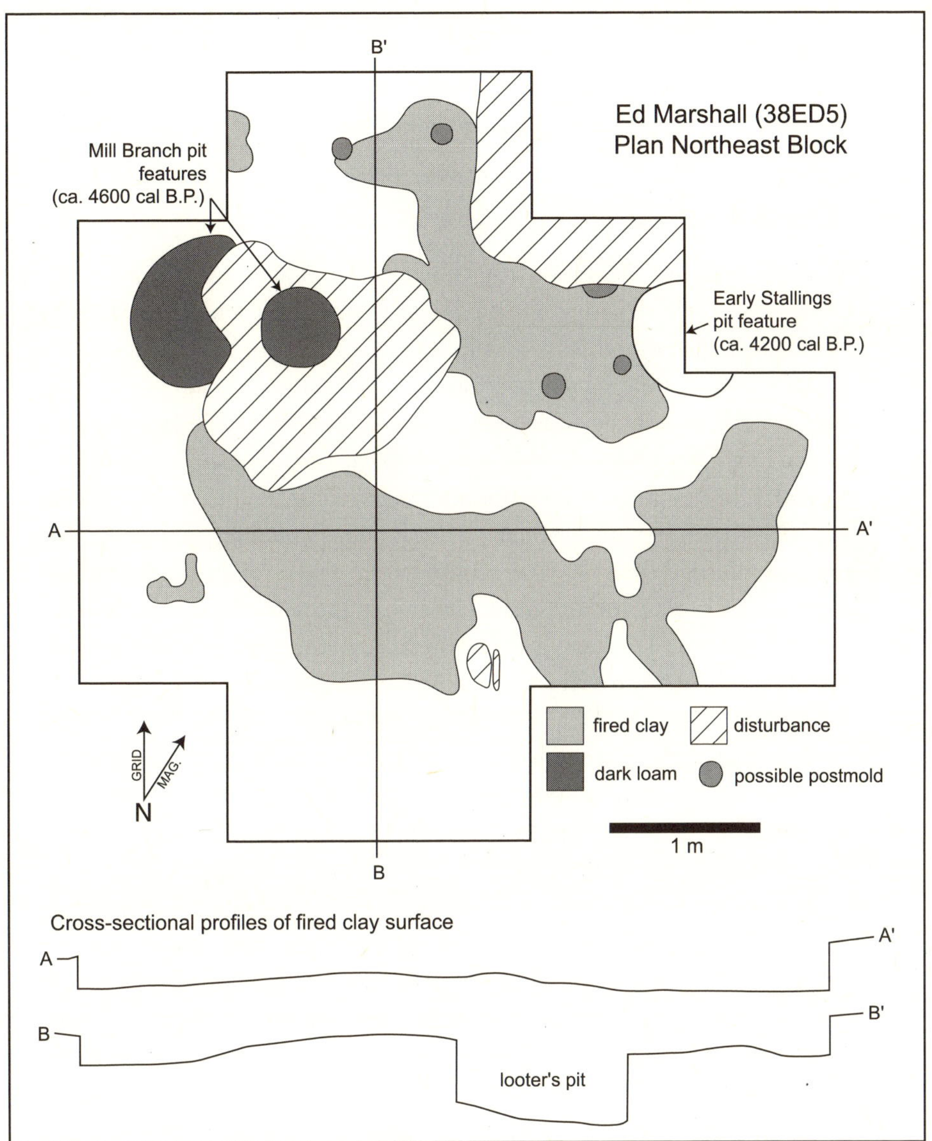

5.2. Fired clay floor uncovered at the Ed Marshall site. The fired clay is patchy, and looters dug through two large portions. Postmolds were too few to estimate the size of the structure; but judging from the clay, we can imagine a minimum dimension of about 4 m for an oval or circular house. Two pit features dating to the Early Stallings period originated from the level of the clay floor, while two other features of Mill Branch age were found at the base of a looter's pit, well below the clay floor.

above-ground granaries), which suggests that concealment of economic gains remained desirable or necessary. I will return to this point in the next chapter. For now, let us consider what other changes in Stallings subsistence can be gleaned from the residues of ancient meals and the technology to prepare them.

In Small Things Eaten

Without question, the most conspicuous aspects of Stallings diet are the by-products of shellfish eating. Strewn about in pits, sheet middens, and occasional large piles, the white shells of molluscs give Stallings sites a distinctive character. Consisting mostly of freshwater clams, these resources have long been regarded as a staple in Stallings diet, indicating that Stallings groups had settled into a more permanent lifestyle than their predecessors.

Today, however, the dietary significance of shellfish and its implications for settlement are matters of great debate. Some would argue that shellfish enabled a settled lifestyle, whereas others see it as a "starvation" food, exploited only in times of dire need. Either way, the amount of inedible waste (shell) from a meal of clams greatly overshadows the edible portion, so shellfish are undoubtedly overrepresented. When we add to this bias that most of the shells are less than 5 cm long, we can begin to question the actual dietary contribution of these invertebrates. Moreover, recent dating of the great shell piles at Stallings Island shows that Paris Island and Mill Branch groups occasionally ate clams too, so there is nothing uniquely Stallings about shellfishing.

When the fill of Stallings excavations is screened, shellfish begin to pale in comparison to the bones of vertebrates. Identifying these bones is the job of faunal specialists Renee Walker, Sharyn Jones O'Day, and, most recently, Meggan Blessing. To date, these three analysts have examined over two hundred thousand bones from Stallings features. Many can be identified to the level of family or genus, sometimes even species. Stallings middens contain a wide variety of fauna, including the familiar white-tailed deer. New to the mix are those small, inconspicuous remains that only fine screening reveals. Fish bones are particularly well represented: no less than 51 percent and as much as 93 percent of the identifiable bone in any given sample. The bones of catfish and sunfish consistently dominate, followed by lesser numbers of suckers and gar. Bones of freshwater drum, bowfin, perch, sturgeon, and shad occur in minor traces.

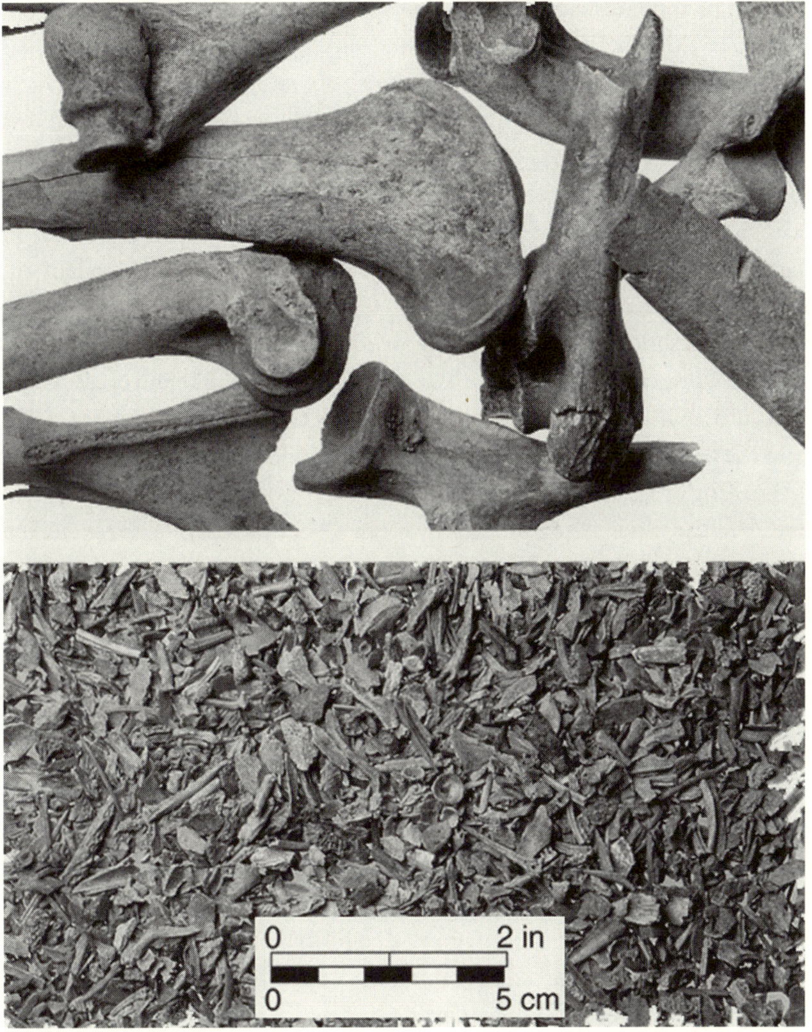

5.3. In the premodern era, when sites were excavated without fine screening, minute food remains from sites went unnoticed, such as the fish bone seen in the bottom photograph. Only large bony remains, such as the deer bone shown in the upper photograph, were routinely recovered. This gave the impression that hunting was an everyday food pursuit, as was shellfishing, an activity that also left conspicuous evidence (photos by the author).

The Victor Mills vertebrate assemblage consists of notoriously small fish. Of the 6,700 bones identified by Renee Walker, 6,200 were fish, mostly catfish and sunfish, whose size was well under the minimum lengths of today's laws. Presumably these small fish were taken with dip nets from the shallows fronting Victor Mills; as noted earlier, they may represent the fare of a temporary encampment. More typically, at the other sites, juvenile sunfish and catfish are accompanied by specimens of greater size in Stallings habitation contexts. Capturing these involved technology familiar to any modern angler: hook, line, and sinker.

Bone fishhooks are among my favorite artifacts from Stallings sites. Although we rarely find whole specimens, fragments of shanks and occasionally tips turn up in shell midden whenever we have the chance to use fine screens and the patience to sort the resulting matrix. Finding a fishhook has become something of a challenge to the many students who have sorted Stallings matrix, because it is easy to lose sight of a thin sliver of worked bone among the hundreds or thousands of nondescript bone fragments in a given sample.

Fishhooks were made from a variety of elements, mostly from the bones of white-tailed deer. Deer toe bones were especially useful for this purpose. With morphology conducive to hook-making, phalanges were carved out with a stone tool to retain one lateral margin and the distal edge. This entire manufacturing process has been documented at Shell Mound Archaic sites in the middle Tennessee River valley, where toe-bone hooks were found concentrated in the upper strata of midden deposits. Other sorts of hooks were found throughout shell-midden sites in Alabama and Tennessee. The distal ends of deer ulnae and other spatulate elements were often slotted and then cut to produce blanks that were ground to form hooks. As a by-product, the bifurcated end of an ulna used for this purpose occasionally provides the only remaining evidence of hook-making.

Both finished hooks and the waste products of hook-making have been recovered from all Stallings contexts in the middle Savannah region. In addition to the methods of manufacture documented in the Midsouth, the Savannah assemblages reveal one additional technique involving multiple blanks. At Stallings Island, one fragment of modified deer bone retains a series of hook blanks along the length of the element. This method suggests a level of production that maximizes the number of hooks that could be made from an element of bone. Admittedly, this is but one example and thus may not be

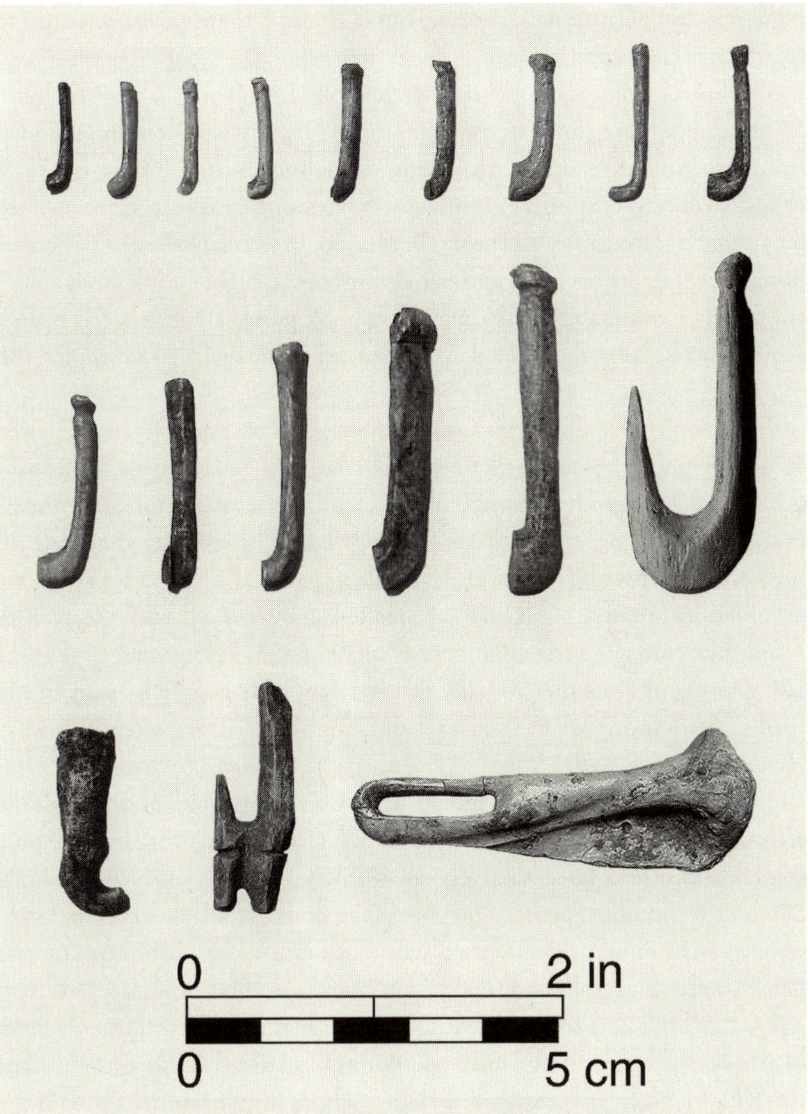

5.4. Fragments of bone fishhooks and by-products of hook-making from Stallings Island and Mims Point. The bottom row shows examples of hook blanks made from a deer toe bone (left), a split long bone (center), and the lower leg bone of a turkey (right). The split long bone has remnants of two hook blanks.

representative of the typical process; but it also may signify more widespread efforts to increase production.

Fishhooks from Stallings sites range from 1.5 cm to 4.2 cm in length. Most common are those in the small range, less than 2.0 cm long. Shank thickness generally varies with length, as the longest hooks have the most robust shanks. Occasional examples of short, stout hooks attest to the need for strength among some of the smaller hooks. In virtually all cases of broken hooks, the fracture occurred at the midpoint of the curved portion, an apparent point of vulnerability. The matching hook points are very rarely found, presumably because they ended up embedded in the mouths of escaping fish or simply were lost in the water as they snapped.

Complementing the hooks from Stallings sites are examples of presumed fishing weights. These are pellet-shaped to flat, oval objects made from soapstone, often with grooves incised circumferentially or broader, shallow notches for the attachment of cordage. Stallings Island has produced at least 40 such objects. Three distinct size classes are apparent. The majority are small, weighing less than 115 g. Only the smallest among them were grooved to accept fine cordage. Lesser numbers of medium (137–175 g) and large (over 200 g) weights are either roughly waisted or weakly grooved. Many of the smaller ones and some of the larger ones are recycled soapstone slab fragments.

Matching the hooks with the weights, we can imagine a hook-and-line technique for fishing involving tackle similar to that used today by cane-pole anglers and others after relatively small catches. The larger weights imply different technology, perhaps not involving hooks at all. Indeed, the larger weights were more probably used to anchor either nets, fish traps, or trot lines. The largest hooks and small, stout hooks are good candidates for trotline fishing, but nets and traps without hooks may have been routinely used. In any case, the technology enabled Stallings folks to fish without constant surveillance, essentially expanding their energies in fish capture through the use of facilities. Also, the technology implicates vigorously flowing water, as might be expected in the riffles and chutes of the shoals, as well as deep channel water. This is a substantial departure from the dip-netting or hook-and-line fishing of near-shore fishing, an activity that even small children could have handled.

Nets or traps fitted with weights might also be part of the technology of turtle capture. Turtles figured significantly in diet throughout the Late

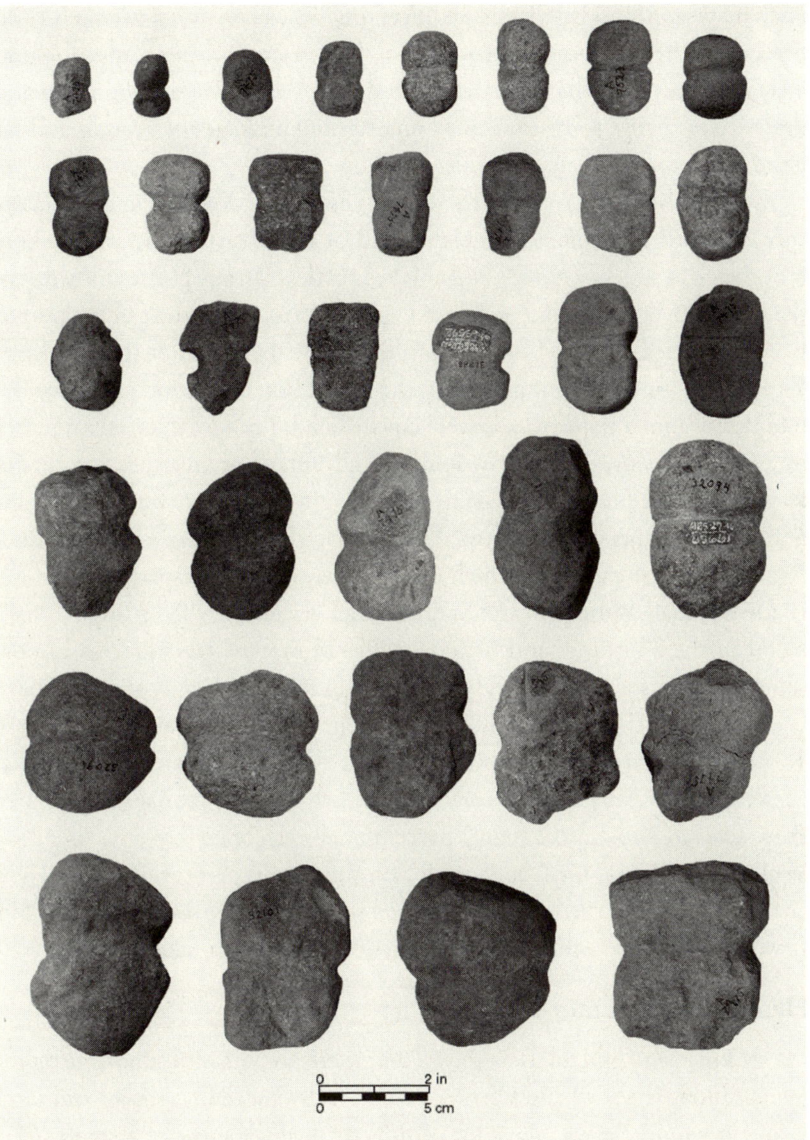

5.5. Line and net weights from Stallings Island. All were made from soapstone, several recycled from perforated cooking slabs; the second from the left in the third row from the top retains the perforation of a recycled slab (photo by Asa Randall; used with permission of the Peabody Museum, Harvard University).

Archaic period, and by Classic Stallings times they constitute as much as 20 percent of the vertebrate remains. Like shellfish, turtles are disproportionately represented by the bones left behind; yet even so, the sheer number and diversity of turtles show that these unassuming packages of protein and fat became increasingly important through time.

Most of the turtle remains in Stallings assemblages are from the aquatic species. These are split between the mud or musk turtles and the basking types, such as sliders, cooters, and chicken turtles. On any given sunny day in the Broad River of Columbia, South Carolina, basking turtles can be spotted by the hundreds on the boulders forming a shoals habitat at the Fall Line. Escaping substantial impoundment, the Broad River is a good proxy for the middle Savannah before dams were constructed. I can imagine any number of capturing techniques that would take advantage of unsuspecting turtles as they energized in the warm sun. Traps would be effective but perhaps unnecessary if the people could stealthily approach basking turtles from behind. Again, this is something in which children may have participated.

Other small animals in the Stallings diet are familiar from any Archaic menu in the Southeast and include squirrels, rabbits, raccoons, and opossums. Muskrats are surprisingly common at Stallings Island and may have been valued for their pelts more than for their meat. The remains of waterfowl or other birds represent a significant minority of bone assemblages. Ducks, geese, and especially turkeys turn up routinely in large faunal samples, but they never compose more than 2 percent of all vertebrate remains. Together, small mammals and birds account for only about 10 percent of assemblages analyzed. Fish and turtles clearly formed the bulk of the diet if measured in raw quantity alone, and the vast majority of the fish were small.

Hunting Deer, Hunting Fish

Careful recovery and analysis shows that there are lots of fish and turtle remains among the shell, but what exactly does this mean in terms of real food value? It would clearly take a lot of fish to equal the meat of a single deer, so we cannot simply compare numbers of bones to reconstruct diet. More realistic data are found in the estimated meat yield from particular species. Such calculations verify that deer eclipsed all other meat resources. Still, humans do not live by deer alone, and the newfound data reveal aspects of the routine, daily components of Stallings diet. No doubt the occasional deer kill provided a bounty of high-protein food; but as Stallings groups became increasingly stationary in their riverine settlements, aquatic foods appear to have become their staple resource. It follows that the killing of a deer became increasingly eventful.

Deer hunting had been the dietary anchor of Archaic populations since the end of the Ice Age, but it is hard to gauge its relative value through time. Outside of shell-midden contexts, the actual proportion of deer in the diet may be overrepresented, because deer bone in general is more resistant to decay and easier to recover than, say, fish bone. When preservation and recovery biases are eliminated, differences in the relative frequency of deer bone may be meaningful. For instance, Early Stallings assemblages of the middle Savannah contain fewer deer bones per volume excavated than do those of Classic Stallings age. I can envision a number of hypotheses to explain this difference. Perhaps the leading one is that Early Stallings groups had less collective experience hunting in the middle Savannah compared to either their successors or people of the indigenous Paris Island and Mill Branch phases. If we accept that Early Stallings groups who began to move into the middle Savannah at ca. 4450 B.P. trace their heritage to coastal and Coastal Plain environments, then it may have taken some time for them to adjust to their new surroundings, at least in terms of tracking deer. Recall that the Coastal Plain habitat at the time when Early Stallings groups moved upriver was dominated by pine forests, which are not terribly conducive to deer populations. Modern hunters in the province today rely on the deer's attraction to edge habitat and baited fields, features that have certainly been enhanced through historic and contemporary land-use practices.

Deer-hunting technology likewise registers subtle changes through time. The flaked-stone technology of Stallings people shows less formalization than that of their Piedmont counterparts, perhaps owing to decreased reliance on deer. Bifaces with stemmed haft elements dominate assemblages throughout, but the diversity of size, shape, and raw materials of Stallings assemblages increases through time. By Classic Stallings times the inventory included all sorts of stemmed bifaces, many with asymmetrical blades and rudimentary or haphazard stems. Missing from these assemblages are well-made lanceolate forms that were clearly designed to be projectiles, such as the Allendale points of pre-Stallings times. Bifaces were instead drafted into a variety of cutting functions. If the asymmetry of blades is not enough to make this argument, consider the whole biface that was found with its antler haft at the Ed Marshall site. Such finds are exceedingly rare, but they attest to the

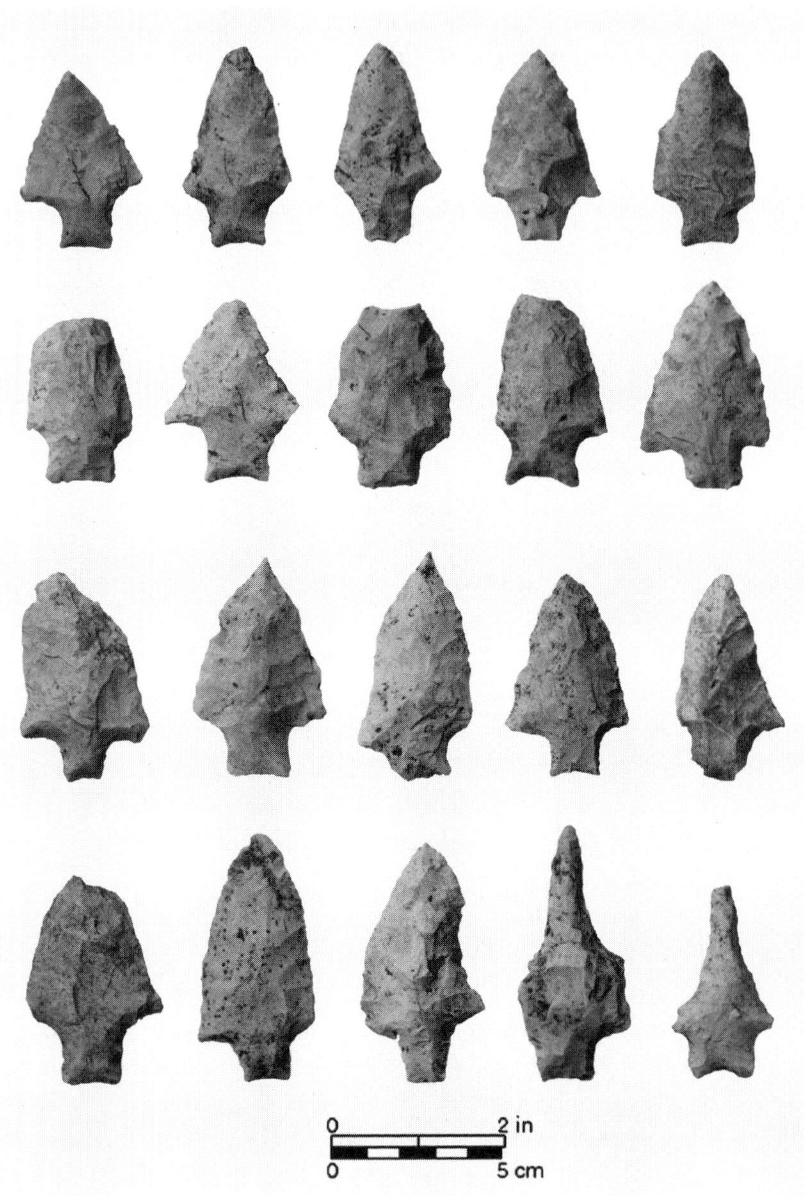

5.6. Classic Stallings hafted bifaces from Mims Point (38ED9), Edgefield County, South Carolina.

5.7. Planview and sideview photographs of a knife found in an Early Stallings context at the Ed Marshall site. The chert blade is a stemmed form, fitted to the slot that was cut into the end of a deer antler tine with its tip removed. The blade and handle were found detached but only centimeters apart and in the "anatomically correct" arrangement. The fit between the stem and the haft is so perfect as to erase any doubt that the blade and handle were at one time attached, apparently even when it entered the ground. The marks of rodent gnawing show that the tool was abandoned on the ground, but more telling are the tooth marks on the handle just below the blade. These are likely to be the work of a dog that got into someone's toolkit and absconded with something to chew.

utility of edged tools as hafted, hand-held implements. Impact fractures indicating projectile functions do not occur on Early Stallings or Classic Stalling bifaces.

Deer were still hunted throughout Stallings times, so how did the hunters dispatch them? The answer comes from the deer bone itself. Stallings assemblages are rife with modified bone and antler, many shaped into formalized tools with specific functions. Socketed antler tines are among the more common items. In an analysis of the Claflin collection, Meggan Blessing recorded 14 such tools and several additional items that were cut and snapped but

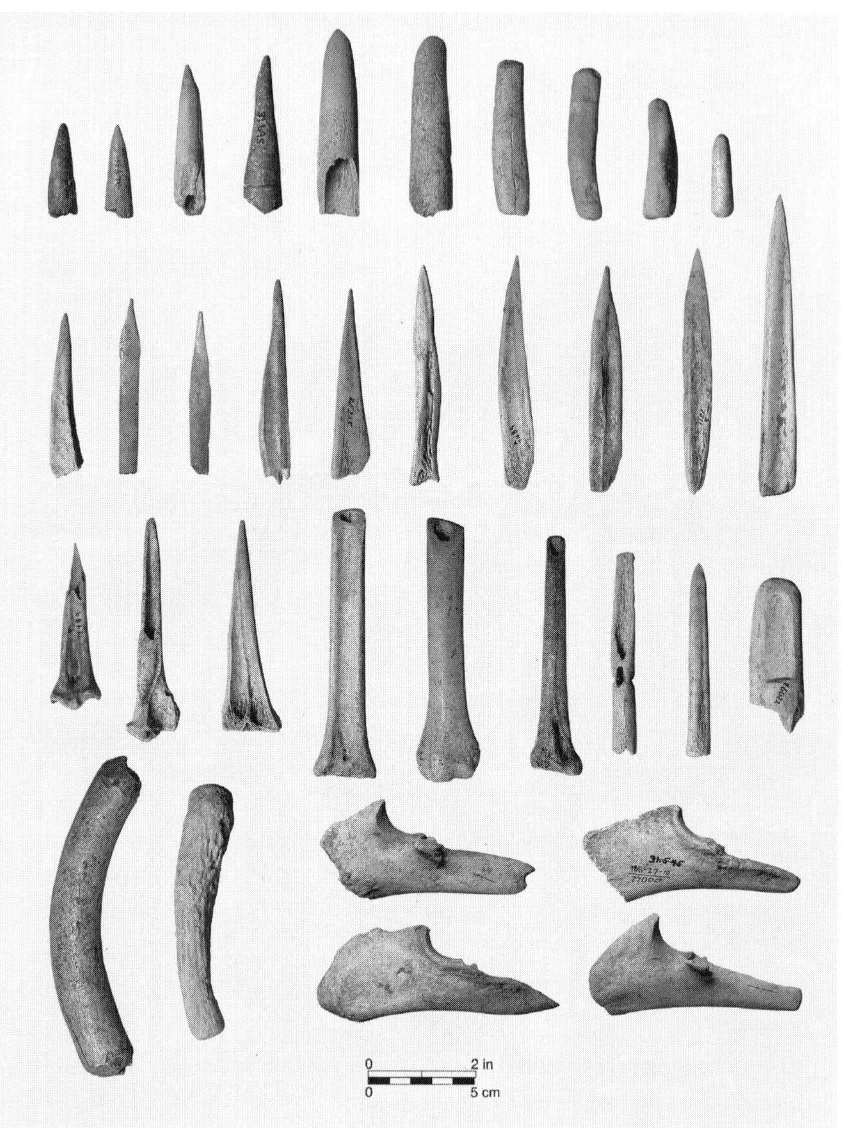

5.8. Various bone and antler implements from Stallings Island, Georgia. The top row includes antler time projectiles and blunt-ended punches; the second row from the top includes a variety of awls made from split long bone; the third row features three awls with joints for handles, followed by three gouge-like tools, an unidentifiable implement with holes drilled on top and sides, one additional awl, and a fragment of a spatulate-tipped implement; the bottom items include two antler beams, the left one possibly a handle, the right one a billet, followed on the right by four deer ulnae with different tips (photo by the author; used with permission of the Peabody Museum, Harvard University).

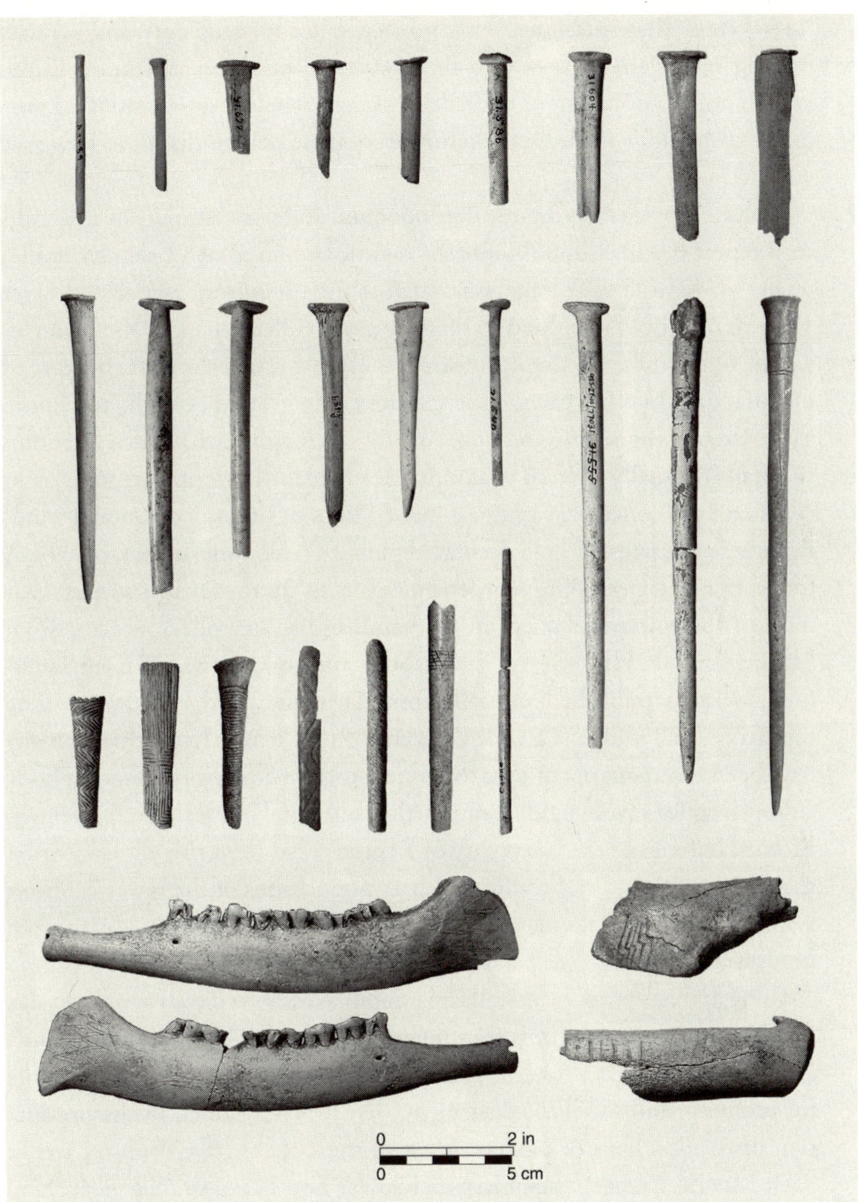

5.9. Bone pins and other ornate bone and antler implements from Stallings Island, Georgia. Bone pins were often fitted with T-tops (top two rows) and less often decorated with geometric designs (third row) or painted (third row, right). Subtle designs were also carved into the surfaces of other objects, such as the deer jaws on the lower left (possibly part of a mask) and the deer ulna and antler spearthrower part on the lower right (photo by the author; used with permission of the Peabody Museum, Harvard University).

unsocketed. These presumably are projectiles for hunting deer, and perhaps other game. It stands to reason that a cultural tradition with roots in the stone-poor environment of the Atlantic Coast would continue to use a projectile technology made exclusively from organic parts—that is, so long as it worked.

Stallings toolmakers drafted deer bone and antler for a variety of uses. Add to the points and fishhooks already mentioned an array of slender implements made from split long bone, such as the ubiquitous awl or pin. Over 150 awls have been identified by Blessing in the collection of 350 bone implements. Often these are simply informal tools that retain the spiral fracture of manufacture. In other cases, bone splinters were ground carefully to achieve a consistently round cross section. Awl-like forms given this much attention to detail are usually referred to as pins. Mostly plain, bone pins are sometimes adorned with concentric arrays of incised lines or other decoration, including painted designs. Whole decorated pins are rare; none, in fact, have been found in our excavations, while fragments turn up routinely. I suspect that most of the whole specimens in the hands of private collectors came from Stallings burials. Flaunting his success at looting, one individual from Statesboro, Georgia, published in a collectors' magazine a plate of elaborate bone pins from shell middens on the Ogeechee River. It is a shame that so many have been taken out of context, for bone pins, like Stallings pottery, embody cultural values involving decoration that ultimately reflect group identity. Richard Jefferies of the University of Kentucky has been able to reconstruct the social boundaries of Middle Archaic populations of the lower Midwest from the geographical variations of bone pin design, notably the way that pin heads were shaped.

Bone and antler tools in Stallings assemblages are typically more prosaic. In addition to pins and awls they include a variety of blunt-end tools, such as billets and punches for stone-tool making, spatulate-shaped implements for scraping, and modified deer ulnae that probably aided in the production of textiles, nets, or baskets. Most of these items have counterparts in Shell Mound Archaic assemblages across the Southeast, so there is nothing special about Stallings organic tools. In her analysis of the Clafin collection, however, Blessing identified an antler tool form that appears to be unique to Stallings assemblages: a special sort of socketed point.

As we have seen, socketed or cut-and-snapped antler tines are common items in Stallings assemblages and have been found in Paleoindian and

5.10. Socketed and beveled antler points from Stallings Island, Georgia. Although socketed antler tines are not uncommon in Archaic shell-midden assemblages across the eastern United States, these more robust forms, made mostly from the beam of the antler, may have served a specialized function in Classic Stallings times (photo by the author; used with permission of the Peabody Museum, Harvard University).

Archaic contexts at sites across the continent. Apparently, these naturally pointed objects were ideal projectiles for many people. Unique to Stallings assemblages are socketed points made from the beam of the antler, not the tine. To achieve this form, Stallings toolmakers not only had to cut and hollow the base of the beam but had to carve its entire surface to remove the irregularities and achieve smooth cross sections. What is more, the working ends of these items were shaped with a distinctive bevel. Because only the cortical portion of the beam was hard enough to withstand heavy-duty service, toolmakers had to form the point along only one side of the beam. The result was a form that is canted when viewed from the side. Many such forms also have asymmetrical tip morphology, a sure sign of tip maintenance. Clearly, the socketed antler point was a highly curated, formalized tool and, as such, likely fulfilled a specialized function.

In seeking ideas about how socketed antler beams were used, Blessing scoured the literature for similar items but found few candidates. She did, however, uncover a number of ethnohistoric and ethnographic accounts of spearfishing with points made from organic media. Comparing this to a list of fishes large enough to spear, she hypothesized that these items were used to dispatch sturgeon or shad.

Ever since William Claflin noted seeing "quantities" of sturgeon bone at Stallings Island, local archaeologists have assumed that anadromous fish formed a significant part of the Stallings diet. Anadromous fish are species that migrate from the sea into freshwater rivers to spawn. In addition to the Atlantic sturgeon, anadromous species that migrate up the Savannah River include members of the herring family, notably the American shad. Anyone familiar with the annual salmon runs of the Northwest Coast knows how bountiful a resource anadromous fish can be. In fact, many Northwest Coast tribes depended on salmon not only for its immediate food value but as a storable commodity. In addition, salmon runs were times of great feasting among the clans, who banded together cooperatively to harvest and process fish. Many anthropologists believe that the richness and the reliability of this resource were the main reason why so many Northwest Coast groups achieved a level of sedentism and cultural complexity well beyond that of hunter-gatherers elsewhere.

Here, it seemed, was an appropriate ethnographic analog for the development of Stallings Culture. The shoals of the middle Savannah River afforded ample opportunity to construct fish weirs for exploiting spring fish runs. Once in place, such facilities would have drawn people back year after year, nurturing interdependence among households and the development of technologies of mass processing and storage. Such an economic foundation would have supported sedentary communities, emergent leaders, and elaborate ceremonialism—the very traits believed to set Stallings apart from other groups of the region.

It all seemed to fit except for one pesky detail: no hard, bony evidence for anadromous fish. Despite Claflin's observation from the 1920s, absolutely no sturgeon or shad bone was detected in an analysis of Stallings Island bone by Dan Weinand and Elizabeth Reitz of the University of Georgia. Because these samples were not adequately screened, it might seem possible that the evidence slipped through our hands. This is clearly not the case, however, in the samples that Renee Walker examined from Victor Mills and Mims Point.

An occasional appearance notwithstanding, sturgeon or shad simply were not routinely collected by Stallings folks at these two sites, at least not in ways that resulted in preserved deposits of bone. Instead of seeing sturgeon, Weinand and Reitz surmised, Claflin may have observed the remains of soft-shell turtles. Indeed, the shell segments of this reptile species resemble some of the bony elements of sturgeon.

I came to accept that sturgeon and shad simply did not factor into Stallings diet in any significant fashion, but all that changed when we had the chance to view the Claflin collection from Stallings Island. Among the many modified bone and antler items were two unusual forms. One lone piece is a large sturgeon skull-bone that was ground along the edges and perforated at one end. Another few items consist of the Y-bone, an odd element that is unique to sturgeon anatomy. Both the skull fragment and the Y-bones represent fish of substantial size. Mature female Atlantic sturgeon today average 8 feet long and range up to 14 feet long. Males are smaller than females, and the short-nosed species, which may also be represented in the Stallings collections, is smaller than the Atlantic. Even so, these are all big fish by any standards. There are, in fact, historical accounts of Native Americans spearing them. James Adair, in his 1775 treatise on southeastern Indians, recalls fishing trips that he witnessed on the Savannah River, where sturgeon were speared with green cane harpoons launched from canoes.

Our discovery of sturgeon elements at Stallings Island vindicated Claflin to some extent, but were sturgeon really all that common a menu item? Did they occur in the "quantities" that Claflin insinuated? Apparently not, for although Blessing has now identified sturgeon in just about all Stallings-period assemblages, she has never found more than a trace. The same is true of American shad. In the case of this smaller fish, poor preservation looms large. I once saw several fishermen land American shad in the lower Savannah on a spring morning and later watched them cook some of their catch. After removing the roe sack, guts, and head, they deep-fried the whole bodies of these four-pound fish in a large vat of oil. The cooked product was eaten entirely. The already fine bones in the meat were rendered soft and digestible by the hard-frying process. I read later that shad cooked in ovens at low temperatures for long time can also be eaten entirely. Perhaps the potential hard evidence for shad consumption by Stallings folks, like the meat itself, passed through the human digestive tract and entered the archaeological record as

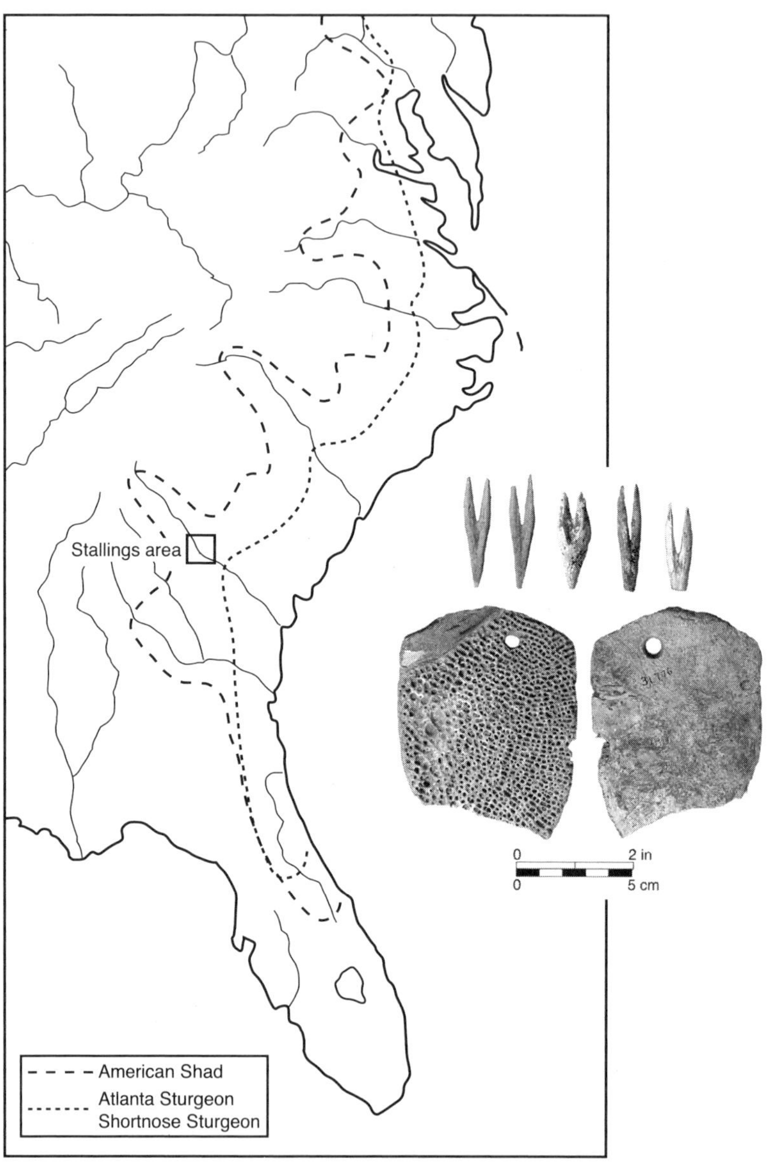

5.11. Map of the migratory range of shad and sturgeon in rivers of the Atlantic Seaboard. Shown with this map are elements of sturgeon recovered from Stallings Island, Georgia. Of the five "Y-bones" illustrated, the two on the right appear to have been copies of this sturgeon element made from split deer bone. This would suggest that the Y-bones were drafted into either technological or ornamental uses. The large skull bone shown in obverse and reverse views was ground along its edges and drilled in the manner of a soapstone cooking stone. Its use is uncertain (photo by the author; used with permission of the Peabody Museum, Harvard University).

feces. It is too bad that our excavations of Stallings sites have not uncovered many paleofeces.

Irrespective of the actual dietary contribution of sturgeon and shad to Stallings diet, fish remains routinely include examples of other large fish, notably catfish, some estimated to be in excess of 50 pounds. Little of the hook-and-line technology that has survived in archaeological contexts could have been used to land 50-pound fish. Short of spearing them or waiting for a dead catfish to float ashore, Stallings anglers must have had ways of capturing large fish that, like shad bones, escape archaeological detection.

One hypothesized method for capturing big catfish was inspired by a documentary film on "noodling." This is a technique to catch large fish holed up under logs, banks, or other accessible nooks in relatively shallow water using nothing but the fisherman's arm. The Oklahoma noodlers captured on film were after flatheads, and the ones they captured ranged well over 50 pounds. Noodlers with missing fingers and other parts of their hands serve as testimony to the dangers of this technique. Occasional holes are occupied by snapping turtles, snakes, and other biting critters who do not take kindly to having their space invaded. The fish themselves pose something of a threat, because they literally swallow the arm; the fish can take and keep a noodler down if it is as strong or stronger. So competitive was noodling among Oklahomans that they instituted an annual tournament to crown the best noodler. Elsewhere this same technique for luring big catfish with one's appendages is known as "tickling" or "grappling."

James Adair once again gives us hope that our hypothesis for noodling is viable. He writes that the Indians "have a surprising method of fishing under the edges of rocks, that stand over deep places of a river. There they pull off their red breeches . . . and wrapping it round their arm, so as to reach the lower part of the palm of their right hand, they dive under the rock where the large cat-fish lie to shelter themselves from the scorching beams of the sun, and to watch for prey." Adair goes on to describe the action: "as soon as the fierce aquatic animals see that tempting bait, they immediately seize it with the greatest violence, in order to swallow it. Then is the time for the diver to improve his favourable opportunity: he accordingly opens his hand, seizes the voracious fish by his tender parts, hath a sharp struggle with it against the crevices of the rock, and at last brings it safe ashore."

This is not fishing—this is hunting. Considering that some of the large catfish found in Stallings assemblages have estimated weights of well over 50 pounds, their food value approaches that of a white-tailed deer. They thus have the same potential for food sharing as terrestrial game and perhaps, through sharing, the capacity to be converted to social debt. Symbolically, the capture of large fish may have been the direct equivalent of deer hunting, essentially the symbolic conversion of a long-standing traditional practice. If practiced by men, large fish capture may have been a means to accrue social prestige in communities consisting of unrelated men. It did not require cooperation, but it may very well have enabled the brokering of all sorts of social alliances.

Sturgeon and shad are another kettle of fish altogether. At the upper range of their size limit, sturgeon may have required cooperative efforts to land by spearing. Certainly the mass capture of shad would have taken both communal facilities and collective labor for processing. Stallings culture may never have involved such intensive harvesting, and indeed the total numbers of sturgeon, shad, and large catfish are eclipsed by the assemblage of small fishes. But if Meggan Blessing is right about the function of socketed antler points, sturgeon were hunted like deer, as were large catfish if noodling was practiced back then. If done individually, like deer hunting, sturgeon and catfish hunting produced foods that brought prestige to those eager to share.

Domestic and Political Economies

Issues of prestige take us to the realm of political economy and the influences of social impingements on decisions to allocate limited time and energy to the daily chores. Before we consider that in the following chapter, let us take a summary glimpse at changes in diet and subsistence technology over the course of Stallings time. Was the increased settlement permanence of the middle Savannah attended by subsistence change? Were low-ranking foods added to the menu as returns on traditional foods diminished?

The answer to both questions, frankly, is no. We know now with certainty that shellfish were nothing new or original to Stallings diet in the middle Savannah because indigenous people collected and ate them for centuries before Early Stallings groups moved in. This is new information, and it sharply changes the picture painted by earlier analysts. If anything, shellfish use decreased over Stallings times, even as it shifted from a seasonal to perennial supplement to the diet.

The patently important role of fish in the Stallings diet may also have been matched in the diet of Piedmont neighbors, although few contexts are available for comparison. If the pre-Stallings shell strata of Stallings Island are any indication, fish was just as important to Paris Island and Mill Branch people as it was to Stallings folks. Turtles seem to have increased in use through time, but not so drastically as to suggest a major rupture in traditional practice.

Use of mast resources like acorns and hickory nuts was also deeply traditional and shared among Piedmont and Coastal Plain groups alike. As we have seen, Early Stallings groups adjusted to the limited availability of mast in the Coastal Plain by making regular trips to the middle Savannah to collect, store, and retrieve nuts. Their pit technology for doing so was uniquely Stallings. And, after settling into the area permanently, they converted communal storage to private storage in circular village compounds, another uniquely Stallings practice. Whereas the use of mast resources themselves remained constant, the way in which they were collected and used changed appreciably.

Thus, meaningful subsistence change cannot be found in the choice of daily foods and perhaps not even in their relative contribution to Late Archaic diets. Rather, changes in subsistence over Stallings times centered on the technology of storage and on those resources—deer and large fish—with the potential for food sharing outside the household. Minor yet specialized additions to the fishing tackle, like the beveled antler points, signal greater pursuit of large packages of food, not as daily fare, but perhaps for special events. When we add to this the prevalence of carinated serving vessels and mortuary activities at Stallings Island, we begin to appreciate that the costs of staying put were felt not so much in the daily routines of feeding the family but more in the social costs of being a member of a circumscribed community in which alliances with others, including the dead, required regular maintenance. Living off the land permanently appears not to have been as taxing on the Stallings economy as were the costs of living with one another.

6

Living with Each Other

Life has its hidden costs, and some of the steepest are associated with group membership. Federal and state income taxes, social security taxes, and workers' compensation payments are among the social costs of being an American. We are legally obliged to contribute to these funds. Although many Americans are happy to do so out of a sense of civic duty, others no doubt feel exploited, forced to subsidize those unable to work and the pork-barrel projects that keep politicians in office. Such contrasting perspectives on social welfare are among the great cleavage planes of our nation, a dichotomy that historically has fueled the pendulum swings between conservative and liberal values.

No matter how small and uncomplicated they may appear to be compared to modern nation-states, hunter-gatherer communities have their hidden costs too. When anthropologists collected data on the household economies of hunter-gatherers living in the deserts of southern Africa, they found that basic needs could be met with only about 20 hours of work a week (see chapter 5). This life of "original affluence" seemed counterintuitive for a people who have not only a limited technology but a harsh, unpredictable environment to boot. To be sure, long-term success under such challenging conditions requires insurance against failure. A 20-hour work week is sufficient only because social ties to other people provide a safety net when times get tough. Those social ties—those insurance policies—have their costs.

Anthropologist Polly Weissner studied in great detail the social alliances of Kalahari hunter-gatherers in an exchange milieu known as *hxaro*. She observed that social alliances created and maintained by hxaro trade offset the risk of acting alone by providing social security in times of need. Social safety nets run the gamut from food sharing among part-time co-residents to seeking temporary refuge in the territories of allies. Weissner documented how women establish and maintain hxaro partners through the gifting of headbands with ornate, personalized beaded patterns. Women and men alike spend considerable time crafting things for hxaro exchange, traveling to neighboring lands, and visiting partners. These, Weissner showed, are the hidden costs of the "original affluent society." When we add to the 20 hours of domestic chores the time spent making and keeping social alliances, we have a full work week. Humble though it may seem, this is the political economy of foraging; it ensures social reproduction, long-term population success, and some semblance of continuity in cultural practice.

Hxaro for people of the Kalahari is an institution, not simply quirky, idiosyncratic behavior, and it thus qualifies as an apparatus of social reproduction (as do schools and churches today). The big difference, many would acknowledge, is that hxaro is organized by egalitarian principles, ensuring autonomy for all who abide by its rules of reciprocity. Nor does it involve a class of nonworkers or a privileged elite—people who have to be "paid" for their insurance services. Lacking such oppressive features, hxaro is downright enjoyable for most, and people eagerly seek opportunities to visit old partners and establish alliances with new ones.

Among non-Western cultures worldwide, institutions of social reproduction are found in ritual practices that are at once enjoyable and beneficial to all. Quite often they include rituals involving food. Indeed, feasting is among the most common mechanisms of social integration, as people come together to share in the preparation and consumption of food and drink. Feasting surrounds rites of passage, ceremonies of political alliance, and commemorative events. Even today we imbibe and gorge at all sorts of social gatherings, many of which, like Thanksgiving, are vital to the social reproduction of extended family ties. We also occasionally give gifts to reaffirm our social commitment to one another. In feasting and gifting we share with people worldwide a common bond of sociality, an essential need to be a part of the family and community.

No matter how enjoyable and gratifying they may be, throwing big parties and giving things away are costly strategies for making and keeping friends. Insofar as the recipients of an individual's generosity reciprocate, the costs of such actions are equilibrated. But clearly the balance of giving is tenuous, as the social debt created by every act of generosity must be acknowledged and obliged. With the means to throw many parties and give many gifts, a person is able to accumulate a great deal of social debt. It is in this potential that social scientists have found the means by which small-scale, egalitarian societies develop into more complex societies, with privileged individuals who require subsidies and thus impinge on the workloads of others. Feasts in particular have attracted much interest because of their potential to involve large numbers of people in social obligation. When several individuals compete to throw the biggest parties and obligate increasingly larger groups of people through generosity, the dynamic of feasting has enormous power to alter society and impact the environment. Ironic though it may seem, rituals predicated on generosity often become institutions of selfishness and aggrandizement: would-be leaders, in order to outcompete rivals, find it increasingly necessary to exploit the labor and goodwill of their constituencies. Such circumstances require ideological mechanisms—some type of propaganda—to mask the hidden costs of hosting feasts.

Classic Stallings culture may be among the many cases of economic intensification driven by ritual acts involving food. This is certainly the trend in recent interpretations of their coastal counterparts, whose large, ring-like accumulations of shell indicate events of mass consumption. Moreover, the manner in which shell accumulated at coastal sites suggests that feasts may have been competitive, perhaps driven by the demands of privileged individuals. I believe that these fledgling circumstances of social complexity are of historical relevance to our understanding of Classic Stallings culture.

The Sociality of Shell Rings

I have introduced coastal shell rings in the prologue and again in chapter 2. These unusual accumulations of shell are among the Southeast's least-understood archaeological phenomena. Archaeologists have vacillated between two contrasting perspectives on the function of shell rings. On the one hand, shell rings have been regarded by some as simply locations of habitation. They typically contain features, artifacts, and food remains other than shell, and some excavations suggest that the rings formed through the gradual accumulation of refuse around houses arrayed in a circle. A few archaeologists have even gone on to suggest that circular arrangements are inherently egalitarian: everyone has a front-row seat, so to speak. On the other hand, some archaeologists regard rings as ceremonial sites, created and used to conduct the rituals of social reproduction. They have noted differences between ring sites and coeval sites with amorphous middens. These latter sites often contain more diverse material and food assemblages than do shell rings, which, together with the lack of formalized site plans, suggests mundane living.

Both perspectives on the function shell rings have their supporting evidence, for shell rings indeed vary wildly, leaving little room for broad generalizations. Shell deposits generally conforming to circular or semicircular shapes range from tens to hundreds of meters in diameter. Some are fully enclosed; others are open. Most have interiors devoid of midden and features, but a few contain evidence of central activities. None have produced solid evidence for houses, but most include the sorts of features that we expect of domestic sites, such as shellfish steaming pits. They are found along both the south Atlantic and Gulf coasts as well as in coastal South America and therefore could not have been the work of one people.

Field expeditions to shell rings over the years have gradually clarified many of the questions about ring function and structure. Research on rings in the Southeast has burgeoned lately, with projects headed by Mike Russo and Rebecca Saunders and, most recently, by Victor Thompson. The work of Russo and Saunders has been especially instrumental in addressing the sociality of shell-ring sites. They have found in shell rings suggestive evidence for both feasting and social differentiation. Among the more revealing projects in this respect is their work at the Fig Island complex on the south coast of South Carolina.

Fig Island consists of three "rings" distributed over some five hectares in an estuary off Edisto Island. Fig Island 2 is the closest to an actual ring, at some 77 m in diameter and about 2.5 m above the underlying marsh surface. Fig Island 3 is an arcuate midden about 50 m in maximum dimension that was connected to Fig Island 2 by a shell causeway. The largest feature, Fig Island 1, is a deposit 157 m long, 111 m wide, and some 5.5 m tall consisting of one large, steep-sided half-circle enclosing a small plaza and at least two small "ringlets" attached to the arc and enclosing additional small plazas. The sheer complexity of Fig Island 1 challenges the imagination, but even the circular Fig Island 2 is actually structurally asymmetrical. As Russo notes, the ring is hexagonal in plan, with an opening to the southwest at the midpoint of one of its six sides. Opposite the opening are the widest and tallest segments of the enclosure; behind them is the causeway linking it with Fig Island 3, whose highest and widest aspect lies at one end of the arc.

As in most of the Atlantic coastal rings, oysters make up the bulk of the Fig Island rings, and fish bones are the most common vertebrate remains. These same foods predominate in amorphous middens, so nothing about the types of foods found at Fig Island distinguishes it from other sites in the coastal zone. Rather, the difference between shell rings and other midden sites is in the manner in which oyster shell was deposited. At Fig Island large lenses of whole, jumbled shell were deposited at the bases and at various places

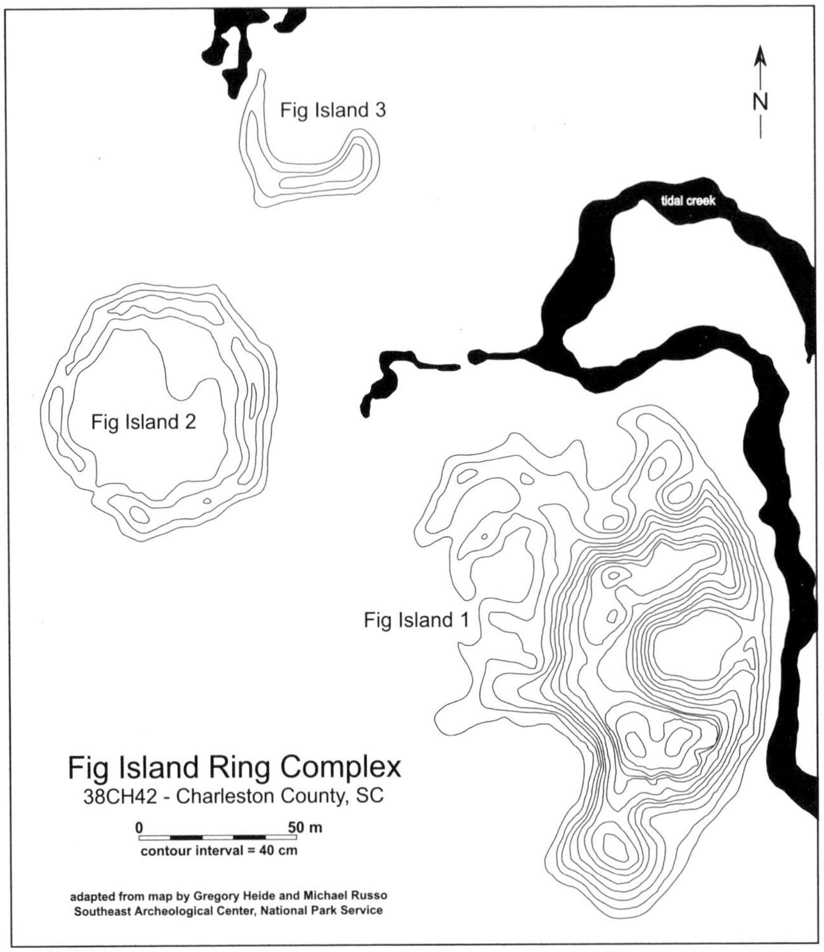

6.1. Topographic map of the Fig Island shell ring complex, Charleston County, South Carolina (adapted from a map provided by Mike Russo).

throughout the cores of the ring. Lenses of soil or crushed shell atop these dumps testify to stable surfaces that intermittently interrupt sequences of accumulation. Each of these episodes of dumping is too large to have been the remains of daily meals by households, and in some cases paired shells suggest that oyster was deposited without being eaten at all. Besides Fig Island, large dumps of whole, clean shell have been documented at Ford Shell Ring and Sea Pines on Hilton Head; shell rings on Sapelo Island; Rollins in northeast Florida; and Joseph Reed in southeast Florida.

Saunders admits that the evidence for feasting remains circumstantial, because much of the oyster at shell rings could have accumulated through daily consumption by resident groups. The large dumps of clean, whole shell are compelling evidence, however, that oyster shell was a building material as well as the by-product of a primary food source. Other lines of evidence, including the pottery of shell rings, support the view that large dumps of shell resulted from large-scale feasts. Virtually all the pottery at Fig Island consists of open, shallow bowls that apparently were not used over fire. Saunders suggests that these were serving bowls, and the high proportion of decoration on these vessels indicates use in extrahousehold contexts of consumption. As Jim Michie pointed out long ago, shell rings often contain a greater percentage of decorated wares compared to amorphous middens. Coupled with other differences in material culture, Michie viewed this contrast as a functional one, with rings being the location of special activities.

If rings indeed were the locations of feasts, can we determine if feasts were cooperative or competitive? Competitive feasts imply some level of social differentiation, so that certain individuals had the wherewithal, or at least the desire, to accumulate greater amounts of surplus than would-be competitors. This is the line of argumentation proffered by Mike Russo. He regards variations in the height and breadth of segments of rings as a measure of differential status. Such variations indeed appear patterned across sites, with the highest and broadest segments of rings typically opposite ring openings or other meaningful features. The large, arcuate shell formations of Florida, for instance, have peaks at central positions. Inasmuch as shell accumulated episodically at shell rings, segments with exceptional height and breadth attest to redundant uses of space: certain segments routinely received more shell than others. If this resulted from fixed spatial arrangements of personnel occupying rings over generations, then the roles that these people played in society may have transcended their lifetimes. Even if these variations did not result from the activities of specific types of personnel, the resultant accumulations are testimony to patterned uses of space. Rings were indeed places structured by proscriptions about the specific locations of certain activities and deposits.

The links among shell piles, feasting, and social status are tenuous at best; but I, for one, find the argument compelling. The trouble in convincing others is that direct evidence for differential social status is not literal; nor is it found in the residues of routine life. Nothing in the archaeological record of the Late Archaic societies who made and used rings points directly to the existence of big men, big women, or any sort of chiefly elite. Rather, the evidence for social differentiation is structural and corporate, not necessarily tied to particular people or lineages. It is found in the way in which these societies represented themselves in the contexts of ritual, in those moments of idealized cultural practice that laid bare their core beliefs about the world around them and their place in it. In the case of shell-ring feasting, the long-term result was patterned variation in shell accumulations; in the context of feasting certain individuals may have asserted roles of authority to coordinate the actions of others. The people no doubt all knew their place in ritual practice, and differences in roles may not have been contested or competitive. Means of rotating the privileged roles of ritual practice among participating families or lineages could have precluded the emergence of institutionalized leaders. But then again, some people may not have had the knowledge and economic means necessary to pull off a big feast and have the resultant by-products piled up in culturally meaningful ways. The seeming contradiction between evidence for highly structured collective action and the lack of institutionalized leadership persists as a nagging anthropological puzzle. It also may have been a nagging contradiction for those who lived through it.

Classic Stallings Socializing

The actions that led to the impressive shell formations of Fig Island provide a historical backdrop for the development of Stallings Culture in the middle Savannah region. The first piles of shell at Fig Island were laid down around 4600 B.P., and the final episodes of mounding occurred around 4200 B.P. This is the time of great culture change in the middle Savannah, as groups of Early Stallings affiliation started to move into the Fall Zone on a seasonal basis and shortly thereafter established relatively permanent settlement. As I have argued, Classic Stallings culture arose from the interactions between those interlopers from the Coastal Plain and the indigenous Mill Branch culture. I doubt that the denizens of Fig Island had any direct involvement in this process. The pottery from Fig Island is quite different from either Early or Classic Stallings wares of the middle Savannah. The sandy paste and periwinkle-punctate designs of Fig Island sherds give it a distinctive look and feel, typical of the coastal Thoms Creek tradition that evolved alongside Stallings wares. Despite the differences in pottery, the Fig Island tradition of piling oyster shell in a ring-like formation was shared by those making and using

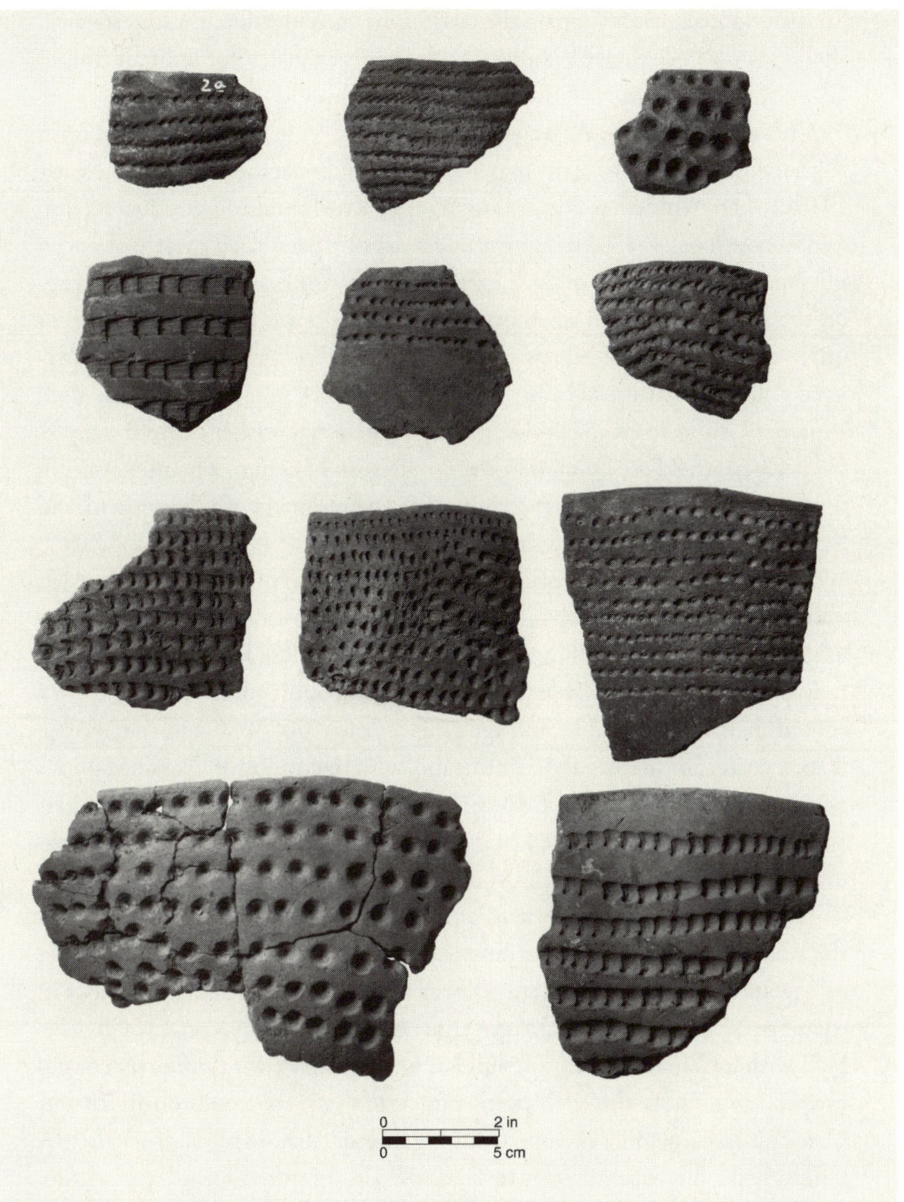

6.2. Sherds of fiber-tempered pottery collected from the Chesterfield shell ring, Beaufort County, South Carolina. The drag-and-jab sherds shown here are very similar to sherds from Stallings Island, while the shell-point punctate sherds reflect a distinctively coastal design tradition.

Stallings pottery elsewhere on the coast. One such location, the Chesterfield shell ring on Port Royal Island, provides solid evidence for a direct link to Classic Stallings culture in the middle Savannah.

Chesterfield is a horseshoe-shaped ring some 55 m in diameter and open to the west. Its arcuate form may have been fully enclosed before the early 1930s, when Woldemar Ritter and Warren K. Moorehead conducted limited excavations. Their testing revealed a deposit composed mostly of oyster interspersed with layers of dark earth and periwinkle shell. Like most rings on the Atlantic Coast, the interior of Chesterfield was devoid of midden or other obvious traces of human activity. The pottery that Ritter and Moorehead collected was mostly fiber-tempered and was, in fact, the sample used by James Griffin to establish the Stallings type series. Other pottery samples from Chesterfield are curated at the Charleston Museum. My inspection of these sherds years ago convinced me that the residents of Chesterfield and Stallings Island spent time with one another.

More than any other assemblage of fiber-tempered pottery from the coast, punctated sherds from Chesterfield bear very strong stylistic and technological affinity to Classic Stallings pottery from the middle Savannah. Only one radiocarbon assay is available from Chesterfield, but it comes directly from a sooted sherd. With a calibrated age range of ca. 4100–3850 B.P., the 3660 ± 50 B.P. radiocarbon assay fits comfortably with the timing of Classic Stallings occupations at Mims Point, Ed Marshall, and Stallings Island. Chesterfield is among the closest coastal shell rings to these middle Savannah sites, approximately 200 km as the crow flies and nearly directly downriver.

Is it possible that Chesterfield and middle Savannah sites were actually the seasonal encampments of a single, transhumant population? Similarities in age and pottery would seem to bear this out, but certain differences in the respective pottery assemblages argue otherwise. Every sherd at Chesterfield with a Classic Stallings design has a counterpart with uniquely coastal properties, notably the shell-point punctate that is so common in Thoms Creek assemblages like the one from Fig Island. Although it is true that the Chesterfield sherds are similar to Classic Stallings pottery in paste and wall thickness, Chesterfield vessels were at least occasionally used over fire while those from Stallings Island and neighboring sites were not. Finally, none of the drag-and-jab rim sherds from Chesterfield have left-oriented punctations, while assemblages from the middle Savannah (as discussed in chapter 4) consistently express rates of about 20 percent.

On balance, the evidence points to affinity and interaction between the two populations, but they nonetheless remained distinct people. The circular village arrangements at Stallings Island, Mims Point, and Ed Marshall were most likely influenced by interactions with shell-ring residents. To be sure, Chesterfield and other shell rings on the Georgia-Carolina coast are not much bigger than the projected size of middle Savannah compounds. If similarities in community structure between the two types of sites extend to other realms of sociality, then it is reasonable to expect locations like Stallings Island to bear evidence for feasting and spatial differentiation like that seen on the coast.

Influenced though they were by coastal tradition, circular villages in the middle Savannah were not shell rings and actually contain relatively little shell. Among those investigated to date, only Stallings Island and Lake Spring boast large quantities of shell; but even there much of it, perhaps most of it, accumulated earlier at the hands of indigenous Piedmont groups. What is more, the thick lenses of shell at Stallings Island are filled with broken artifacts, fire-cracked rock, charcoal, the remains of various vertebrates, and innumerable terrestrial snails. Unlike the rapid accumulation of mostly oyster at shell rings, the shell-rich strata encircling the side slopes of Stallings Island appear to have formed through the gradual removal of everyday trash. If feasting took place as side-slope middens formed, it did not involve the sort of site formational pattern that we see at shell rings. Rather, evidence for feasting at Stallings Island is found in pits, not in piles.

The large storage pits that are unique to Stallings culture in the middle Savannah were typically filled with refuse after they were abandoned. When pits were directly associated with structures (as at Mims Point and Stallings Island), the fill that accumulated contained all manner of domestic refuse, including many diagnostic artifacts and diverse food remains. When such pits were employed for storage away from structures (as appears to be the case at Victor Mills), they were filled with cultural material specific to the activities of storage and processing stored foods, such as grinding slabs, fire-cracked rock, flat-bottomed pots, soapstone slabs, nutshell, and charcoal. I imagine that earth removed to make new storage facilities was usually deposited in pits that had become spoiled and were abandoned. This would explain why pits at Victor Mills contained so few artifacts.

The refuse-filled storage pits at Mims Point and Stallings Island both have artifact- and bone-rich fill indicative of household refuse, but several Stallings

Pit Features at Stallings Island, Georgia

upper left: Cosgroves' back-filled trench intercepts unexcavated pit; upper right: pit excavated and back-filled in 1929 (left) next to another pit (right) that was left unexcavated; left: a basin-shaped pit sectioned in half; bottom left: profile of a basin-shaped pit over a silo (i.e., deep storage pit); bottom right: Feature 17, a silo with layers of shell, wood charcoal, and charred nutshell near base.

6.3. Examples of refuse-filled pits at Stallings Island excavated by the 1999 University of Florida expedition. The largest pits shown here are common to Classic Stallings assemblages in the region and likely started off as storage pits (photos by the author).

Island pits have layers of material that suggest relatively rapid and specialized in-filling. Feature 17 is a case in point. This large silo at Stallings Island has several distinct layers of fill: near the base is a layer of freshwater clam shell with some vertebrate remains, notably fish; over that is a 10-cm layer of charcoal with an abundance of charred hickory nutshell; over that is a diverse fill with abundant fish bone, including large gar, suckers, bass, and catfish. A nearly identical pit feature was excavated by the Cosgroves. Related to these are smaller features with enormous quantities of fish bone, like Feature 10. The base of Feature 2 was lined with the shells of unusually large clams.

Not all Stallings Island pits are so distinctively filled with refuse, but enough of these stratified and specialized fills have been observed to know that it was not at all uncommon. Pit fill such as this, however, is uncommon at other Stallings sites in the immediate vicinity; in fact, none of the scores of pits that we excavated at Mims Point, Ed Marshall, or Victor Mills matched this pattern. When we add that Stallings Island is the only middle Savannah location with a large number of carinated vessels and human interments, the pit fill unique to this site appears even more significant. Considering all these lines of evidence, a reasonable assertion at this juncture is that Stallings Island was the locus of occasional feasting, and it seems reasonable as well to suggest that feasting was directly associated with mortuary activities.

Feasting with the Dead?

Archaeologists have admonished C. C. Jones for singling out Stallings Island as an "Island of the Dead"; but from a modern vantage point, I believe that he was right. Differences in the preservation of human bone aside, Stallings Island is one of only two shell-bearing sites in the middle Savannah with more than an occasional burial. The other is Lake Spring, about 20 km upriver from Stallings Island. Both sites contain large shell middens, dense artifact assemblages, and scores of human burials, and both have burials dating to prepottery times as well as Stallings times. Stallings Island is the larger of the two, and its assemblage of pottery includes a much higher proportion of carinated vessels. What is more, the burials at Stallings Island include a subset of individuals interred in the center of a circular village, a practice not duplicated at other village sites in the immediate area or at any of the coastal shell rings.

Stallings Island was indeed a special place, a locus of human interment going back to at least 5200 B.P., centuries before Early Stallings groups moved into the area. When they got to the middle Savannah, Early Stallings groups avoided Stallings Island. They established settlements all around the island but never directly on it. Two centuries later their descendants (those of Classic Stallings identity) reestablished Stallings Island as a locus of burials, this time in the context of circular village life and perhaps occasional feasting. It is tempting to conclude that all three aspects of Classic Stallings culture—circular villages, burial, and feasting—were intrinsically linked to this location as a center of social reproduction.

Making this case requires that we first sort through the inventory of Stallings Island burials to locate those of Classic Stallings age. This is a hard task, as some of the burials not only predate Stallings times but also date as recently as the seventeenth century. In the block excavation of their 1929 expedition, the Cosgroves exhumed 62 human interments. Another 10 were uncovered in a unit at the north end of the site. Including the 12 burials Claflin excavated earlier, the total curated assemblage of burials is 84. Untold additional burials were exhumed by Jones and any number of looters in recent decades. Although it is risky to estimate the entire burial population at Stallings Island, a minimum count of 200–300 individuals appears reasonable.

Among the burials that the Cosgroves dug were four with pottery of Mississippian age. In our 1999 expedition we observed, but did not remove, an additional grave with several historic-era Indians disturbed by looters. Burials of pre-Stallings age are more difficult to identify due to lack of pottery, but a few with bannerstones attest to either Paris Island or earlier interments. Stallings people and their predecessors did not routinely inter their deceased with diagnostic artifacts, so we have little direct evidence for attributing individual graves to specific Archaic phases. Although shell beads were recovered from nine of the interments, these spanned graves of pre-Stallings, Stallings, and Mississippian age.

Fortunately, the Cosgroves opened up such a large area in the center of the site that the distribution of graves relative to diagnostic pit features enables us to infer that one particular cluster of burials was almost certainly of Classic Stallings affiliation. Indeed, the distribution of burials in the block shows an unequivocal nonrandom pattern for location within the projected plaza of a circular village. Of the 58 burials in the Cosgroves' block, 32 fall inside the projected plaza, and another 12 are situated in the projected compound of surrounding houses. Of the 32 burials in the central area, 2 were interred in urns during the Mississippian era and must be eliminated as intrusive fea-

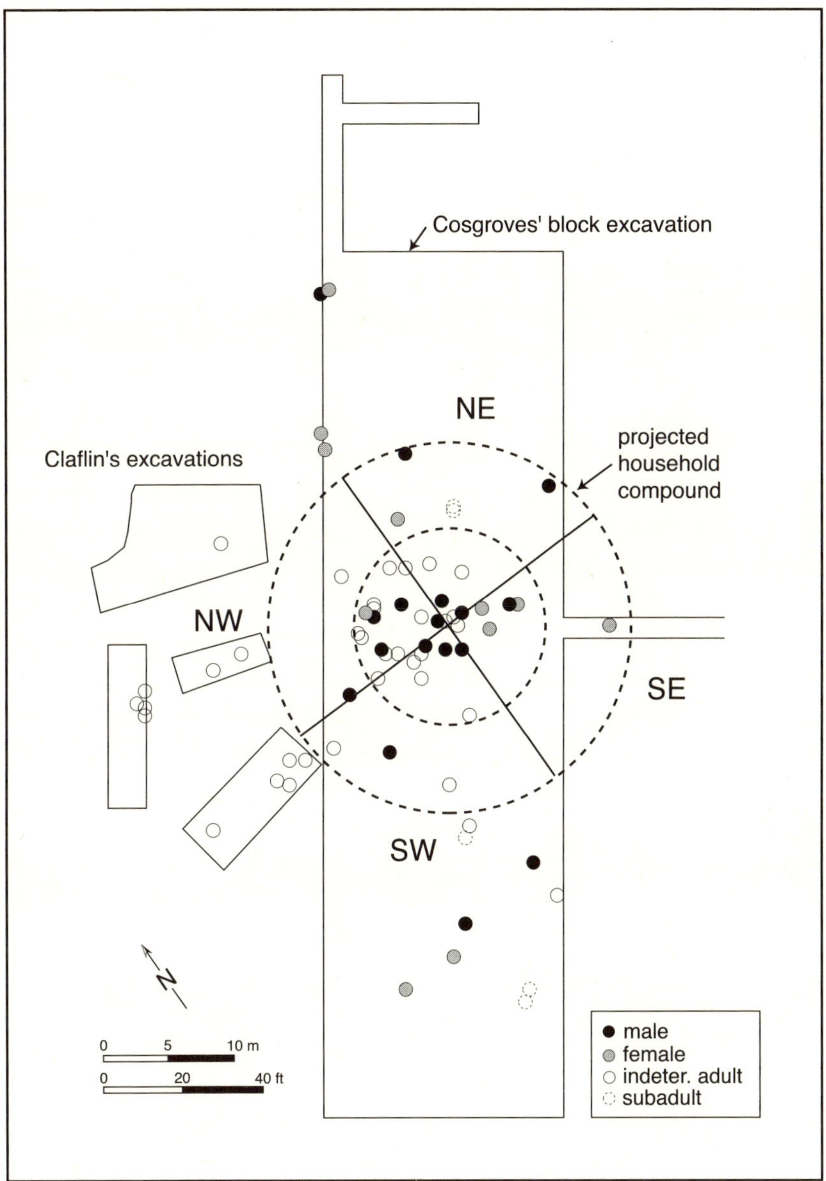

6.4. Schematic drawing of human interments at Stallings Island in and around the proposed location of a circular household compound with an interior "plaza" (adapted from report by William Claflin).

tures; I am confident that the remaining 42 burials in the circular compound actually date to Classic Stallings times.

Although the Cosgroves did not always record information on the age and sex of Stallings Island burials, the observations that they did record reveal some tantalizing patterning. First, the projected plaza population consists entirely of adults. An infant and a juvenile occupied locations on the outer eastern edge of the plaza, and a second infant was placed on the outer western edge of the larger circle, but none were located in the central area. Granted, the size of the subadult population is small; but given the disproportionate number of burials in the projected plaza, some representation by subadults is expected based on chance alone.

Second, females tend to be located in the southeast quadrant of the projected plaza, an area otherwise bereft of burials. Overall, individuals recorded as female are underrepresented in the plaza compared to those identified as male. This same discrepancy holds for the larger group of burials within the circular compound, with 82 percent of males contained therein, compared to 55 percent of females.

A cluster of five burials in the very center of the projected plaza includes no identified females and two identified males. An additional four males, one female, and an unsexed adult occupy area within 3 m of the center. All but one of these individuals were in a flexed position, and five have their heads oriented toward the center. The exception to flexing is a seated burial in the northwest quadrant. Three other examples of seated burials were found in the outer periphery of the projected plaza: one each in the northeast, southeast, and southwest quadrants.

Small sample size and problems of ascription aside, these tendencies in spatial arrangement offer ample reason to suggest that mortuary space at Stallings Island was highly structured and thus possibly indicative of social identity. Even if the patterns that I suggest characterize the internal configuration of Stallings burials are imagined and not real, the unequivocal clustering of burials in an area surrounded by Classic Stallings pit features remains significant. Aside from cultural affiliation, what does this tell us about social identity? Were those buried at Stallings Island privileged individuals? Were those buried in the central plaza the most privileged?

Apart from where individuals were buried, grave treatment is of little help in answering these questions. Those buried in the very center of the plaza appear to have patterned orientation, but no burial includes special grave goods.

Only one of the nine individuals with strands of beads was interred in the plaza; most such graves were located to the west of the Cosgroves' block in excavations made by Claflin and date to the Paris Island/Mill Branch era.

Like the shell-ring evidence for differential status and feasting, the Stallings Island record is ambiguous yet nevertheless tantalizing. We are certainly justified in asking why Stallings Island was so different from the other Classic Stallings communities (such as Mims Point and Ed Marshall) and why certain individuals were buried in the center of the Stallings Island village, as opposed to its periphery.

Relevant to this first question is the history of communities in the middle Savannah long before Classic Stallings culture arose. In these earlier centuries, ca. 5100–4700 B.P., Paris Island residents collected large quantities of shellfish and interred their dead at Stallings Island. As far as we know, these activities took place at an unprecedented level for Piedmont groups. This apparent intensification coincides with the appearance of Early Stallings groups in the middle Coastal Plain of the Savannah River valley, at locations like Rabbit Mount and Fennel Hill. Given connections between these newcomers and Piedmont indigenes, it is reasonable to conclude that shellfishing and specialized mortuary practice were precipitated by such interaction. Indeed, many have long regarded the inception of shellfishing at places like Stallings Island as a direct consequence of developments on the coast.

However, this was not the only factor influencing the actions of Paris Island residents. Rare though it is, evidence for shellfishing and interment of the dead with shell goes back at least to 6500 B.P. At Mims Point we encountered a single female, 25–30 years of age, tightly flexed and placed in a narrow grave with abundant shell. Domestic features and numerous stone tools dating to this time attest to a bona fide late Middle Archaic occupation at Mims Point, not simply an isolated grave. Interestingly, none of the mundane features of Middle Archaic age contained shell, suggesting that the very first use of shellfish in the middle Savannah was for mortuary purposes.

Thus, Mims Point provides solid precedent for the use of shell in graves well before Paris Island, Mill Branch, and Stallings cultures existed. In the larger scheme of Eastern Woodlands prehistory, this is hardly surprising. Shellfishing and burials in shell began as early as 8,300 years ago in the middle Tennessee River valley. And it is no coincidence that the Morrow Mountain tradition responsible for these earliest practices was the same stream of culture that begot Middle Archaic populations of the Carolina Piedmont. Despite its antiquity, this seed of tradition, transplanted hundreds of kilometers and many centuries from its source, did not germinate in earnest until a second cultural influence from the Midsouth crept in sometime after 5,800 years ago. This second wave in the Savannah valley, welling up from Benton and related traditions from the west, became manifested in the local Allendale phase. Together, then, the deep roots of shellfishing and mortuary practice of Middle Archaic times and the more recent wave of similar practices emerged in the context of interactions between Piedmont indigenes and Coastal Plain interlopers, ca. 5100 B.P.

With the stage set for rapid cultural change, what exactly led to the particular practice of centering graves in the Classic Stallings compound at Stallings Island? A plausible answer to this question is found in the patterns of intergroup alliance that formed as two streams of history converged. If the practice of unilocal postmarital residence discussed in chapter 4 predated Classic Stallings times, then Early Stallings groups consisted of adult females with Allendale heritage and adult males of Paris Island heritage. It is also likely that Allendale marriages in the early years involved recruitment from coastal populations; if these later groups also abided by matrilocal postmarital residence rules, however, Allendale men would have relocated to the coast after marriage. What little information we have on this matter supports both patterns: Paris Island bannerstones and soapstone show up in Early Stallings assemblages of the Coastal Plain, and Allendale points occasionally turn up at coastal locales like Hilton Head Island. If the acquisition of all such classes of material culture was predominately a male activity, then the flow of goods was from west to east, upriver to downriver. The major flow in the opposite direction was pottery or at least the idea of pottery, which, we might presume, was largely female technology. Shell beads also moved from the coast to the interior, but we have no basis for ascribing this class of material culture to either of the genders.

By the time Allendale groups, now Early Stallings groups, became large enough to split into subregional populations and marry among themselves, we begin to find the material patterns of new and distinct cultures, most notably Mill Branch culture. Cultural differences between Mill Branch and Stallings are accentuated at this point. I can imagine at least two alternative scenarios to explain this development. Mill Branch culture may have become distinctive as a consequence of cultural resistance. Locked out of marriages with Stallings people, bearers of Mill Branch culture may have become retrenched into cultural tradition and sought alliances elsewhere. I believe the abandonment of river sites and eventually the entire middle Savannah area by Mill Branch descendants points in this direction. And yet, before these events transpired in the final centuries of the Mill Branch phase (4450–4200 B.P.), interactions between personnel of Early Stallings and Mill Branch affiliation likely involved occasional marriages. Again, if the postmarital practices of Classic Stallings culture were already in place, Mill Branch men would have relocated from natal communities upon marriage to join their wives' communities.

Both processes—intermarriage and resistance or avoidance—likely worked in tandem, with some members of Mill Branch culture accommodating change, others eschewing it. The final gasp of Mill Branch culture in the middle Savannah coincides precisely with the emergence of Classic Stallings culture. This "event" was centered on Stallings Island, the locus of traditional practice extending well past Mill Branch times into the Paris Island phase. Stallings Island was the crucible of culture change, and its ingredients were apparently multiethnic. I believe that Classic Stallings culture became deliberately unique as a means of integrating its disparate elements. The emergent Classic Stallings tradition incorporated elements of indigenous and "foreign" culture by virtue of its convergent history. It quickly became insular and self-reproducing, with marriage alliances eventually restricted to Stallings factions on the Ogeechee River, Brier Creek, and perhaps coastal groups at Chesterfield and elsewhere.

None of this can be read literally in the archaeological record of the middle Savannah, so it remains hypothetical and admittedly hard to test. This scenario is inspired more by the reality of ethnographic cultures than by archaeological data. It is in these contemporary accounts that we can appreciate how social formations based on intergroup marriages pose something of an economic as well as social challenge.

The economic challenge in marriage alliances among hunter-gatherers worldwide resides in the obligations between in-laws. Unilocal postmarital arrangements redistribute the supplies of labor among intermarrying groups, with one spouse of the new marriage leaving his or her natal community and joining the village of the in-laws. In a survey of ethnographic hunter-gatherer populations, Robert Kelly shows that such intermarriages often do not involve any material exchanges between the allied families. In about 20 percent of the 113 cases Kelly reviewed, however, marriage arrangements involved some form of bridewealth; another 16 percent involved bride service. Both forms of exchange are intended to alleviate the instability inherent in intergroup marriages by offsetting some of the hidden costs of marriage from wife-givers to wife-takers. The opposite sort of arrangement, akin to dowry, is rare among hunter-gatherers, occurring in only two of the cases in Kelly's inventory.

Every instance of bride service or bridewealth involving young Stallings men was presumably matched by an equal flow of alliance exchange coming from without. Unequal forms of marriage alliance are not uncommon among hunter-gatherers, however, and they create and reproduce social ranking among families or lineages. For instance, in unequal bridewealth, wife-givers appropriate the labor of husbands and their families by threatening to take back the wife. Men potentially find themselves working more for their affines than for their blood relatives, who, in order to offset their loss of labor, require work from their sons-in-laws.

Although the potential for unequal alliances to spiral out of control is obvious, they often do not do so in small-scale societies. This has much to do with the power of ritual to alleviate tensions by integrating people into a common bond of spirituality. Herein lies the significance of Stallings Island and feasting associated with the dead. More than a memorial to death, mortuary ritual was a time to invite the in-laws over for a visit. We may never know whether men were returned to their natal communities for interment or buried in the villages of their affines. In any case, men were apparently the focus of this ritual. This is understandable, given their potentially tenuous social positions in communities defined by the generational continuity of the women they married. Men were "outsiders" in Classic Stallings society, but in mortuary ritual they were literally brought to the center. This is true not only in the placement of men centrally in the plaza but also in the use of "male" items (like bannerstones) traditionally in the graves of women and perhaps later as a form of bridewealth. In death the association of men with deep tradition was rendered unambiguous.

Rituals of death involved innovations like feasting with large fish and carinated vessels, which shows that traditions were constantly changing to accommodate changes in social affiliations and identity and to incorporate the social identities of the opposite gender, the opposing culture. The metaphorical association of men with tradition and women with innovation was a constitutive theme of Classic Stallings culture, likely a source of enduring contradiction.

We return now to the issue posed at the outset of this chapter: the hidden costs of group membership. Rife with contradiction, Classic Stallings society required ritual to stay afloat; and the costs of ritual practice were real, if not substantial. It is difficult to judge the relationship between the price of ritual and the budgets of day-to-day living in Stallings communities. We do know, however, that after three centuries the ritual ways of Classic Stallings culture and its presence at the central site of ritual were no longer possible. Whether it was the lack of sufficient resources to sustain these rituals or internal strife that made it difficult to succeed under even good circumstances, Classic Stallings people abandoned Stallings Island and eventually the middle Savannah after 3,800 years ago. The circumstances surrounding this event are the subject of the final chapter of their history.

7

Twilight on the Savannah

After a long history of development and a short time of florescence, Stallings Culture of the middle Savannah River valley came to an abrupt halt. Its demise at about 3,800 years ago was indeed quick, seemingly catastrophic. The timing of this event is certain, but its circumstances or causes are poorly understand. One of the Southeast's great archaeological puzzles is how and why one of the region's most celebrated hunter-gatherer societies met its end.

Actually, the bearers of Stallings Culture never fully disappeared: they simply starting doing things differently and in other places and thus became archaeologically recognized as a different people. Most notably, sites along the Savannah River were completely abandoned for a new life in the adjacent hill country. The ensuing pattern of upland settlement involved much smaller and more dispersed communities than those of Classic Stallings times. Communities were no longer arrayed in circular fashion. Carinated vessels fell into disuse. Other technology and stylistic expression changed, too. Lacking as they did the opportunities and demands of a river way-of-life, descendants of Stallings Culture adapted their toolkits and labor arrangements to their new surroundings.

Acknowledging that life carried on in new ways for the once insular and stationary Stallings people hardly satisfies curiosity about the reasons for this change. Were riverine communities forced from their homes by severe weather, perhaps flooding or drought? Did they seal their own fate by overtaxing the very resources on which they had come to depend? How about relations with neighboring groups? Were they at war or at peace? What about nutrition and disease, or labor relations?

Possible causes for the demise of Stallings Culture are many. Conclusive evidence is not so plentiful. So far, no obvious traces of environmental disaster have been uncovered. I doubt that such evidence has gone unnoticed, for much of it would be highly conspicuous. Flooding, for example, often leaves erosional surfaces and layers of sediment in the profiles of archaeological sites. The consequences of recent flooding were documented by Claflin at Stallings Island. Our own work at Ed Marshall uncovered similar evidence.

River floods had eroded large portions of the shell midden at Ed Marshall and redeposited it in two channel chutes. The channel fill was chock-full of Stallings artifacts, fooling us into thinking that we had discovered the telltale signs of an ancient catastrophe. But the very bottom of this deposit told the true story. Among all the flaked stone tools and bone pins of Stallings age were two pieces of clear bottle glass, undeniable evidence for early-twentieth-century events. These may very well be the same floods that Claflin recounted in his 1931 report.

Flooding undoubtedly was a regular nuisance for prehistoric river people, but the severity of floods has increased markedly in historic times. The vast acreage cleared for farming in the eighteenth and nineteenth centuries released tons of Piedmont clay into river drainages like the Savannah. Unable to carry these sediments all the way to the ocean, the Savannah River periodically unloaded its burden in the first convenient spot downriver—the Fall Zone.

The flood situation during Stallings time does not appear to have involved catastrophic events. Evidence for flooding includes normal depositional episodes, such as levee and point bar accretion, but not severe erosion. Stallings residences probably took seasonal floods in stride, moving temporarily to one of the numerous ridge-top sites overlooking the river, like Mims Point.

If a single catastrophic event cannot be blamed for the demise of Stallings, what about more gradual change? Perhaps slow, incremental declines in the availability of key food resources were at first tolerated but eventually led to crisis levels. We might not expect such a process to be apparent in the ways people went about making a living—that is, not before it was too late. But it ought to show up in the food resources they exploited.

Did Stallings Communities Suffer from Diminishing Returns?

A popular model for understanding changes in the hunter-gatherer diet is adapted from the economic study of energy budgets among nonhuman foragers. Optimal foraging theory is premised on the assumption that—for organisms to survive—strategies of feeding must result in energy returns (benefits) that are as great or greater than the costs of acquisition. Quite simply, critters that expend more energy than they capture cannot last long. The Darwinian process of natural selection ensures that populations whose members routinely operate below optimal levels do not survive, at least not in the face of competition by more efficient populations.

Hypothetically, given an array of choices for allocating limited time and energy to food acquisition, foragers will select foods that provide the highest return on investments and ignore foods with lesser returns. This is usually measured in calories, which are generally taken as a proxy for reproductive energy. Of course, taste, prestige, taboo, and the hidden costs of *social* reproduction, among other cultural factors, impinge on the decisions of human foragers, lessening the interpretive value of optimal foraging theory among cultural beings. Still, it is a useful place to begin any study of culture change, because it helps to define relevant variables in the food economy or (as in the case of Stallings Culture) to eliminate many of these variables as possible causes for change.

After several years of intermittent fieldwork, the Stallings Archaeological Project turned its attention to the analysis of food remains and related materials, with the express intent of assessing the ecological circumstances surrounding abandonment of the middle Savannah River valley. With support from the National Science Foundation, I assembled a team of six graduate students at the University of Florida to develop the requisite data. Three data sets were derived directly from the remains of Late Archaic meals: vertebrate fauna, freshwater mussels, and ethnobotanical remains. A fourth set of data consisted of subsistence technology, including pits, hearths, groundstone, and worked bone/antler, as well as the usual flaked stone and pottery. The final data set consisted of terrestrial snails, which we recovered by the tens of thousands but always disregarded as incidental material. Few, if any, of the oodles of snails found in features and middens were the remains of meals; these creatures simply lived off the organic waste of human activities. It turns out that these commensal species are especially good indicators of microenvironment, so I was hopeful that any measurable changes in local climate or ground cover would be registered in changes in the sorts of snails that climbed into Stallings features over time.

The research hypotheses were clear. If members of Classic Stallings culture, by virtue of increasingly permanent settlement in the middle Savannah, outstripped the environment's capacity to sustain them, then we ought to find evidence for the following factors in the centuries leading up to abandonment. First, subsistence economies over time would have diversified to include lower-ranked foods. This is known as the diet-breadth model, mathematically designed in the fashion of marginal value theorum. Second, the increased use of low-ranking foods would have resulted from diminishing returns on high-ranking resources. Following from the diet-breadth model, preferred foods—those with the greatest net caloric value—would become increasingly costly, because they became increasingly scarce. This leads us back to the consequences of sedentism in the third hypothesis: diminishing returns on high-ranking resources resulted from overexploitation by Stallings communities. Put more simply, Stallings people exhausted the environment. Finally, I proposed that the technological innovations of Stallings culture, pottery, storage, and the like contributed to, rather than alleviated, economic stress.

In testing these hypotheses, we had available for comparison a series of pit features and midden deposits with good preservation spanning the centuries in question. Those of prepottery age provided a baseline for conditions in the middle Savannah ca. 5100–4450 B.P. Later features of Early and Classic Stallings age provided the opportunity to monitor subsistence change over time. These otherwise straightforward comparisons through time were a bit complicated because Paris Island/Mill Branch and Stallings cultures had somewhat different histories and thus potentially different cultural rationales for food selection and related subsistence choices. Central to any explanation of change are the particular histories and cultures of those under study. We might call such an approach historical ecology, as opposed to the evolutionary ecology of optimal foraging theory. Clearly, in this case of two distinct cultural histories, we cannot assume a universal set of shared motives in dietary selection. Stallings people were newcomers to the middle Savannah, people with no prior (or at least recent) experience making a living in a shoals, Fall-Zone habitat. Insofar as Stallings communities recruited through marriage allies of Paris Island and then Mill Branch culture, they benefited from the collective knowledge of people with centuries of experience in such a land.

The results of our analyses, summarized below, show no dramatic change in diet or in the relative abundance or quality of resources of daily fare. Diversity at first decreased during Early Stallings times then slowly increased. These changes may be largely a consequence of the Stallings people's adjustments to new environmental circumstances and eventually the economic consequences of permanent settlement. It is unlikely that they totally wiped out the local environment, however. The independent data afforded by snails and wood charcoal reveal only subtle changes in vegetation cover, although land snails indeed register the inception of relatively permanent villages and the on-site land clearing that this likely entailed.

We have already dispelled the misconception that Stallings people in the middle Savannah were the first to collect and eat freshwater mussels. That credit goes to the indigenous groups of the lower Piedmont. If anything, shellfish use diminished through time. We were initially convinced that the size of shellfish dropped as middle Savannah groups intensified their use. In a pilot study, Pat O'Day found a 30-percent reduction in clamshell length from those recovered from the basal stratum of the side-slope midden at Stallings Island (the onset of shellfishing at ca. 5100 B.P.) to those collected in an overlying stratum dating to ca. 4900 B.P. Shells from Classic Stallings features some six centuries later, however, showed a slight increase in average shell length.

O'Day conducted additional analyses to document two very important, if subtle, changes in capture populations of shellfish. He sectioned over 1,400 shells from a variety of strata and features to compare growth rates with size. Freshwater mussels lay down shell continuously as they grow, with bands of growth appearing as alternating translucent and opaque layers. O'Day found that clams tended to grow faster through time, a response not uncommon for populations under heavy predation.

The increase in shellfish size during Classic Stallings times that we observed in the pilot study was accentuated in these expanded samples. Valve lengths of Classic Stallings shells average about 28 percent greater than those from the basal side-slope stratum of Stallings Island. Importantly, these larger mussels also exhibit the greatest morphological variation. Unlike the earliest capture populations of shellfish, which have consistent ratios of valve width to length, the Classic Stallings mussels are much more variable. As far as we can tell this is not genetic variation but rather differences attributed to the microenvironments of mussels, particularly stream flow velocity. High variations in width to length shell ratios suggest that capture populations were taken from a variety of habitats, ranging from relatively fast-flowing to sluggish water. While such differences in stream flow might be expected to occur within any given stretch of the middle Savannah, it seems more likely that Classic Stallings shellfishers sought out the biggest clams in more remote locations, such as tributary streams and backwater sloughs, as well as the nearby shoals.

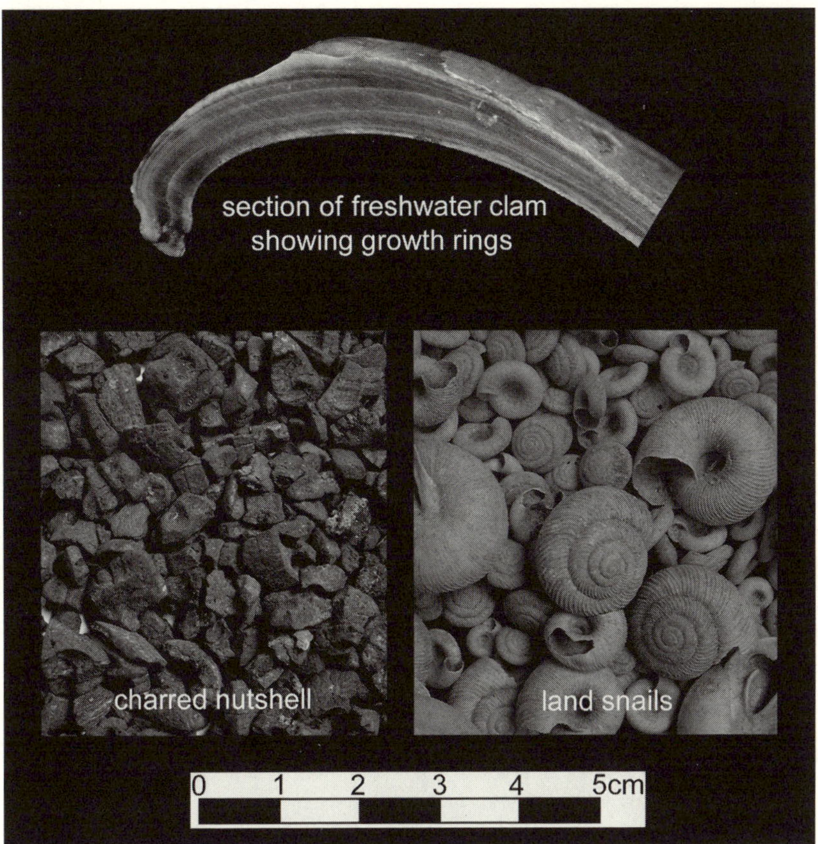

7.1. Examples of the types of minute evidence used to explore the impact that Stallings people may have had on their environment. The upper photo is a thin-section of freshwater clam, showing growth rings of alternating dark and light bands. The bottom left shows some of the charred and cracked nutshell from Stallings pit features, while the bottom right features a few of the many types of land snails that are used to reconstruct ancient groundcover (photos by author).

The Stallings people's penchant for larger clams is not restricted to Classic times: Pat O'Day's samples from Early Stallings contexts show nearly as large, if not as diverse, capture populations. Moreover, selection is not merely a function of depositional contexts, with the largest clams found primarily in pits and smaller clams primarily in midden. The sheet midden sample from Victor Mills matches nicely the coeval pit samples from Ed Marshall. The greatest differences overall are seen in comparisons of Stallings assemblages from any context with those of Paris Island/Mill Branch age. Given the cultural differences of these two groups, they may have approached the collection of shellfish slightly differently. For example, Early Stallings groups may not have trained their attention on the shoals habitat for clams because they came from a Coastal Plain environment lacking such a habitat. Backwater sloughs were more familiar to them and thus were sought out whenever possible.

Following the hypotheses stated earlier, data on uses of vertebrate fauna were expected to show increased diversity as lower-ranked species were added to the diet under diminished returns on first-line resources. Here the assumption that dietary selection by indigenous Piedmont groups reflects the baseline mix of high-ranking resources has to be tempered with two caveats: the cultural-historical difference already cited and the fact that Paris Island and Mill Branch groups utilized the middle Savannah riverine sites only seasonally. Early Stallings groups may also have made only seasonal use of the locale in their early sojourns in the middle Savannah, but we do not know if their seasonal use matched or complemented those of the indigenous groups. Eventually they settled in, so that by Classic Stallings times we are looking at perennial use of the riverine environment. It follows that comparing the vertebrate fauna from early and late periods may be a bit problematic.

Early results from the usual site-specific analyses of animal bone pointed to a pattern of increased diversity coupled with resource depression in the fishes. The Mill Branch sample from Ed Marshall consisted mostly of fish but also included appreciable quantities of deer, small mammals, turkeys, and waterfowl—overall a relatively diverse array of animal foods. The fish were perhaps not so diverse as a group, with catfish and sunfish combined making up nearly 60 percent of the assemblage. Large-mouth bass and sucker were distant seconds, and gar, drum, herring/shad, crappie, and bowfin provided only trace amounts. The side-slope midden at Stallings Island attests to at least occasional use of sturgeon this early.

The Stallings vertebrate assemblages actually show diminished diversity at first and then gradually increasing diversity. The drop in diversity is undoubtedly biased toward temporary use of the middle Savannah. The large sample from Victor Mills, for instance, consist of mostly fish (93 percent), with catfish and sunfish accounting for 86 percent of this group. As discussed in chapter 5, the fish from Victor Mills are consistently small, the sort of catch that could be taken with dip nets near shore and thus consistent with the "fast food" requirements of a temporary encampment. The Early Stallings component at Ed Marshall is perhaps a better measure of diet once these interlopers moved into the area permanently. Greater use of small mammals, deer, and turtles is coupled with more diversity among the fish, with bass, crappie, and gar making up more than trace frequencies.

Classic Stallings samples return to the high levels of dietary diversity seen in the Paris Island/Mill Branch samples, with some notable differences in the proportions of particular resources. Turtles now constitute upward of 20 percent of all vertebrate bone. Although fish continue to dominate all assemblages, the prevalence of catfish and sunnies gives way to a more even mix, including significant increases in the use of sucker, gar, and drum. Coupled with this growing diversity is evidence for diminished size of some species of sunfish. The average size of vertebrae, for instance, drops 20 percent from 3.6 mm in Paris Island/Mill Branch times to 2.9 mm during Classic Stallings times. Reduced growth rates and delayed maturation have been documented in species of sunfish as responses to prolonged predation. Although changes in fishing technology must be taken into consideration, these preliminary findings provide sufficient grounds for hypothesizing that increased dietary diversity was accompanied by resource depression in at least one of the major food groups.

As the overall size of the most common fish dropped, the use of especially large fish increased. Large catfish and the occasional sturgeon attest to a divergence from the overall pattern. As discussed in chapters 5 and 6, feasting and other social contexts of consumption may have been the impetus for seeking out and capturing unusually big fish. If so, the Classic Stallings vertebrate assemblage shows a divergence between daily fare and special meals. Like the selection for larger clams just discussed, such preferential use likely entailed labor and technology costs that exceeded those of daily practice.

Plant remains add another dimension to the story. Beth Auten spent the better part of two years sorting through the enormous quantities of feature and midden matrix that we collected to locate and identify the nutshell, wood charcoal, and seeds of Late Archaic plant use. Hickory nutshell was far and away the most common type of plant remains observed, occurring in all feature and midden contexts, occasionally in enormous numbers. Feature 17 at Stallings Island, for instance, contained over 13,000 charred fragments, and that was just a sample of the fill of this large pit. Overall, Auten found that hickory use increased through time, a trend that coincided with the inception of storage technology at Victor Mills, ca. 4600 B.P. The enormous nutshell density of Feature 17 signified persistent reliance on hickory through Classic Stallings times.

With the onset of storage and apparent evidence for intensification beginning in Early Stallings times, Auten sought evidence for changes in the way hickory was processed. She calculated average weights for nutshell fragments and found that those of Early Stallings times are consistently greater than those of Paris Island/Mill Branch times. Average weights for Classic Stallings feature vary from low to high, which shows that the difference between early and later sample is not simply a function of time and preservation. Context mattered, however: basins of all ages typically have consistent assemblages of nutshell, while silos vary in density if not nutshell size. The lowest density was found in the pits at Victor Mills, the highest at Stallings Island. Being a temporary encampment occupied primarily to store and process nuts, Victor Mills apparently did not involve the routine use of nutshell for fuel, at least not so much as locations of intensive habitation such as Stallings Island and Mims Point.

Because it is hard and dense, hickory nutshell makes a great fuel. If it had not been regularly drafted for such use, we would probably not find it in most archaeological contexts. Like some barbecue chefs today, Stallings people may have used hickory to impart flavor to food. If the choice of nutshell for fuel was instead a matter of economy, however, then perhaps other fuels had fallen into short supply. We hypothesized that through time, as settlement in the middle Savannah became more permanent, Stallings chefs would find it difficult to collect sufficient fuel among the usual dead wood lying about. If they actually had to fell trees for fuel as well as architecture and watercraft, then through time we might find changes in ground cover. Specifically we expected a gradual increase in the proportion of pine as hardwoods were reduced through land clearing. This is the usual pattern of recruitment and replacement in a location like the Fall Zone, where a mix of pines and hardwoods prevails. Our hypothesis was bolstered by the fact that Stallings people persisted in the use of indirect stone boiling, a method of cooking that is more fuel consumptive than direct-heat cooking. Asa Randall and Kara Bridgman (members of our research team working with technology) set about investigating variations in plant processing and cooking technology relevant to this hypothesis. I also asked them to see if the manufacture and use of grooved axes accelerated with the onset of permanent settlement during Stallings times.

All lines of data on technology point to increasingly intensive subsistence practices, but the only "smoking gun" for changing fuel consumption came from the fuel itself. With help from paleoethnobotanist Lee Newsom, Beth Auten identified wood charcoal from 12 samples crosscutting each of the sites and the three periods in question Pine charcoal dominated all samples, making up as much as 92 percent of identifiable fragments. Most of this came from the yellow pine or southern hard pine group, species whose wood is dense and hard compared to other pines. The few hardwood samples identified came from ash, mulberry, blueberry, and grapevine; only a very small amount of it came from hickory or oak. Our hypothesis was quickly falsified, as selection for fuels clearly did not match the prevalence of hardwoods evident in the consumption of mast resources.

If we were to gauge accurately any impacts that humans may have had on the environment, we needed data on vegetation cover that were independent of human selection for food and fuel. I had hoped that pollen could be extracted from the soil of Stallings sites but was disappointed with the results of a pilot study on samples from Mims Point. I had never considered the interpretive potential of land snails until Peter Hallman arrived in Gainesville in 1999. He had spent a good deal of time out west learning how to identify land snails and using them as a proxy for vegetation cover. For some species, there is good correlation between snail distribution and environmental contexts. Various species are sensitive to changes in moisture, ground cover, temperature, and substrate. Especially noteworthy are the effects of deforestation on the variety and abundance of species whose niche is forest litter. Archaeologists working across the globe have used changes in snail assemblages to monitor the emergence of agricultural practices involving extensive land clearing.

The work that Peter Hallman began in 1999 continues today as he sorts and identifies the literally hundreds of thousands of snails that we collected from features and midden samples. Some of the species consist of snails as large as a golf ball, but most are very small—smaller than the head of a pin in some cases. The number of genera and species present is mind-boggling. Because so few data exist on the environmental niches of many of these species, Hallman and project consultant Evan Peacock set out to collect modern control samples from sites throughout the middle Savannah. The work of preparing and identifying these modern assemblages is as painstaking as the sorting of ancient samples. These efforts are ongoing; only preliminary results are available to date, but here is what we know so far.

The most common species of land snail across all samples is *Discus patulus*, a species that likes moist and shaded forest habitat. Its frequency tends to decrease through time as other species tolerant of open conditions, such as members of the family Pupillidae, gained in frequency. Hallman's initial data suggested that this was a slow, gradual trend of increasingly open habitat, presumably a function of local deforestation. As more data accumulated it appeared that this trend was much more complicated. Ground cover during Paris Island/Mill Branch occupations was at first dense forest but quickly opened up locally through the pre-Stallings occupations of Stallings Island and Ed Marshall. With abandonment of these sites after 4450 B.P., dense forest cover returned to sites of habitation, only to be reduced again with intensive occupations of Classic Stallings times. All three locations of circular villages were particularly clear of dense forest litter. This, of course, is not surprising, given the presumed permanence and formality of circular villages.

Species intolerant of open conditions persisted throughout the entire period in question, which shows that the middle Savannah was never completely denuded of vegetation. Forest-litter-loving snails found refuge in the margins of areas opened for habitation and could quickly return to dominance in the snail assemblages of settlements that were abandoned for more than a few years. Still, Hallman's data help us to monitor the relative intensity of settlement and indeed provide independent verification for the sorts of permanent villages inferred from the arrangement of features at Classic Stallings sites.

On balance, the combined data derived from clams, vertebrate remains, nutshell, wood charcoal, and land snails do not clearly support the notion that Stallings communities overexploited their environment. Minor variations in frequency and quality of foods and fuel notwithstanding, there is nothing in the archaeological record in the middle Savannah that screams environmental crisis or economic failure.

Instead of examining worsening conditions that forced people away from riverine settlements, we might consider how environmental conditions elsewhere attracted their attention. This is the approach of geoarchaeologist Mark Brooks of SCIAA. In the 1980s Brooks and his former geology professor Don Colquhoun reconstructed sea-level changes on the South Carolina coast, which had both positive and negative consequences for prehistoric residents of the low-country. Taking this research one step further, Brooks examined the response of Coastal Plain river systems to changes in sea level. Several lines of evidence suggested that upland tributaries of the upper Coastal Plain became less erosional and more depositional at about 3,800 years ago. This transition to modern floodplains improved habitat not only for aquatic plants and animals but also for mast resources and organisms up the food chain, like turkey and deer—on balance, not a bad alternative to life on the big river.

More recent research by Mark Brooks and pond ecologist Barbara Taylor suggests that sustained upland settlement was possible long before the establishment of modern floodplains. Their study subjects are Carolina bays, the enigmatic upland wetlands that dot the Coastal Plain province of the South Atlantic region. Brooks and Taylor have marshaled abundant ecological and archaeological data to demonstrate that many bays were well watered throughout human prehistory. Accordingly, bays offered reliable supplies of freshwater and aquatic food resources, as well as microhabitats for broadleaf trees in an otherwise pine-dominated landscape.

Hence life in the uplands was not only possible throughout prehistory, but at times highly desirable. The immediate descendants of Stallings Culture thought so, as did a variety of other prehistoric groups. But members of Classic Stallings culture did not. Instead, they remained tightly tethered to riverine sites for about three centuries. Something besides food and water must have kept them there, for these basic resources indeed were plentiful elsewhere.

Putting Stallings decisions into a broader context, we have to consider cultural factors that transcend subsistence economics. Among them are the symbolic power of places of origin or ancestral homes. As we have seen, Stallings Island was one such place, both the resting place of the ancestors and a locus of social gatherings that commemorated the dead in feast and ritual. The middle Savannah was a great place to make a living off the land, but was that the main reason why Classic Stallings communities dug in and stayed put for so many generations?

A Matter of Life and Death

Stallings burials provide not only a reminder of the symbolic influence of place but our best insight into the consequences of a stationary lifestyle. As the old adage goes, you are what you eat. For the skeletal biologist, this is more than a metaphorical quip. Registered in the bony tissue of ancient people is evidence of diet and health. Bones also record the personal histories of trauma, work habits, and degenerative disease. There is perhaps no better source of data on how adapted a people were to their environmental, social, and cultural circumstances.

Collecting such data on Stallings burials was the job of bioarchaeologist Kristin Wilson. As she quickly learned, the data would be few. Although over 80 skeletons were recovered in the early excavations of Stallings Island, three factors intervened to reduce the sample to only a few dozen individuals. First, only half of the skeletons recovered from the 1928–29 expedition of the Cosgroves were curated at the Peabody Museum at Harvard, sponsor of the dig. Second, several of the curated skeletons dated to later prehistoric occupations. Third, many of the skeletons were incomplete, owing in large measure to the methods of excavation, which were woefully inadequate by today's standards.

To increase her sample, Wilson traveled to Washington, D.C., to examine skeletons from the 1951 excavation of Lake Spring, the large shell-midden site 20 km upriver from Stallings Island. The 11 individuals from Lake Spring curated at the Smithsonian Institution were mostly Late Archaic in age but of uncertain cultural affiliation. Radiocarbon dating and careful review of provenience data revealed that most of the individuals were pre-Stallings Late Archaic. Although this did little to bolster the Stallings sample, it provided an important point of reference for the biological health of Stallings predecessors, people who maintained a more mobile lifestyle.

The contrasts in biological health between pre-Stallings and Stallings subgroups are illuminating. Compared to their predecessors, Classic Stallings individuals exhibited higher levels of dietary stress, trauma, and degenerative illness. Particularly curious is the relatively high level of iron-deficiency anemia in the Stallings group. Freshwater shellfish offer above-average levels of iron, so iron deficiency is unexpected among habitual shellfish eaters. To explain this dilemma, Wilson pointed to a number of systemic factors that may have compromised the metabolic uptake of iron. Among them are the effects of parasitic infections—ailments common among people who, for lack of mobility, find themselves in constant association with accumulating garbage.

In addition to showing how much worse off Stallings individuals were than their forebears, Wilson's research suggests that the brunt of Stallings life was not shared equally. Incidences of infection and trauma were much more common among Stallings women than among men. Despite the limited sample size, the contrast between the sexes is remarkable. If, as I argued earlier, Classic Stallings society was organized by matrilocal postmarital residence, women would have been permanent residents of riverine shell-midden sites and hence more subject to parasitic infection, while the men they married included members of more mobile neighboring groups.

The differences between men and women in terms of biological health underscore that an individual's experience as a participant in Classic Stallings Culture depended on social identity. Health consequences along lines of gender suggest that significant disparities may have been felt at the household level. More broadly, with a system of unilineal descent, disparities within households may have extended to the realm of kin group or lineage. For instance, were men routinely serving the economic needs of households to which they were related only through marriage, or did they continue to serve the households of their blood line? This is hardly a trivial matter for societies whose economic well-being and long-term survival depend on the social alliances of descent and marriage.

The bulk of the evidence points to the likelihood that Stallings culture fell victim to its own social rules. If so, we might expect that its dissolution in the middle Savannah involved a series of fissioning events along the cleavage planes of kinship groups. Some such groups continued to reproduce elements of Stallings culture elsewhere, others returned to more traditional lifestyles, and still others entered into radically different alternatives. Compared to the distinctive qualities of Classic Stallings culture, the ensuing social formations left an archaeological record of disparate elements and marked diversity.

Life Goes On

Groups bearing accoutrements of Classic Stallings culture persisted in the centuries following abandonment of the middle Savannah in a variety of guises, none of which involved the intensive use of shellfish. Although our

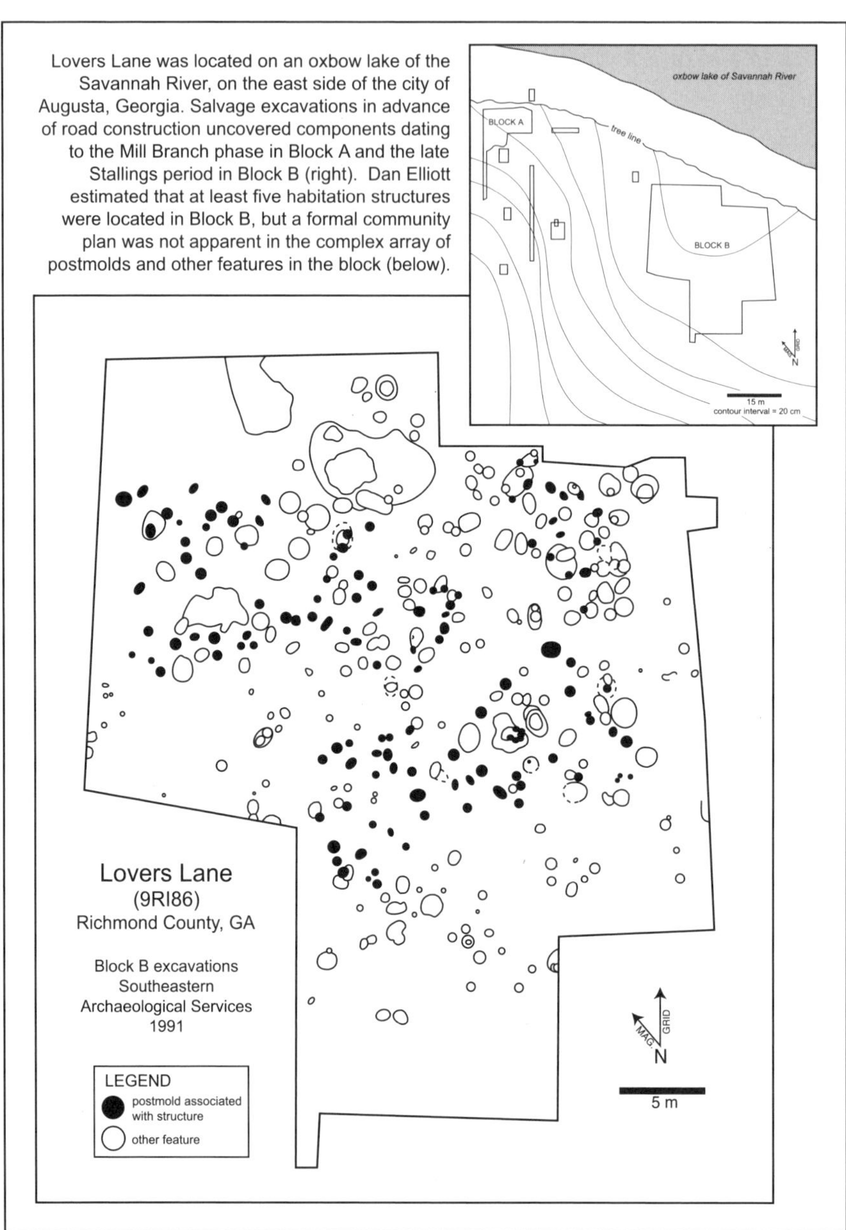

7.2. Map and plan drawing of the features found in Block B at Lovers Lane (9RI86), Richmond County, Georgia, by Dan Elliott and colleagues at Southeastern Archaeological Services, Inc., of Athens, Georgia (adapted from report by Dan Elliott and colleagues).

known sample of the settlements of all these descendant populations is thin, two very distinctive patterns emerge from the data that we do have.

First, a band of "post-Classic" Stallings settlements existed at various locations roughly 25 km from Stallings Island. Among the more significant along the river is the enigmatic Lovers Lane site in Augusta. This is the very location (discussed in chapter 3) where Dan Elliott found evidence for Mill Branch–period bannerstone production. Lovers Lane also housed a sizable Stallings assemblage in an area east of the Mill Branch settlement. Nearly 400 features were recorded in a large block stripped by Elliott, including postholes, earth ovens, large basins, and two human cremations. Pottery from these features and general midden context includes examples of Classic Stallings drag-and-jab designs and a greater proportion of separate punctate. Soapstone cooking slabs are relatively infrequent. Charcoal from five features gave age estimates ranging from ca. 4200 to 3550 B.P., making it difficult to pinpoint actual episodes of occupation. Patterning in the distribution of postholes enabled Elliott to infer a series of irregularly shaped structures. The collective pattern does not assume any sort of linear, arcuate, or circular arrangement; nor are the structures associated with individual storage pits. Rather, the assemblage of features and the associated material culture look like Classic Stallings culture in disarray. No doubt some of this seeming chaos is simply a function of intermixing among similar but not identical components. I suggest that much of it is the expected outcome of a formalized society that came unglued.

In the opposite direction—upriver from Stallings Island at a distance equal to the downriver locus of Lovers Lane—the Lake Spring site stood sentinel. Now inundated by the waters of Clark Hill Lake, Lake Spring is the northernmost shell midden of any good scale. Like Stallings Island, the site also contained a Paris Island/Mill Branch component and a sizable burial population. The fate of Classic Stallings occupants at Lake Spring may have paralleled the fate of those on Stallings Island, but I am certain that it was a different community of people, rather than the seasonal village of a group moving up and down the river. Without more dates we will never know if the Lake Spring community was coeval with those of the middle Savannah. It is possible that occupation at Lake Spring continued after Stallings Island and related sites were abandoned; it is even feasible that some of those abandoning Stallings Island relocated to Lake Spring.

Other locations with components of Stallings affinity about 25 km from

Stallings Island lie among the upland landforms on either side of the river. Sites in the Hitchcock Woods area near Aiken, South Carolina, and the Mill Branch type site in Warren County, Georgia, contain relatively small assemblages of drag-and-jab and related Stallings pottery. Radiocarbon dates from both locales suggest that occupations spanned Classic Stallings times and likely persisted a short while after riverine sites were abandoned. I have long wondered if some of these upland occupations were merely the seasonal camps of riverine groups, but the pottery suggests otherwise. Upland wares are typically much sandier than Classic Stallings pottery at riverine sites and occasionally bear traces of direct-heat cooking. In all cases upland assemblages have relatively low density and diversity, typical of the sort of short-term encampments of a seasonally mobile people. We may never know exactly how these sites relate to riverine locales at the apogee of Stallings Culture, but one interpretation is a pattern of dispersed, mobile settlement following the abandonment of riverine shell-midden sites. Equally viable is the idea that small-scale, mobile groups bearing some of the emblems of Stallings Culture, especially the pottery style, existed alongside river-oriented groups throughout Stallings history. Either way, these inconspicuous sites are woefully understudied, too often deemed insignificant, and highly vulnerable to even shallow ground disturbances, such as logging and farming.

A second pattern of more distant settlement is seen in an array of sites 75–100 km from Stallings Island. Sites downriver are restricted to upland locales along major tributaries of the Savannah River. Over a period of a decade, volunteers with the Augusta Archaeological Society, under the guidance of George Lewis, excavated one such site along Tinker Creek in Aiken County. The Tinker Creek site was the locus of repeated occupation since the Early Holocene, including one dating to ca. 3950 B.P., the height of Classic Stallings times. The Tinker Creek assemblage matches Stallings pottery in its decoration; but like the closer upland sites, it consists of sherds with sandy, fiber-tempered paste. I suspect that the people making these pots would have self-identified as a community different from, though clearly related to, those of the river. I also suspect that some of these distant upland sites postdated the abandonment of the river.

Going across the grain of major river drainages, at locations roughly 100 km east and west of Stallings Island, lie two clusters of settlement whose origins are uncertain but whose development likely flourished in the centuries following abandonment of the middle Savannah. In the Midlands of

South Carolina near Columbia, where the Broad and Saluda Rivers join to form the Congaree, myriad sites spanning all of prehistory attest to intensive use of this Fall Line locale. Among them are the type site for Thoms Creek pottery. Going in the opposite direction, sites with Stallings fiber-tempered pottery cluster at locations in the lower Piedmont along the Oconee River of Georgia. Age estimates for settlement in these distant clusters are sketchy, but some fiber-tempered pottery assemblages in the Oconee include soapstone vessel sherds, a class of artifact never found with Classic Stallings pottery in the middle Savannah. Associations between fiber-tempered pottery and soapstone vessels are duplicated at sites in the Big Bend of the Ocmulgee documented by Frankie Snow, as well as a couple of sites investigated by David Anderson before the construction of the Richard B. Russell Reservoir. Calibrated radiocarbon age estimates for these associations fall between 3800 and 3650 B.P., although the sample of assays is woefully small. Nonetheless, more widespread dating of sooted vessel sherds confirms that soapstone vessels were not used in the middle Savannah before 3800 B.P. and date only a few centuries older in the oldest examples from north Georgia. Thus, the association between fiber-tempered pottery and soapstone vessels is a distinctively postabandonment phenomenon.

Despite its postabandonment timing, the circumstances surrounding the inception of soapstone vessel technology in north Georgia trace to earlier events in the middle Savannah. As discussed in chapter 6, people of Mill Branch disappeared from the middle Savannah region just as Classic Stallings culture rose to prominence at ca. 4200 B.P. Those outside this ethnogenetic outcome appear to have relocated westward into north Georgia. One outcome of this relocation was the Black Shoals phase as defined by Bill Stanyard. Dating to ca. 3800–3600 B.P., the Black Shoals phase is essentially Mill Branch with soapstone vessels but still no pottery. There may be some simple, pragmatic explanation for why this enclave of Late Archaic living persisted another three centuries without adopting pottery technology, but I am inclined to believe that soapstone had value well beyond its effectiveness in cooking. This is the moment in time when the production and exchange of soapstone vessels intensified to the point of becoming subcontinental in scale.

In the ensuing centuries the importation and consumption of soapstone vessels were key processes contributing to the magnificent Poverty Point culture of northeast Louisiana. Arguably the grandest expression of Archaic

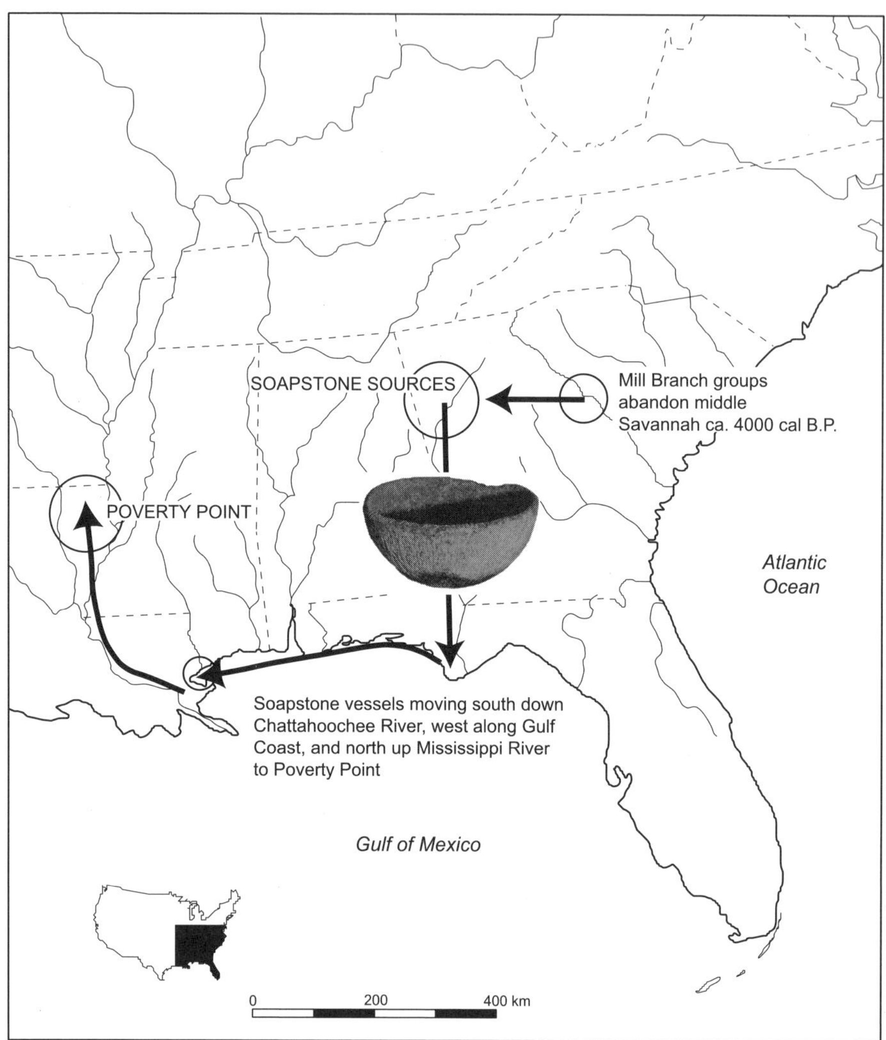

7.3. Model of the development of soapstone vessel exchange triggered by the abandonment of the middle Savannah River valley by descendants of Mill Branch culture. The route featured here down the Chattahoochee River, across the Gulf Coast, and up the Mississippi River is only one of several possible routes.

culture, Poverty Point, with its elaborate mounds, long-distance exchange, and symbolic art, is a long way literally and figuratively from the goings-on in the middle Savannah, yet its involvement with long-distance trade guaranteed that it had cultural reverberations equally vast. By all accounts, soapstone vessels began flowing down the Chattahoochee River to the Gulf Coast as early as 4150 B.P., were handled and sent west by Gulf communities in Choctawhatchee Bay and the Pearl River delta, and wound up at locales of Poverty Point culture. While not all soapstone vessels made in Georgia headed west, and not all soapstone vessels in northeast Louisiana came from Georgia, the mere fact that Poverty Point itself was the recipient of thousands of vessels from sources no closer than eastern Alabama is proof enough to me that trade in soapstone had the potential to affect the distribution and social relations of participating groups across the entire Southeast.

Putting this all into perspective, the rise of soapstone vessel exchange may have been among the straws that broke the Stallings back. Quite simply, the allure of alliances with people connected with the traders who were connected with the traders who were connected to Poverty Point may have been all that was needed to persuade people to break tradition, relocate to strategic locales, and redefine themselves via new allies. This would have been an especially attractive option if the quality of local conditions, environmental and social, was in decline.

The allure of Atlantic coastal alliances may have had a similar, if weaker, effect. At the time Classic Stallings people abandoned the middle Savannah, shell rings on Hilton Head Island were occupied by people who apparently used both fiber- and sand-tempered wares. Lesser shell-bearing sites in the area—like Fish Haul, dug by Michael Trinkley, and Daws Island, documented by Jim Michie—have evidence of occupations either coeval or postdating the middle Savannah abandonment. Daws Island is especially curious because of the prevalence of plain fiber-tempered wares and soapstone cooking slabs dating as late as 3550 B.P. Like some of the other remote locations, Daws Island has the appearance of a "devolved" Stallings culture, when decorated pottery again is in the minority.

As noted in the previous chapter, a functional dichotomy between shell rings and more mundane middens appears to have been in place on the coast, with the former contexts sporting more elaborate material culture. While this dichotomy remains to be adequately defined with good samples, there is clearly a trend toward lesser stylistic elaboration through time, at least on the

South Carolina coast. By the time the last shell rings formed off the coast of Charleston County after ca. 3550 B.P., middens were thin, communities were small, and pottery was largely plain. Local settlement appears to have grown less permanent and local abandonment more common. It may be more than coincidental that the heyday of shell-ring living terminates with the rise of Poverty Point. As is the fate of modern people today, I expect that the contours of Late Archaic history were shaped by processes well beyond those that were locally controlled or understood. It was most likely convenient and perfectly natural for people to blame their fate on that which could not be controlled, as they do today.

The Second Fall of Stallings Culture

The story of Stallings decline unfolds on another front. As if its demise 3,800 years ago was not enough, Stallings Culture faces a second fall these days at the hands of looters and relic seekers. In their reckless digging to collect a few stone tools or bone pins, looters compromise the contexts and associations that enable archaeologists to reconstruct the details of ancient lifeways. Each of the many Stalling sites that I have discussed in these chapters has been badly vandalized, and some continue to be.

Fortunately, we have been able to salvage a great deal of information from the scraps left by looters. Our success in this regard is due in great measure to the hard work of dozens of volunteers as well as the institutional support of outfits such as the National Geographic Society, the American Philosophical Society, the National Science Foundation, the U.S. Forest Service, the U.S. Department of Energy, Augusta State University, the University of Florida, and, most critically, the South Carolina Institute of Archaeology and Anthropology and its Savannah River Archaeological Research Program. The financial support of these agencies and programs has provided a firm foundation for sustained research, but it is not enough. Many more sites (some the recent or impending victims of rampant urban sprawl around Augusta) await attention. The collections of many other sites reside in boxes awaiting the analytical attention that they deserve. Each of our salvage operations in the field resulted in thousands of artifacts and even greater quantities of feature matrix that require painstaking sorting and analysis. Laboratory costs outweigh field costs at least tenfold, especially in human time. Radiocarbon, faunal, and floral analyses are particularly costly but increasingly necessary to further our understanding of ancient human life.

Resources to support research such as this are finite. Even more limited these days are students eager to carry the torch of Stallings research. The archaeological records of later Woodland and Mississippian cultures hold greater sway in attracting the attention of fledgling professionals. I hope that in this exposition of Stallings Culture I have changed the minds of those who believe that nothing much of interest happened before Mississippian chiefdoms erected mounds on the Savannah 1,000 years ago. Stallings is an ancient case study in nascent social complexity that failed to multiply and grow. As such it ought to provide a great contrast for the emergent institutions of Mississippian culture that thrived long enough to leave an indelible mark on the landscape of the middle Savannah, as they did elsewhere in the Southeast. Like social formations that came before, Mississippian chiefdoms met their demise too, sometimes as a consequence of European contact, sometimes on their own. David Anderson has taught us that those of the middle Savannah met an abrupt end at ca. A.D. 1450 after a period of political competition and prolonged drought, but before Spanish explorers arrived. Their circumstances were far different from those of Stallings people, and yet they shared parallel experiences of colonization, fluorescence, and local collapse, in both cases elapsing over only a few centuries.

The many centuries that separate these historical "moments" deflect attention from the fact that they were both enacted in the same theatre. Places like Stallings Island were key stages in these plays. Through practices of tradition and reinvented tradition, such places condensed history and human experience, collapsing time across the millennia to form meaningful bridges between then and now. In this sense the fall of Stallings Culture was merely the beginning of something new. The people who returned to Stallings Island some 500, 2,500, and 3,500 years later would all define its meaning in the things that they did there and in the way they thought about this place and its past. The ongoing process of culture-making ensures that Stallings Island will always be significant to people who take the time to appreciate all that has happened there before.

Epilogue

Stallings Island, A.D. 1439

Redstalk looked up to the sky and held his breath as he lowered his dead daughter into the shallow pit. To gaze upon her lifeless body as she entered the grave was to impede her passage to the Upper World. Smoke from the funerary fire enveloped father and daughter, cloaking them in the hope of transcendence. The rite, the medicine, the incantation all had to be true, had to be right. It was Redstalk's final hope. His daughter, like so many children in recent years, had succumbed to the sickness of the cold winter. The short days had never been so harsh, the preceding summer's harvest never so poor. The people prayed and sacrificed for relief, but none of the usual rites seemed to work. So Redstalk brought his daughter to the island to enjoin its power in death, to reach back to the Ancients for help, to resurrect the tradition that his people had forsaken.

As the chief of the secondary people, Redstalk had little clout with the Ancients. His lineage was young and foreign, subordinate to the primary people, whose ancestry was rooted in all things old and original. Redstalk's rival, the old chief Whitehorn, could recite at will the many generations of his ruling lineage. At its apex was the chief of the Ancients, a man of great skill in diplomacy and magic. He moved deftly and boldly between the Upper and Lower Worlds. He brought prosperity and honor to his people. He fended off mortal foe and dark spirits. He persuaded rain to fall and floodwaters to recede. He made men loyal to their women and punished those who strayed from tradition. He was father to the people, treating them with unconditional allegiance and receiving from them unquestioned compliance.

Stallings Island was the ultimate source of chiefly authority and sacred power, the birthplace of the Ancients and the fitting abode of ancestor spirits. But its enormous power made it no place for lesser people. In the story of their origins, as Whitehorn would tell it, Stallings Island was abandoned when the red-tailed bird dropped seed from the sky to spawn the great cornfields of the low-country. Those who migrated down the great river prospered in its bounty. They built great mounds of earth to emulate their chiefly birthplace and to lift their leaders high above the World of the People. The chiefs traveled widely, built strong alliances with chiefs elsewhere, and acquired the medicines of sacred authority, objects of shell, copper, and mica. Through divine leadership, the People grew larger in number, their stores deeper in grain.

After seven generations of chiefs, the People became too numerous as one and had to split into two. The division was inevitable, because over time fewer could claim legitimate descent from the Ancients because of all the intermarriage with Others. Surely few anticipated that alliances with foreign people would one day erode traditional practices, but eventually the divide between the old and the new became clear and indeed became a source of persistent tension. So unbalanced were the People that one day a great wind blew in from the sea, flooding the fields and villages, and driving the Children of the Ancients back to their homeland and the ways of tradition. There at the Shoals, in the shadow of the Great Island, they re-created the world they once knew, this time fiercely guarding tradition from corruption and change. Corn was now part of that tradition, and the Children of the Ancients came to the shore of the Great Island every summer to lay stalks at its feet. Only Holy Men and the Chief could ascend its banks to the top, where the Ancients once lived in body and still resided in powerful spirit. In times of unbalance the sacred ones would stay atop the Shell Mound for days in sweat, purifying their spirits for journeys of wisdom and clairvoyance. They found great power in many of the objects left behind on the Island, like those of polished stone and shell in the graves of the Ancients. Nothing was more sacred than the power of the Ancients in this place and these things.

That was Redstalk's hope indeed. His people and the Children of the Ancients had suffered terribly in recent years. The usual summer rains had stopped long ago. Local communities could barely get by with the meager corn they coaxed from dry floodplains. More and more of Redstalk's people moved deep along upland tributaries, where they spent more time harvesting acorns and hickories than they did farming. No manner of persuasion could convince even his closest allies to stay on the river. The primary chief and Redstalk's rival, Whitehorn, held greater sway over his kindred. They did not question his decision to relocate once again downriver, to the place where the floodwaters spread widest. But even there the farming was tough, and there was little time to build mounds and prepare for ceremonies. Soon even

Whitehorn's authority dwindled. Change this time would be irreversible, as more and more families fled the region to join communities far away.

Under these dire circumstances, Redstalk had nothing to lose by bringing his daughter to the Island. The sacra of Whitehorn's lineage, the objects of the Ancients, were fair game now. Like all people of his time, Redstalk happened upon such objects in his daily life. But he, like others, never collected or kept these things, for that would invite accusations of witchcraft. The objects of the Island were especially taboo; those from the graves of the Ancients could strike a man dead. No one but Whitehorn had the strength and wisdom to handle such power, not even his own People. Nonetheless, Redstalk had learned indirectly the ways of Ancient power; after all, he was chiefly too. Whitehorn's authority meant nothing now. Whatever power he could muster to protect his people from sickness and death was not enough. Redstalk always thought that he could do better.

The traditional shell beads of healing hung from his daughter's neck as Redstalk lowered her into the grave. Without looking down he reached into a leather pouch for a bundle of deer toes and placed them beside her body, followed in sequence by a bone fishhook, five antler batons, four beaver incisors, a net sinker made of soapstone, a large blade of dark chert, and two bone awls. He laid the final offering, a large shell cup, at her left shoulder.

Redstalk was hopeful that this was the assemblage of balance, the complement of things traditional and new, of things sacred and mundane. His daughter's passage to the Upper World would go unimpeded, uncontested. Her sacred journey would evoke new life for his People. The power of the Ancients and their homeland, their Shoals and Great Island, were hers now. With it she would replenish the earth and its People. In her death, life would once again flourish.

Peabody Museum, May 2003

The objects that lay before me were mesmerizing. I knew that several of the burials at Stallings Island were Mississippian in age but never before appreciated the extent to which these later people used ancient objects in mortuary rites. I had always assumed that the occasional bannerstone or Archaic biface in Mississippian graves was simply the happenstance of digging into an old midden. One cannot dig at Stallings Island without uncovering something old, and no doubt this held true for Mississippian undertakers too. But the reinterment of ancient objects was perhaps not so random, at least not in this case. Before me lay the objects from the grave of a child, some distinctively old, others uniquely new. They sent my mind reeling.

My graduate students and I had journeyed to Harvard's Peabody Museum with the intent of analyzing as much of the Claflin collection as we could in two weeks. Most of the items recovered from the 1929 expedition to Stallings Island were bequeathed to the Peabody upon the death of Claflin's widow, and the curatorial staff had done an excellent job preparing it for research and curation. Meggan Blessing spent her time with the more than 600 bone and antler tools in the collection, while Asa Randall and I pored over large assemblages of bifaces, bannerstones, axes, and soapstone objects. On this trip we did not plan to examine the mortuary objects that had been so thoroughly inventoried by Peabody staff in compliance with the Native American Graves Protection and Repatriation Act. But on the last day of our two-week visit, with an hour or so left before our departure, I pulled the one tray known to contain a special stone tool and gazed upon an assemblage of diverse objects.

The objects of shell, bone, antler, and stone came from Burial 13 of the Cosgroves' expedition. It was the interment of a young child, placed in an extended position on its back, with its head to the southwest. It was found at the very edge of the Cosgroves' large block, about 20 m away from the main cluster of burials of Classic Stallings age. The inclusion of a shell cup was evidence that the child was probably Mississippian, but some of the other objects were those of more ancient people. Many such objects—the bone awls, deer-bone fishhook blanks, and shell beads—were things that perhaps transcended time, threads of continuity that linked the ancient past with the present. Looking at these objects caused me to ponder the role of Stallings Island in the making of history. Obviously the island has figured into the lives of people throughout time as a place to live and occasionally as a place to die and be buried. But was it also a place whose history was rewritten over and over as human needs and circumstances dictated?

This one instance of human compassion, of human remembrance, embraced so much history, so much time. It acknowledged the past; it anticipated the future. It reproduced and perhaps even transformed tradition to fit whatever circumstances lay before those who participated in the act. This was the same process of inventing tradition that people of Classic Stallings identity engaged in 4,200 years ago, stipulating the island as their land and its dead as their ancestors. Americans engaged in the same process when they bestowed upon Stallings Island National Landmark status and embraced it as their own. And I, as an archaeologist, engaged in this same process while writing this book. Other stories of Stallings Island and its people will flourish in permutations yet to come so long as humans continue to beckon the past to rationalize the present and erect guideposts for the future.

Glossary

Archaic period: the time between the end of the Ice Age (ca. 12,000 B.P.) and the beginning of the Woodland period (ca. 3000 B.P.), when eastern North America was populated by diverse hunter-gatherer societies.

bannerstone: a pecked and polished stone object of varied form that is drilled longitudinally through its midsection for attachment to a shaft; many such objects were fitted to spearthrowers (atlatls) and are thus referred to as atlatl weights; especially ornate or oversized examples may have been used for strictly ceremonial purposes.

biface: a stone implement that has been flaked (chipped) on both sides; flaked-stone knives, projectile points, and drills are usually bifacial.

block excavation: a technique of archaeological excavation designed to open large areas for the purpose of exposing community patterning and other horizontal spatial relationships at sites.

bride service: services rendered by bride-takers (husbands and their families) to compensate for loss of daughters in marriage.

bridewealth: payments made by bride-takers (husbands and their families) to compensate for loss of daughters in marriage.

calibration: a means of adjusting radiocarbon age estimates to actual calendar years using some independent measure of absolute age, usually the annual growth rings of trees.

carinated vessel: a bowl-shaped vessel with a rim that turns inward at a sharp angle.

cross-dating: a method of estimating the age of a stratum, a feature, or an object with reference to the known age of a comparable stratum, feature, or object found elsewhere.

debitage: the waste by-products of flaking or chipping stone, otherwise known simply as "flakes."

drag-and-jab punctation: a technique of decorating Stallings and Thoms Creek pottery with a stylus that is inserted in the wet clay of a vessel surface to make consecutive punctations along a line formed by "dragging" the stylus between points of punctation.

ethnogenesis: the formation of a "new" culture or ethnic group through the interaction of two or more previously distinct populations.

feature: a nonportable "artifact" at an archaeological site (such as a pit, burial, or hearth) that is treated as a discrete context (a time capsule) and often, but not always, provides good opportunity for age estimates and reconstruction of site function and structure.

grid: a system of spatial reference for an archaeological survey or excavation based on Cartesian coordinates.

hafted: attached to a handle; bifaces often have modifications for hafting, such as notches or stems.

heat-treating: a method for improving the quality of stone used for making flaked-stone tools by applying heat (also known as thermal alteration).

matrilocal: the custom of residence whereby the bride and her husband live in the vicinity of her mother's community after marriage.

midden: an accumulation of food refuse and other waste by-products of human activity.

Mississippian: generally applied to the populations dating from ca. A.D. 900 until European contact in eastern North America that had a chiefly level of sociopolitical organization, an intensive corn-based agricultural economy, and a politico-religious system involving the construction and use of flat-topped mounds.

patrilocal: the custom of residence whereby the husband and his bride live in the vicinity of his father's community after marriage.

plowzone: an upper zone of homogenized soil that is produced by repeated tilling, which disturbs the spatial arrangement and integrity of archaeological deposits near the surface; generally about 20–25 cm thick.

postmarital residence: customs that prescribe where a couple will live after marriage.

punctation: the chief form of decoration on Stallings and Thoms Creek pottery, formed by the insertion of a stylus (stick, reed, or bone) into the wet clay of a vessel surface before it was fired.

radiocarbon dating: a method of obtaining age estimates for organic materials found in archaeological sites, such as charcoal or bone, based on the amount of radioactive decay in carbon that the organism (for example, a tree or an animal) ingested while it was alive.

sedentism: a nonmigratory or "settled" lifestyle.

shell midden: an accumulation of food refuse and other waste by-products of human activity that includes a substantial amount of shell from mollusks.

shell ring: a shell midden or mounded shell arrayed in a circular or semicircular fashion; ranges in size from a few tens to hundreds of meters in diameter.

sherd: a fragment of a broken pottery vessel.

soapstone: a metamorphic rock rich in talc that is usually soft enough to scratch with a fingernail; used to make bannerstones, cooking stones, vessels, and other items.

stone boiling: a technique of cooking that involves stones that are heated in fire and transferred to a container holding water or some other liquid; as they cool, stones may have to be removed, reheated, and returned to the vessel to achieve the desired result.

stratigraphy: the arrangement of strata (layers) in an archaeological or geological deposit.

superpositioning: the simple principle, borrowed from geology, that layers at the bottom of an undisturbed stratified sequence must be older than those above.

test unit: a unit of systematic excavation, usually square or rectangular (for example, 1 by 1 m or 1 by 2 m), usually oriented to a grid, and usually excavated in levels (incrementally, such as in a 10-cm layer at a time from top to bottom).

unilocal: the custom of residence whereby a couple is expected to live after marriage in the vicinity of either the husband's or the wife's side of the family.

Woodland: the period between the end of the Archaic period (ca. 3000 B.P.) and the beginning of the Mississippian period (after A.D. 900), when eastern North America was populated by peoples who routinely made and used pottery and experimented with horticulture.

For Further Reading

Adair, James. 1930. *Adair's History of the American Indians,* edited by Samuel Cole Williams. Promontory Press, New York. (Orig. pub. 1775.)

Anderson, David G., and Joe Joseph. 1988. *Prehistory and History along the Upper Savannah River: Technical Synthesis of Cultural Resource Investigations, Richard B. Russell Multiple Resource Area.* Russell Papers, Interagency Archeological Services Division, National Park Service, Atlanta.

Bullen, Ripley P., and H. Bruce Greene. 1970. Stratigraphic Tests at Stalling's Island, Georgia. *The Florida Anthropologist* 23:8–21.

Caldwell, Joseph R. 1958. *Trend and Tradition in the Prehistory of the Eastern United States.* American Anthropological Association, Memoir 88. Menasha, Wis.

Claflin, William H., Jr. 1931. *The Stalling's Island Mound, Columbia County, Georgia.* Peabody Museum of American Archaeology and Ethnology Papers 14(1). Cambridge, Mass.

Coe, Joffre L. 1964. *The Formative Cultures of the Carolina Piedmont.* Transactions of the American Philosophical Society 54(2). Philadelphia.

Crook, Morgan R. 1991. Chronology of a Stratified Archaic Sequence in the Central Savannah River Valley. *Early Georgia* 19(2):21–33.

Crusoe, Donald L., and Chester B. DePratter. 1976. A New Look at the Georgia Coastal Shellmound Archaic. *The Florida Anthropologist* 29(1):1–23.

Elliott, Daniel T., R. Jerald Ledbetter, and Elizabeth A. Gordon. 1994. *Data Recovery at Lovers Lane, Phinizy Swamp and the Old Dike Sites Bobby Jones Expressway Extension Corridor Augusta, Georgia.* Occasional Papers in Cultural Resource Management 7. Georgia Department of Transportation, Atlanta.

Elliott, Daniel T., and Kenneth E. Sassaman. 1995. *Archaic Period Archaeology of the Georgia Coastal Plain and Coastal Zone.* Georgia Archaeological Research Design Paper No. 11. University of Georgia, Athens.

Fairbanks, Charles H. 1942. The Taxonomic Position of Stalling's Island, Georgia. *American Antiquity* 7:223–31.

Ford, James A. 1969. *A Comparison of Early Formative Cultures in the Americas.* Smithsonian Contributions to Anthropology 11. Smithsonian Institution, Washington, D.C.

Griffin, James B. 1943. An Analysis and Interpretation of Ceramic Remains from Two Sites near Beaufort, South Carolina. *Bureau of American Ethnology Bulletin* (Washington, D.C.) 133:159–68.

Jones, Charles C., Jr. 1861. *Monumental Remains of Georgia.* John M. Cooper and Company, Savannah, Ga.

———. 1873. *Antiquities of the Southern Indians, Particularly the Georgia Tribes.* D. Appleton and Company, New York.

Kelly, Robert L. 1995. *The Foraging Spectrum: Diversity in Hunter-Gatherer Lifeways.* Smithsonian Institution Press, Washington, D.C.

Ledbetter, R. Jerald. 1995. *Archaeological Investigations at Mill Branch Sites 9WR4 and 9WR11, Warren County, Georgia.* Technical Report No. 3. Interagency Archeological Services Division, National Park Service, Atlanta, Ga.

Russo, Michael. 1996a. Southeastern Mid-Holocene Coastal Settlements. In *Archaeology of the Mid-Holocene Southeast,* edited by Kenneth E. Sassaman and David G. Anderson, pp. 177–99. University Press of Florida, Gainesville.

———. 1996b. Southeastern Preceramic Archaic Ceremonial Mounds. In *Archaeology of the Mid-Holocene Southeast,* edited by Kenneth E. Sassaman and David G. Anderson, pp. 259–87. University Press of Florida, Gainesville.

Sassaman, Kenneth E. 1993a. *Early Pottery in the Southeast: Tradition and Innovation in Cooking Technology.* University of Alabama Press, Tuscaloosa.

———. 1993b. *Mims Point 1992: Archaeological Investigations at a Prehistoric Habitation Site in the Sumter National Forest, South Carolina.* Savannah River Archaeological Research Papers 4. Occasional Papers of the Savannah River Archaeological Research Program. South Carolina Institute of Archaeology and Anthropology, University of South Carolina, Columbia.

———. 1997. Refining Soapstone Vessel Chronology in the Southeast. *Early Georgia* 25(1):1–20.

———. 1998a. Crafting Cultural Identity in Hunter-Gatherer Economies. In *Craft and Social Identity,* edited by C. L. Costin and R. P. Wright, pp. 93–107. Archeological Papers of the American Anthropological Association, No. 8. Arlington, Va.

———. 1998b. Distribution, Timing, and Technology of Early Pottery in the Southeastern United States. *Revista de Arquelogía Americana* 14:101–33.

———. 2000. Agents of Change in Hunter-Gatherer Technology. In *Agency in Archaeology,* edited by M. A. Dobres and J. Robb, pp. 148–68. Routledge, London.

———. 2001. Hunter-Gatherers and Traditions of Resistance. In *The Archaeology of Tradition: Agency and History before and after Columbus,* edited by T. R. Pauketat, pp. 218–36. University Press of Florida, Gainesville.

Sassaman, Kenneth E., and David G. Anderson. 1995. *Middle and Late Archaic Archaeological Records of South Carolina: A Synthesis for Research and Resource Management.* Savannah River Archaeological Research Papers 6. Occasional Papers of the Savannah River Archaeological Research Program. South Carolina Institute of Archaeology and Anthropology, University of South Carolina, Columbia.

Sassaman, Kenneth E., Meggan E. Blessing, and Asa R. Randall. 2006. Stallings Island Revisited: New Evidence for Occupational History, Community Patterning, and Subsistence Technology. *American Antiquity* (in press).

Sassaman, Kenneth E., and Wictoria Rudolphi. 2001. Communities of Practice in the Early Pottery Traditions of the American Southeast. *Journal of Anthropological Research* 57(4):407–25.

Sassaman, Kenneth E., Kristin Wilson, and Frankie Snow. 1995. Putting the Ogeechee in Its Place. *Early Georgia* 23:20–40.

Saunders, Rebecca, ed. 2002. *The Fig Island Ring Complex (38CH42): Coastal Adaptation and the Question of Ring Function in the Late Archaic.* Report prepared for the South Carolina Department of Archives and History under Grant #45-01-16441. On file, South Carolina Department of Archives and History, Columbia.

Stanyard, William F. 2002. *Archaic Period Archaeology of Northern Georgia.* Georgia Archaeological Research Design Paper No. 13. University of Georgia, Athens.

Stoltman, James B. 1966. New Radiocarbon Dates for Southeastern Fiber-Tempered Pottery. *American Antiquity* 31:872–74.

———. 1972. The Late Archaic in the Savannah River Region. *Florida Anthropologist* 25(2):37–62.

———. 1974. *Groton Plantation: An Archaeological Study of a South Carolina Locality.* Monograph of the Peabody Museum No. 1. Harvard University, Cambridge, Mass.

Trinkley, Michael B. 1980. A Typology of Thom's Creek Pottery for the South Carolina Coast. *South Carolina Antiquities* 12:1–35.

———. 1985. The Form and Function of South Carolina's Early Woodland Shell Rings. In *Structure and Process in Southeastern Archaeology*, edited by R. S. Dickens and H. T. Ward, pp. 102–18. University of Alabama Press, Tuscaloosa.

Williams, Stephen, ed. 1968. *The Waring Papers: The Collected Works of Antonio J. Waring, Jr.* Papers of the Peabody Museum of Archaeology and Ethnology, Vol. 58. Harvard University, Cambridge, Mass.

Wood, W. Dean, Dan T. Elliott, Teresa P. Rudolph, and Dennis B. Blanton. 1986. *Prehistory of the Richard B. Russell Reservoir: The Archaic and Woodland Periods of the Upper Savannah River.* Russell Papers. Interagency Archeological Services Division, National Park Service, Atlanta, Ga.

Index

Kenneth E. Sassaman is associate professor of anthropology at the University of Florida in Gainesville. Before coming to UF in 1998, Ken worked for 11 years with the Savannah River Archaeological Research Program, where his interest in Stallings archaeology was cultivated and supported. He has written many articles and reports on Stallings culture, including *Early Pottery in the Southeast* (1993), and is preparing a new book on the Archaic cultures of the eastern United States. His ongoing fieldwork is now centered in the St. Johns River valley of northeast Florida.